FROM
A CORNISH WINDOW

FROM
A CORNISH WINDOW

by
Sir Arthur Quiller-Couch

CAMBRIDGE
AT THE UNIVERSITY PRESS
1928

CAMBRIDGE UNIVERSITY PRESS

Cambridge, New York, Melbourne, Madrid, Cape Town, Singapore, São Paulo, Delhi

Cambridge University Press
The Edinburgh Building, Cambridge CB2 8RU, UK

Published in the United States of America by Cambridge University Press, New York

www.cambridge.org
Information on this title: www.cambridge.org/9780521736794

First published by J. W. Arrowsmith 1906
Reprinted 1912
Published as a pocket edition by Cambridge University Press 1928
This digitally printed version 2008

A catalogue record for this publication is available from the British Library

ISBN 978-0-521-73679-4 paperback

DEDICATION

MY DEAR WILLIAM ARCHER,

Severe and ruthlessly honest man that you are, you will find that the levities and the gravities of this book do not accord, and will say so.

I plead only that they were written at intervals, and in part for recreation, during years in which their author has striven to maintain a cheerful mind while a popular philosophy which he believed to be cheap took possession of men and translated itself into politics which he knew to be nasty. I may summarise it, in its own jargon, as the philosophy of the Superman, and succinctly describe it as an attempt to stretch a part of the Darwinian hypothesis and make it cover the whole of man's life and conduct. I need not remind you how fatally its doctrine has flattered, in our time and in our country, the worst instincts of the half-educated: but let us remove it from all spheres in which we are interested and contemplate it as expounded by an American Insurance

'Lobbyist,' a few days ago, before the Armstrong Committee:

The Insurance world to-day is the greatest financial proposition in the United States; *and, as great affairs always do, it commands a higher law.*

I have read precisely the same doctrine in a University Sermon preached by an Archbishop: but there its point was confused by pietistic rhetoric; the point being that in life, which is a struggle, success has in itself something divine, by virtue of which it can be to itself a law of right and wrong; and (inferentially) that a man is relieved of the noble obligation to command himself so soon and in so far as he is rich enough or strong enough to command other people.

But why (you will ask) do I drag this doctrine into a dedication? Because, my dear Archer, I have fought against it for close upon seventeen years; because seventeen years is no small slice of a man's life—rather, so long a time that it has taught me to prize my bruises and prefer that, if anybody hereafter care to know me, he shall know me as one whose spirit took its cheer in intervals of a fight against detestable things; that—let him rank me in talent never so low beside my contemporaries who preached this doctrine—he shall at least have no excuse but to acquit me of being one with them in mind or purpose; and lastly, because in these times few things have brought me such comfort (stern comfort!) as I have derived from your criticism, so hospitable to ideas, so inflexible in judging right from wrong. As I have lived lonelier it has been better for me, and a solace beyond your guessing, to have been reminded that criticism still lives amongst us and has a Roman spirit.

A. T. QUILLER-COUCH

THE HAVEN
FOWEY

3 *April* 1906

PREFACE TO THIS EDITION

I risk—with a particular apology presently to be made to the reader—letting the following pages stand as they were written years ago for the old *Pall Mall Magazine*, on the instance of its editor, the late Lord Frederic Hamilton.

My particular apology is that the volume includes (and more or less literally repeats) some pages on Mr Bertram Dobell's *trouvaille* of an oddly disarranged imprint of Goldsmith's *The Traveller*. I took this and added it to a new edition of my *Adventures in Criticism* issued by the Cambridge University Press. It belonged to the same period, or thereabouts, of my writing. I had at the time no notion of this new edition; and no quarrel lies anywhere save between me and the reader, whom I ask to forgive.

I am aware that these pages mix up the serious with the ludicrous in a somewhat bewildering way; but hope that beneath some apparent and purposed frivolities the same gentle reader will detect that the author, from month to month writing casually, had a sense of the beauty and seriousness of life as well as of its humours.

Q.

June 1928

JANUARY

SHOULD any reader be puzzled by the title of this discursive volume, the following verses may provide him with an explanation. They were written some time ago for a lady who had requested, required, requisitioned (I forget the precise shade of the imperative) something for her album. 'We are in the last ages of the world,' wrote Charles Lamb to Barry Cornwall, 'when St Paul prophesied that women should be "headstrong, lovers of their own will, having albums. ——"'

BEATUS POSSIDENS

I can't afford a mile of sward,
  Parterres and peacocks gay;
For velvet lawns and marble fauns
  Mere authors cannot pay.

And so I went and pitched my tent
  Above a harbour fair,
Where vessels picturesquely rigg'd
  Obligingly repair.

The harbour is not mine at all:
  I make it so—what odds?
And gulls unwitting on my wall
  Serve me for garden-gods.

By ships that ride below kaleid-
  oscopically changed,
Unto my mind each day I find
  My garden rearranged.

These, madam, are my daffodils,
My pinks, my hollyhocks,
My herds upon a hundred hills,
My phloxes and my flocks.

And when some day you deign to pay
The call that's overdue,
I'll wave a landlord's easy hand
And say, 'Admire *my* view!'

Now I do not deny that a part of the content expressed
in these lines may come of resignation. In some moods,
were I to indulge them, it were pleasant to fancy myself
owner of a vast estate, champaign and woodland; able to
ride from sea to sea without stepping off my own acres, with
villeins and bondmen, privileges of sak and soke, infang-
thef, outfangthef, rents, tolls, dues, royalties, and a private
gallows for autograph-hunters. These things, however, did
not come to me by inheritance, and for a number of sufficient
reasons I have not amassed them. As for those other ambitions which fill the dreams of every healthy boy, a number
of them had become of faint importance even before a
breakdown of health seemed definitely to forbid their attain-
ment. Here at home, far from London, with restored
strength, I find myself less concerned with them than are
my friends and neighbours, yet more keenly interested than
ever in life and letters, art and politics—all that men and
women are saying and doing. Only the centre of gravity
has shifted, so to speak.

I dare say, then, that resignation may have some share
in this content; but if so 'tis an unconscious and happy one.
A man who has been writing novels for a good part of his
life should at least be able to sympathise with various kinds
of men; and, for an example or two, I can understand—

1. Why Alexander cried (if he ever did) because he had no second world to conquer.

2. Why Shakespeare, as an Englishman, wanted a coat of arms and a respectable estate in his own native country town.

3. What and how deep are the feelings beneath that *cri du cœur* of Mr Wilfrid Blunt's 'Old Squire'—

> I like the hunting of the hare
>   Better than that of the fox;
> I like the joyous morning air,
>   And the crowing of the cocks.
>
> I covet not a wider range
>   Than these dear manors give;
> I take my pleasures without change,
>   And as I lived I live.
>
> Nor has the world a better thing,
>   Though one should search it round,
> Than thus to live one's own sole king
>   Upon one's own sole ground.
>
> I like the hunting of the hare;
>   It brings me day by day
> The memory of old days as fair,
>   With dead men past away.
>
> To these as homeward still I ply,
>   And pass the churchyard gate,
> Where all are laid as I must lie,
>   I stop and raise my hat.
>
> I like the hunting of the hare:
>   New sports I hold in scorn.
> I like to be as my fathers were
>   In the days ere I was born.

4. What—to start another hare—were Goldsmith's feelings when he wrote—

> And as a hare whom hounds and horns pursue
> Pants to the place from whence at first she flew,
> I still had hopes, my long vexations past,
> Here to return—and die at home at last.

5. With what heart Don Quixote rode forth to tilt at sheep and windmills, and again with what heart in that saddest of all last chapters he bade his friends look not for this year's birds in last year's nests.

6. Why the young man went away sadly, because he had great possessions and could not see his way to bestowing them all on the poor; why, on the contrary, St Paulinus of Nola and St Francis of Assisi joyfully renounced their wealth; what Prudhon meant by saying that 'property is theft'; and what a poor Welsh clergyman of the seventeenth century by proclaiming in verse and prose that he was heir of all the world, and properties, hedges, boundaries, landmarks meant nothing to him, since all was his that his soul enjoyed; yes, and even what inspired him to pen this golden sentence—

You will never enjoy the world aright till the sea itself floweth in your veins, till you are clothed with the heavens and crowned with the stars.

*   *   *   *   *

My window, then, looks out from a small library upon a small harbour frequented by ships of all nations—British, Danish, Swedish, Norwegian, Russian, French, German, Italian, with now and then an American or a Greek—and upon a shore which I love because it is my native country. Of all views I reckon that of a harbour the most fascinating and the most easeful, for it combines perpetual change with perpetual repose. It amuses like a panorama and soothes like an opiate, and when you have realised this you will understand why so many thousands of men around this island appear to spend all their time in watching tidal water. Lest you should suspect me of taking a merely dilettante interest in the view, I must add that I am a Harbour Commissioner.

As for the house, it is a plain one; indeed, very like the house a child draws on a slate, and therefore pleasing even externally to me, who prefer the classical to any Gothic style of architecture. Why so many strangers mistake it with its modest dimensions for a hotel, I cannot tell you. I found one in the pantry the other day searching for a brandy-and-soda; another rang the dining-room bell and dumbfoundered the maid by asking what we had for lunch; and a third (a lady) cried when I broke to her that I had no sitting-room to let. We make it a rule to send out a chair whenever some unknown invader walks into the garden and prepares to make a water-colour sketch of the view.

There are some, too, whose behaviour cannot be re-conciled with the hallucination of a hotel, and they must take the house for a public institution of some kind, though of what kind I cannot guess. There was an extremely bashful youth, for instance, who roamed the garden for a while on the day after the late Duke of Cambridge's funeral, and, suddenly dashing in by the back door, wanted to know why our flag was not at half-mast. There was also a lady who called on the excuse that she had made a life-study of the Brontës, and after opining (in a guarded manner) that they came, originally, from somewhere in Yorkshire, desired to be informed how many servants we kept. I have sometimes thought of rechristening our house The Hotel of the Four Seasons, and thereby releasing its true name (The Haven) to a friend who covets it for his own.

On the whole, however, these visitors disturb the house and the view from my window very little. The upper halves of them, as they pass up and down the road, appear above my garden wall much as the shadows that passed in Plato's cave. They come, enjoy their holiday, and go, leaving the window intent upon the harbour, its own folk and its own business.

*   *   *   *   *

And now for the book, which is really not a book at all, but a chapter of one.

Last autumn I returned from a holiday to find that the publishing season had begun. This was announced by a stack of new books, review copies and presentation copies, awaiting me on my window-seat. I regarded it sourly. A holiday is the most unsettling thing in the world. At the end of it I regain the well-worn chair with a sigh of pleasure and reach for the familiar tobacco-jar, wondering how I could have been fool enough to leave them; yet somehow this lively sense of repurchased habit does not go far enough and compel me to work. Being at home is a game, and so good a game that I play at it, merely rearranging my shelves and, under pretence of dealing with arrears of correspondence, skimming the literary papers and book-catalogues found amid the pile of letters.

It happened that the first postal-wrapper to be broken enclosed a copy of *The Academy*, and *The Academy* opened with this sentence: 'Since our last issue we have received

one hundred and nineteen new books and reprints.' I looked
across to the pile on my window-seat and felt it to be
insignificant, though it interfered with my view of the
English Channel. One hundred and nineteen books in a
single week! Yet who was I to exclaim at their number?—
I, who (it appeared) had contributed one of them? With
that I remembered something which had happened just
before my holiday, and began to reflect on it, for the first
time seriously.

A publisher had asked me for a complete list of my
published works, to print it on the fly-leaf of another of
them. I sat down with the best intention and compiled it
for him, and, in honest oblivion, omitted a couple—of
books, mind you—not of pamphlets, reviews, stray articles,
short stories, or any such trifles, but of books solemnly
written for this and future ages, solemnly printed, bound,
and put into circulation at the shops and libraries. (Here,
for the due impressiveness of the tale, it becomes necessary
to tell you that their author is an indolent and painful
writer, slow at the best of times.)

Well, the discovery that I had forgotten two of my own
books at first amused and then set me thinking. 'Here you
are,' said I to myself, a 'writer of sorts; and it's no use to
pretend that you don't wish to be remembered for a while
after you are dead and done with.'

'Quite right,' the other part of me assented cheerfully.

'Well, then,' urged the inquisitor, 'this is a bad look-out.
If you had been born a Dumas—I am speaking of fecundity,
if you please, and of nothing else—if you had been born
a Dumas, and could rattle off a romance in a fortnight, you
might be excused for not keeping tally of your productions.
Pitiful, dilatory worker that you are, if *you* cannot remember

them, how can you expect the world (good Heavens!) to take the trouble?'

'I suppose it won't,' responded the other part of me, somewhat dashed; then, picking up its spirits again, 'But, anyhow, I shall know where to lay the blame.'

'On yourself?'

'Most assuredly not.'

'Where, then?'

'Why, on the publishers.'

'Ah, of course!' (This with fine irony.)

'Yes, on the publishers. Most authors do this during life, and now I begin to see that all authors do it sooner or later. For my part, I shall defer it to the future state.'

'Why?'

'Obviously because there will be no publishers thereabouts to contradict me.'

'And of what will you accuse them?'

'That they never issued my work in the form it deserved.'

'I see. Poor fellow! You have the "Edinburgh" Stevenson or something of that sort on your mind, and are filled with nasty envy.'

Upon this the other part of me fairly lost its temper.

'The "Edinburgh" Stevenson! The "Edinburgh" Ste——, and you have known me all these years! The "Edinburgh" Stevenson is a mighty handsome edition of a mighty fine writer, but I have no more desire to promenade the ages in that costume than to jump the moon. No, I am not going to break any more of the furniture. I am handing you this chair that you may seat yourself and listen.... Now! The book which I shall accuse my publishers of not having produced will be in one volume——'

'Come, come. Modesty is all very well, but don't overdo it.'

'——folio.'

'Oh!'

'——of three thousand odd pages, printed (blunt type) in double columns, and here and there in triple.'

'O—oh!'

'——with marginalia by other hands, and footnotes running sometimes to twenty thousand words, and, including above six thousand quotations from the best poets— every one, in short, which has given me pleasure of a certain quality, whether gentle or acute, at one time or another in my life.'

'! ! !'

'——the whole profusely, not to say extravagantly, adorned with woodcuts in the text, not to mention fifty or sixty full-page illustrations in copper.'

'By eminent artists?'

'Some of them by eminent artists, for the reason only that I number such among my friends; the rest by amateurs and members of my household who would help, out of mere affection, in raising this monument.'

'They would do it execrably.'

'I dare say; but that would not matter in the least. The book should be bound in leather and provided with service-able clasps, as well as with a couple of inner pockets for maps and charts. The maps should contain plenty of sea, with monsters rising from it—leviathans and sea-serpents— as they do in Speed's map of Cornwall which hangs in the hall.'

'Your book will need a window-seat to hold it.'

'Ah, now you talk intelligently! It was designed for a window-seat, and its fortunate possessor will take care to provide one. Have you any further objections?'

'Only this: that a book of such a size written by one

man (I make the objection as little personal as I can) must perforce contain many dull pages.'

'Hundreds of them; whole reams of dull pages.'

'They will be skipped.'

'They will be inserted with that object.'

'Oh!'

'It is one of the conditions of becoming a classic.'

'Who will read you?'

'Look here. Do you remember the story of that old fellow—a Dutchman, I think—who took a fancy to be buried in the church porch of his native town, that he might hear the feet of the townsfolk, generation after generation, passing over his head to divine service?'

'Well?'

'Well. I shall stand on my shelf, bound in good leather, between (say) *Bayle's Dictionary* and *Sibrandus Schnafnaburgensis, his Delectable Treatise;* and if some day, when the master of the house has been coaxed by his womenfolk to take a holiday, and they descend upon the books, which he (the humbug) never reads, belabour and bang the dust out of them and flap them with dusters, and all with that vindictiveness which is the good housewife's right attitude towards literature——'

'Had you not better draw breath?'

'Thank you. I will; for the end of the protasis lies yet some way off. If, I say, some child of the family, having chosen me out of the heap as a capital fellow for a boobytrap, shall open me by hazard and, attracted by the pictures, lug me off to the window-seat, why then God bless the child! I shall come to my own. He will not understand much at the time, but he will remember me with affection, and in due course he will give me to his daughter among her wedding presents (much to her annoyance, but the

bridegroom will soothe her). This will happen through
several generations until I find myself an heirloom....'

'You begin to assume that by this time you will be
valuable. Also permit me to remark that you have slipped
into the present indicative.'

'As for the present indicative, I think you began it.'

'No.'

'Yes. But it doesn't matter. I begin precisely at
the right moment to assume a value which will be
attached to me, not for my own sake, but on account
of dear grandpapa's book-plate and autograph on the
fly-leaf. (He was the humbug who never read me—
a literary person; he acquired me as a "review copy,"
and only forbore to dispose of me because at the current
railway rates I should not have fetched the cost of
carriage.)'

'Why talk of hindrances to publishing such a book, when
you know full well it will never be written?'

'I thought you would be driven to some such stupid
knock-down argument. Whether or not the book will ever
be finished is a question that lies on the knees of the gods.
I am writing at it every day. And just such a book was
written once and even published; as I discovered the other
day in an essay by Mr Austin Dobson. The author, I grant
you, was a Dutchman (Mr Dobson calls him "Vader
Cats,") and the book contains everything from a long
didactic poem on Marriage (I also have written a long
didactic poem on Marriage) to a page on Children's
Games. (My book shall have a chapter on Children's
Games, with their proper tunes.) As for poetry—poetry,
says Mr Dobson, with our Dutch poet is not by any means
a trickling rill from Helicon: "it is an inundation *à la mode
du pays,* a flood in a flat land, covering everything far and

near with its sluggish waters." As for the illustrations, listen to this for the kind of thing I demand:

Perhaps the most interesting of these is to be found in the large head-piece to the above-mentioned Children's Games, the background of which exhibits the great square of Middleburgh, with its old Gothic houses and central clump of trees. This is, moreover, as delightful a picture as any in the gallery. Down the middle of the foreground, which is filled by a crowd of figures, advances a regiment of little Dutchmen, marching to drum and fife, and led by a fire-eating captain of fifteen. Around this central group are dispersed knots of children playing leap-frog, flying kites, blowing bubbles, whipping tops, walking on stilts, skipping, and the like. In one corner the children are busy with blind man's buff; in the other the girls, with their stiff head-dresses and vandyked aprons, are occupied with their dolls. Under the pump some seventeenth-century equivalent for chuck-farthing seems to be going on vigorously; and, not to be behind-hand in the fun, two little fellows in the distance are standing upon their heads. The whole composition is full of life and movement, and—so conservative is childhood—might, but for the costume and scene, represent a playground of to-day.'

'Such are the pictures which shall emerge, like islands, among my dull pages. And there shall be other pages, to be found for the looking. . . . I must make another call upon your memory, my friend, and refer it to a story of Hans Andersen's which fascinated the pair of us in childhood, when we were not really a pair but inseparables, and before you had grown wise; the story of the Student and the Goblin who lodged at the Butterman's. The Student, at the expense of his dinner, had rescued a book from the butter-tub and taken it off to his garret, and that night the Goblin, overcome by curiosity, peeped through the keyhole, and lo!

the garret was full of light. Forth and up from the book
shot a beam of light, which grew into the trunk of a mighty
tree, and threw out branches over the bowed head of the
Student; and every leaf was fresh, and every flower a face,
and every fruit a star, and music sang in the branches.
Well, there shall be even such pages in my book.'

'Excuse me,' said I, 'but, knowing your indolence, I
begin to tire of the future indicative, which (allow me to
repeat) you first employed in this discussion.'

'I did not,' said the other part of me stoutly. 'And if
I did, 'tis a trick of the trade. You of all people ought to
know that I write romances.'

* * * * *

I do not at all demur to having the value of my books
enhanced by the contributions of others—by dear grandpapa's autograph on the fly-leaf, for example. But it annoys
me to be blamed for other folks' opinions.

The other day a visitor called and discoursed with me
during the greater part of a wet afternoon. He had come
for an interview—'dreadful trade,' as Edgar said of
samphire-gathering—and I wondered, as he took his departure, what on earth he would find to write about: for
I love to smoke and listen to other men's opinions, and can
boast with Montaigne that during these invasive times my
door has stood open to all comers. He was a good fellow,
too; having brains and using them: and I made him an
admirable listener.

It amused me, some while after, to read the interview
and learn that *I* had done the talking and uttered a number
of trenchant sayings upon female novelists. But the amusement changed to dismay when the ladies began to retort.
For No. 1 started with an airy restatement of what I had

never said, and No. 2 (who had missed to read the interview) misinterpreted No. 1's paraphrase; and by these and
other processes within a week my digestive silence had
passed through a dozen removes, and was incurring the
just execration of a whole sex. I began to see that my old
college motto—*Quod tacitum velis nemini dixeris*—which
had always seemed to me to err, if at all, on the side of
excess, fell short of adequacy to these strenuous times.

I have not kept the letters; but a friend of mine, Mr
Algernon Dexter, has summarised a very similar experience
and cast it into chapters, which he allows me to print here.
He heads them—

HUNTING THE DRAG

CHAPTER I

Scene: *The chastely-furnished writing-room of* Mr Algernon
Dexter, *a well-known male novelist. Bust of* Pallas *over
practicable door L.U.E. Books adorn the walls, interspersed with
portraits of female relatives.* Mr Dexter *discovered with* Interviewer. Mr D., *poker in hand, is bending over the fire, above
which runs the legend, carved in Roman letters across the
mantelpiece,* ' Ne fodias ignem gladio.'

INTERVIEWER (*pulling out his watch*): Dear me! Only five
minutes to catch my train! And I had several other questions
to ask. I suppose, now, it's too late to discuss the Higher
Education of Women?

Mr D. (*smiling*): Well, I think there's hardly time. It will
take you a good four minutes to get to the station.

INTERVIEWER: And I must get my typewriter out of the
cloakroom. Good-day, then, Mr Dexter! (*They shake hands
and part with mutual esteem.*)

CHAPTER II
Extract from The Daily Post
MONDAY TALKS WITH OUR NOVELISTS.—No. MCVI.
Mr ALGERNON DEXTER

'And now, Mr Dexter,' said I, 'what is your opinion of the Higher Education of Women?'

The novelist stroked his bronze beard. 'That's a large order, eh? Isn't it rather late in the day to discuss Women's Education?' And with a humorous gesture of despair he dropped the poker.

CHAPTER III
Tuesday's Letter

SIR,—In your issue of to-day I read with interest an account of an interview with Mr Dexter, the popular novelist, and I observe that gentleman thinks it 'rather late in the day' to discuss the Higher Education of Women. One can only be amused at this flippant dismissal of a subject dear to the hearts of many of us; a movement consecrated by the life-energies—I had almost said the life-blood—of a Gladstone, a Sidgwick, a Fitch, and a Platt-Culpepper. Does Mr Dexter really imagine that he can look down on such names as these? Or are we to conclude that the recent successes of 'educated' women in fiction have got on his nerves? To suggest professional jealousy would be going too far, no doubt.

Yours faithfully,

'HIGH SCHOOL.'

CHAPTER IV
Wednesday's Letters

(1) SIR,—I, too, was disgusted with Mr Algernon Dexter's cheap sneer at women's education. He has, it seems, 'no opinion' of it. Allow me to point out that, whatever his opinion may be, Women's Education has come to stay. The

time is past when Woman could be relegated to the kitchen
or the nursery, and told, in the words of the poet Byron, that
these constituted her 'whole existence.' Not so; and if Mr Dexter
is inclined to doubt it let him read the works of George Eliot
(Mrs J. W. Cross) or Marian Crawford. They will open his
eyes to the task he has undertaken.

I am, Sir, yours, etc.,

'AUDI ALTERAM PARTEM.'

(2) SIR,—Mr Algernon Dexter thinks woman's education
'a large order'—not a very elegant expression, let me say,
en passant, for one who aspires to be known as a 'stylist.'
Still a large order it is, and one that as an imperial race we
shall be forced to envisage. If our children are to be started
in life as fit citizens of this empire, with a grasp on its manifold
and far-reaching complexities of interest, and unless the
Germans are to beat us, we must provide them with educated
mothers. 'The child is father of the man,' but the mother has,
me judice, no less influence upon his subsequent career. And
this is not to be done by putting back the hands of the clock,
or setting them to make pies and samplers, but by raising
them to mutually co-operate and further what has been aptly
termed 'The White Man's Burden.' Such, at any rate, though
I may not live to see it, is the conviction of

'A MUS. DOC. OF FORTY YEARS' STANDING.'

(3) SIR,—'High School' has done a public service. A popular
novelist may be licensed to draw on his imagination; but
hitting below the belt is another thing, whoever wears it.
Mr Dexter's disdainful treatment of that eminent educationist,
Mr Platt-Culpepper—who is in his grave and therefore unable
to reply (so like a man!)—can be called nothing less. I hope
it will receive the silent contempt it deserves.

Yours indignantly,

'MERE WOMAN.'

CHAPTER V

Thursday's Letters

(1) SIR,—Your correspondents, with whose indignation I am in sympathy, have to me most unaccountably overlooked the real gravamen of Mr Dexter's offence. Unlike them, I have read several of that gentleman's brochures, and can assure you that he once posed as the advocate of unbounded license for women in Higher Education, if not in other directions. This *volte face* (I happen to know) will come as a severe disappointment to many; for we had quite counted him one of us.

> We that had loved him so, followed him, honoured him,
>   Lived in his mild and magnificent eye,

shall have, it seems, to 'record one lost soul more, one more devil's triumph,' etc. I subscribe myself, sir, more in sorrow than in anger,

PERCY FLADD,

President, H.W.E.L. (Hoxton Women's Emancipation League).

(2) SIR,—Why all this beating about the bush? The matter in dispute between Mr Dexter and his critics was summed up long ago by Scotia's premier poet (I refer to Robert Burns) in the lines—

> To make a happy fireside clime
>   To weans and wife,
> That's the true pathos and sublime
>   Of human life,

and *vice versa*. Your correspondents are too hasty in condemning Mr Dexter. He may have expressed himself awkwardly; but, as I understood him, he never asserted that education necessarily unsexed a woman, if kept within limits. 'A man's a man for a' that'; then why not a woman? At least, so says

'AULD REEKIE.'

(3) SIR,—Let Mr Dexter stick to his guns. He is not the first who has found the New Woman an unmitigated nuisance, and I respect him for saying so in no measured terms. Let

women, if they want husbands, cease to write oratorios and other things in which man is, by his very constitution, *facile princeps*, and let her cultivate that desideratum in which she excels—a cosy home and a bright smile to greet him on the doorstep when he returns from a tiring day in the City. Until that is done I, for one, shall remain

'UNMARRIED.'

P.S.—Could a woman have composed Shakespeare?

(4) SIR,—I had no intention of mixing in this correspondence, and publicity is naturally distasteful to me. Nor do I hold any brief for the Higher Education of Women; but when I see writer after writer—apparently of my own sex—taking refuge in what has been called the 'base shelter of anonymity,' I feel constrained to sign myself,

Yours faithfully,

(Mrs) RACHEL RAMSBOTHAM.

CHAPTER VI

Friday's Letters

(1) SIR,—After reading 'Unmarried's' letter, one can hardly wonder that he is so. He asks if any woman could have written Shakespeare, and insinuates that she would be better occupied in meeting him ('Unmarried') on the doorstep 'with a bright smile.' As to that, there may be two opinions. Everyone to his taste, but for my part, if his insufferable male conceit will allow him to believe it—I would rather have written Shakespeare a hundred times over, and I am not alone in this view. Such men as Mr Dexter and 'Unmarried' are the cause why half of us women prefer to remain single; the former may deny it, poker in hand, but murder will out. In conclusion, let me add that I have never written an oratorio in my life, though I sometimes attend them.

Yours, etc.,

'MERE WOMAN.'

(2) SIR,—Allow me to impale Mr Dexter on the horns of a dilemma. Either it is too late in the day to discuss woman's education, or it is not. If the latter, why did he say it is? And if the former, why did he begin discussing it? That is how it strikes

'B.A. (Lond.).'

(3) SIR,—*Re* this woman's education discussion: I write to inquire if there is any law of the land which can hinder a woman from composing Shakespeare if she wants to?

Yours truly,

'INTERESTED.'

(4) SIR,—Allusion has been made in this correspondence (I think by Mr Dexter) to the grave of that eminent educationist, the late Platt-Culpepper, which is situate in the Highgate Cemetery. My interest being awakened, I made a pilgrimage to it the other day, and was shocked by its neglected condition. The coping has been badly cemented, and a crack extends from the upper right-hand corner to the base of the plinth, right across the inscription. Doubtless a few shillings would repair the damage; but may I suggest, Sir, that some worthier memorial is due to this pioneer of woman's higher activities? I have thought of a plain obelisk on Shakespeare's Cliff, a locality of which he was ever fond; or a small and inconspicuous lighthouse might, without complicating the navigation of this part of the Channel, serve to remind Englishmen of one who diffused so much light during his all too brief career. Choice, however, would depend on the funds available, and might be left to an influential committee. Meanwhile, could you not open a subscription list for the purpose? I enclose stamps for 2s., with my card, and prefer to remain, for the present,

'HAUD IMMEMOR.'

CHAPTER VII

Saturday's Letters

(1) SIR,—H. Immemor's suggestion clears the air, and should persuade Mr Dexter and his reactionary friends to think twice before again inaugurating a crusade which can only recoil upon their own heads. I enclose 5s., if only as a protest against this un-English 'hitting below the belt,' and am,

> Yours, etc.,
>
> 'PRACTICAL.'

(2) SIR,—It is only occasionally that I get a glimpse of your invaluable paper, and (perhaps, fortunately) missed the issues containing Mr Dexter's diatribes anent woman. But what astounds me is their cynical audacity. Your correspondents, though not in accord as to the name of the victim (can it be more than one?), agree that, after encouraging her to unbridled license, Mr Dexter turned round and attacked her with a poker—whether above or below the belt is surely immaterial. 'Tis true, 'tis pity, and pity 'tis 'tis true; but not once or twice, I fear me, in 'our fair island-story' has a similar thing occurred. The unique (I hope) feature in this case is the man Dexter's open boast that the incident is closed, and it is now 'too late in the day' to reopen it. 'Too late,' indeed! There is an American poem describing how a young woman was raking hay, and an elderly judge came by, and wasn't in a position to marry her, though he wanted to; and the whole winds up by saying that 'too late' are the saddest words in the language—especially, I would add, in this connection. But, alaş! that men's memories should be so short! is the reflection of

> 'A MOTHER OF SEVEN.'

[This correspondence is now closed, unless Mr Dexter should wish to reply to his numerous critics. We do not propose to open a subscription list, at any rate for the present.—Ed. *Daily Post.*]

FEBRUARY

'O THAT I were lying under the olives!'—if I may
echo the burthen of a beautiful little poem by
Mrs Margaret L. Woods. I have not yet consulted Zadkiel:
but if I may argue from past experience of February—'fill-
dyke'—in a week or so my window here will be alternately
crusted with Channel spray and washed clean by lashing
south-westerly showers; and a wave will arch itself over
my garden wall and spoil a promising bed of violets; and
I shall grow weary of oilskins, and weary of hauling the
long-line with icily-cold hands and finding no fish. February
—*Pisces?* The fish, before February comes, have left the
coast for the warmer deeps, and the zodiac is all wrong.
Down here in the Duchy many believe in Mr Zadkiel
and Old Moore. I suppose the dreamy Celt pays a natural
homage to a fellow-mortal who knows how to make up
his mind for twelve months ahead. All the woman in his
nature surrenders to this business-like decisiveness. 'O man!'
—the exhortation is Mr George Meredith's, or would be
if I could remember it precisely—'O man, amorously
inclining, before all things be *positive!*' I have sometimes,
while turning the pages of Mrs Beeton's admirable cookery
book, caught myself envying Mr Beeton. I wonder if her
sisters envy Mrs Zadkiel. She, dear lady, no doubt feels
that, if it be not in mortals to command the weather her
husband prophesies for August, yet he does better—he
deserves it. And, after all, a prophecy in some measure
depends for its success on the mind which receives it. Back

in the forties—I quote from a small privately-printed volume
by Sir Richard Tangye—when the potato blight first appeared in England, an old farmer in the Duchy found this
warning in his favourite almanack, at the head of the page
for August:

> And potentates shall tremble and quail.

Now, 'to quail' in Cornwall still carries its old meaning,
'to shrink,' 'to wither.' The farmer dug his potatoes with
all speed, and next year the almanack was richer by a score
of subscribers.

Zadkiel or no Zadkiel, I will suspire, and risk it, 'O that
I were lying under the olives!' 'O to be out of England
now that February's here!'—for indeed this is the time to
take the South express and be quit of fogs, and loaf and
invite your soul upon the Mediterranean shore before the
carnivals and regattas sweep it like a mistral. Nor need
you be an invalid to taste those joys on which Stevenson
dilates in that famous little essay in *'Virginibus Puerisque'*
(or, as the young American lady preferred to call it,
'Virginis Pueribusque'):

> Or perhaps he may see a group of washer-women relieved,
> on a spit of shingle, against the blue sea, or a meeting of flower-
> gatherers in the tempered daylight of an olive-garden; and
> something significant or monumental in the grouping, some-
> thing in the harmony of faint colour that is always characteristic
> of the dress of these Southern women, will come home to him
> unexpectedly, and awake in him that satisfaction with which
> we tell ourselves that we are richer by one more beautiful
> experience.... And then, there is no end to the infinite variety
> of the olive-yards themselves. Even the colour is indeterminate,
> and continually shifting: now you would say it was green,
> now grey, now blue; now tree stands above tree, like 'cloud

on cloud,' massed in filmy indistinctness; and now, at the
wind's will, the whole sea of foliage is shaken and broken up
with little momentary silverings and shadows.

English poets, too, have been at their best on the Riviera:
from Cette, where Matthew Arnold painted one of the
most brilliant little landscapes in our literature, along to
Genoa, where Tennyson visited and

> Loved that hall, tho' white and cold,
> Those nichèd shapes of noble mould,
>   A princely people's awful princes,
> The grave, severe Genovese of old.

[I suppose, by the way, that every one who has taken the
trouble to compare the stanza of 'The Daisy' with that
of the invitation 'To the Rev. F. D. Maurice,' which immediately follows, will have noted the pretty rhythmical
difference made by the introduction of the double dactyl
in the closing line of the latter; the difference between

> Of ólive, áloe, and maíze, and víne,

and

> Máking the líttle one leáp for jóy.]

But let Mrs Woods resume the strain:

> O that I were listening under the olives!
> So should I hear behind in the woodland
> The peasants talking. Either a woman,
> A wrinkled grandame, stands in the sunshine,
> Stirs the brown soil in an acre of violets—
> Large odorous violets—and answers slowly
> A child's swift babble; or else at noon
> The labourers come. They rest in the shadow,
> Eating their dinner of herbs, and are merry.
> Soft speech Provençal under the olives!
> Like a queen's raiment from days long perished,

Breathing aromas of old unremembered
Perfumes, and shining in dust-covered palaces
With sudden hints of forgotten splendour—
So on the lips of the peasant his language,
His only now, the tongue of the peasant.

Say what you will, there is a dignity about these Latin
races, even in their trivial everyday movements. They
suggest to me, as those lines of Homer suggested to
Mr Pater's Marius, thoughts which almost seem to be
memories of a time when all the world was poetic:

Οἱ δ' ὅτε δὴ λιμένος πολυβενθέος ἐντὸς ἵκοντο
'Ιστία μὲν στεῖλαντο, θέσαν δ' ἐν νηὶ μελαίνῃ. . .
'Εκ δὲ καὶ αὐτοὶ βαῖνον ἐπὶ ῥηγμῖνι θαλάσσης.

'And how poetic,' says Pater, 'the simple incident seemed,
told just thus! Homer was always telling things after this
manner. And one might think there had been no effort in
it: that here was but the almost mechanical transcript of a
time naturally, intrinsically poetic, a time in which one
could hardly have spoken at all without ideal effect, or the
sailors pulled down their boat without making a picture in
"the great style" against a sky charged with marvels.'

One evening in last February a company of Provençal
singers, pipers, and tambour players came to an hotel in
Cannes, and entertained us. They were followed next
evening by a troupe of German-Swiss jödelers; and oh, the
difference to me—and, for that matter, to all of us! It was
just the difference between passion and silly sentiment—
silly and rather vulgar sentiment. The merry Swiss boys
whooped, and smacked their legs, and twirled their merry
Swiss girls about, until vengeance overtook them—a vengeance so complete, so surprising, that I can hardly now
believe what my own eyes saw and my own ears heard. One

of the merry Swiss girls sang a love-ditty with a jödeling
refrain, which was supposed to be echoed back by her
lover afar in the mountains. To produce this pleasing
illusion, one of the merry Swiss boys ascended the staircase,
and hid himself deep in the corridors of the hotel. All went
well up to the last verse. Promptly and truly the swain
echoed his sweetheart's call; softly it floated down to us—
down from the imaginary pasture and across the imaginary
valley. But as the maiden challenged for the last time, as
her voice lingered on the last note of the last verse.... There
hung a Swiss cuckoo-clock in the porter's office, and at that
very instant the mechanical bird lifted its voice, and nine
times answered 'Cuckoo' *on the exact note!* 'Cuckoo,
Cuckoo, O word of fear!' I have known coincidences,
but never one so triumphantly complete. The jaw of the
Swiss maiden dropped an inch; and, as well as I remember,
silence held the company for five seconds before we recovered ourselves and burst into inextinguishable laughter.

The one complaint I have to make of the Mediterranean
is that it does not in the least resemble a real sea; and I
daresay that nobody who has lived by a real sea will ever
be thoroughly content with it. Beautiful—oh, beautiful,
of course, whether one looks across from Costebelle to the
lighthouse on Porquerolles and the warships in Hyères
Bay; or climbs by the Calvary to the lighthouse of la
Garoupe, and sees on the one side Antibes, on the other
the Isles de Lérins; or scans the entrance of Toulon
Harbour; or counts the tiers of shipping alongside the quays
at Genoa! But somehow the Mediterranean has neither
flavour nor sparkle, nor even any proper smell. The sea
by Biarritz is champagne to it. But hear how Hugo draws
the contrast in time of storm:

Ce n'étaient pas les larges lames de l'Océan qui vont devant elles et qui se déroulent royalement dans l'immensité; c'étaient des houles courtes, brusques, furieuses. L'Océan est à son aise, il tourne autour du monde; la Méditerranée est dans un vase et le vent la secoue, c'est ce qui lui donne cette vague haletante, brève et trapue. Le flot se ramasse et lutte. Il a autant de colère que le flot de l'Océan et moins d'espace.

Also, barring the sardine and anchovy, I must confess that the fish of the Mediterranean are what, in the Duchy, we should call 'poor trade.' I don't wish to disparage the Bouillabaisse, which is a dish for heroes, and deserves all the heroic praises sung of it:

> This Bouillabaisse a noble dish is—
>   A sort of soup, or broth, or brew,
> Or hotchpotch of all sorts of fishes,
>   That Greenwich never could outdo;
> Green herbs, red peppers, mussels, saffron,
>   Soles, onions, garlic, roach and dace:
> All these you eat at Terré's tavern,
>   In that one dish of Bouillabaisse.

To be precise, you take a langouste, three rascas (an edible but second-rate fish), a slice of conger, a fine 'chapon,' or red rascas, and one or two 'poissons blancs' (our grey mullet, I take it, would be an equivalent). You take a cooking-pot and put your langouste in it, together with four spoonfuls of olive-oil, an onion and a couple of tomatoes, and boil away until he turns red. You then take off the pot and add your fish, green herbs, four cloves of garlic, and a pinch of saffron, with salt and red pepper. Pour in water to cover the surface of the fish, and cook for twenty minutes over a fast fire. Then take a soup-plate, lay some slices of bread in it, and pour the bouillon over the bread. Serve the fish separately. Possibly you incline to add, in

the immortal words of the late Mr Lear, 'Serve up in a
clean dish, and throw the whole out of window as fast as
possible.' You would make a great mistake. The marvel
to me is that no missionary has acclimatised this wonderful
dish upon our coasts, where we have far better fish for
compounding it—red mullet, for instance, in place of the
rascas; and whiting, or even pollack or grey mullet, in
place of the 'poissons blancs.' For the langouste, a baby
lobster might serve; and the saffron flavour would be no
severe trial to us in the Duchy, who are brought up (so
to say) upon saffron cake. As for Thackeray's 'dace,' I disbelieve in it. No one would add a dace (which for table
purposes has been likened to an old stocking full of mud
and pins: or was that a tench?) except to make a rhyme.
Even Walton, who gives instructions for cooking a
chavender or chub, is discreetly silent on the cooking of a
dace, though he tells us how to catch him. 'Serve up in a
clean dish,' he might have added, 'and throw him out of
window as fast as possible.'

'O that I were lying under the olives!' And O that to
olive orchards (not contiguous) I could convey the newspaper men who are almost invariably responsible when a
shadow of distrust or suspicion falls between us Englishmen
and the race which owns and tills these orchards. 'The
printing-press,' says Mr Barrie, 'is either the greatest
blessing or the greatest curse of modern times, one sometimes forgets which.' I verily believe that if English newspaper editors would nobly resolve to hold their peace on
French politics, say for two years, France and England
would 'make friends' as easily as Frenchmen and Englishmen 'make friends' to-day[1]. One hears talk of the behaviour

[1] This was written some time before the *entente cordiale*.

of the English abroad. But I am convinced that at least
one-half of their bad manners may be referred to their
education upon this newspaper nonsense, or to the certainty
that no complaint they may make upon foreign short-
comings is too silly or too ill-bred to be printed in an
English newspaper. Here is an example. I suppress the
name of the writer—a lady—in the devout hope that she
has repented before this. The letter is headed—

THE AMENITIES OF RAILWAY TRAVELLING
IN FRANCE

SIR,—As your newspaper is read in France, may I in your
columns call attention to what I witnessed yesterday? I left
Dinard by the 3.33 p.m. train *en route* for Guingamp, having
to change carriages at Lamballe. An instant before the train
moved off from the station, a dying man belonging to the
poorest class was thrust into our second-class carriage and the
door slammed to. The poor creature, apparently dying of some
wasting disease, was absolutely on the point of death, and his
ghastly appearance naturally alarmed a little girl in the carriage.
At the next station I got down with my companion and
changed into a first-class compartment, paying the difference.
On remonstrating with the guard (*sic*), he admitted that a
railway carriage ought not to be turned into an hospital, but
added, 'We have no rules to prevent it.'

I ask, sir, is it decent or human, especially at such a time,
to thrust dying persons in the last stage of poverty into a
second-class carriage full of ladies and children?

There's a pretty charity for you! 'A dying man belonging
to the *poorest class*.'—'*Our* second-class carriage'—here's
richness! as Mr Squeers observed. Here's sweetness and
light! But England has no monopoly of such manners.
There was a poor little Cingalese girl in the train by which

I travelled homeward last February from Genoa and
through the Mont Cenis. And there were also three Englishmen and a Frenchman—the last apparently (as Browning
put it) a person of importance in his day, for he had a bit
of red ribbon in his buttonhole and a valet at his heels.
At one of the small stations near the tunnel our train halted
for several minutes; and while the little Cingalese leaned
out and gazed at the unfamiliar snows—a pathetic figure,
if ever there was one—the three Englishmen and the
Frenchman gathered under the carriage door and stared
up at her just as if she were a show. There was no nonsense
about the performance—no false delicacy: it was good,
steady, eye-to-eye staring. After three minutes of it, the
Frenchman asked deliberately, 'Where do you come
from?' in a careless, level tone, which did not even convey
that he was interested in knowing. And because the child
didn't understand, the three Englishmen laughed. Altogether
it was an unpleasing but instructive little episode.

No: nastiness has no particular nationality: and you will
find a great deal of it, of all nationalities, on the frontier
between France and Italy. I do not see that Monte Carlo
provides much cause for indignation, beyond the *tir aux
pigeons*, which is quite abominable. I have timed it for
twenty-five minutes, and it averaged two birds a minute—
fifty birds. Of these one escaped, one fluttered on to the roof
of the railway station and died there slowly, under my eyes.
The rest were killed within the enclosure, some by the
first barrel, some by the second; or if they still lingered,
were retrieved and mouthed by a well-trained butcher dog,
of no recognisable breed. Sometimes, after receiving its
wound, a bird would walk about for a second or two,
apparently unhurt; then suddenly stagger and topple over.

Sometimes, as the trap opened, a bird would stand dazed.
Then a ball was trundled at it to compel it to rise. Grey
breast feathers strewed the whole enclosure, in places quite
thickly, like a carpet. As for the crowd at the tables inside
the Casino, it was largely Semitic. On the road between
Monte Carlo and Monaco, as Browning says—

> It was noses, noses all the way.

Also it smelt distressingly: but that perhaps was its mis-
fortune rather than its fault. It did not seem very happy;
nor was it composed of people who looked as if they might
have attained to distinction, or even to ordinary usefulness,
by following any other pursuit. On the whole, one felt
that it might as well be gathered here as anywhere else.

'O that I were lying under the olives!' But since my
own garden must content me this year, let me conclude
with a decent letter of thanks to the friend who sent me,
from Devonshire, a box of violet roots that await the spring in
a corner which even the waves of the equinox cannot reach:

TO A FRIEND WHO SENT ME
A BOX OF VIOLETS

> Nay, more than violets
> These thoughts of thine, friend!
> Rather thy reedy brook
> —Taw's tributary—
> At midnight murmuring,
> Descried them, the delicate,
> The dark-eyed goddesses,
> There by his cressy beds
> Dissolved and dreaming
> Dreams that distilled in a dewdrop
> All the purple of night,
> All the shine of a planet.

Whereat he whispered;
And they arising
—Of day's forget-me-nots
 The duskier sisters—
Descended, relinquished
The orchard, the trout-pool,
The Druid circles,
Sheepfolds of Dartmoor,
Granite and sandstone,
Torridge and Tamar;
By Roughtor, by Dozmaré,
Down the vale of the Fowey
Moving in silence,
Brushing the nightshade
By bridges Cyclopean,
By Glynn, Lanhydrock,
Restormel, Lostwithiel,
Dark woodland, dim water,
    dreaming town—
Down the vale of the Fowey,
Each in her exile
Musing the message—
Message illumined by love
As a starlit sorrow—
Passed, as the shadow of Ruth
From the land of the Moabite.
So they came—
Valley-born, valley-nurtured—
Came to the tideway,
The jetties, the anchorage,
The salt wind piping,
Snoring in equinox,
By ships at anchor,
By quays tormented,
Storm-bitten streets;

Came to the Haven
Crying, 'Ah, shelter us,
The strayed ambassadors!
Lost legation of love
On a comfortless coast!'

Nay, but a little sleep,
A little folding
Of petals to the lull
Of quiet rainfalls,—
Here in my garden,
In angle sheltered
From north and east wind—
Softly shall recreate
The courage of charity,
Henceforth not to me only
Breathing the message.

Clean-breath'd Sirens!
Henceforth the mariner,
Here on the tideway
Dragging, foul of keel,
Long-strayed but fortunate,
Out of the fogs, the vast
Atlantic solitudes,
Shall, by the hawser-pin
Waiting the signal—
'Leave-go-anchor!'
Scent the familiar
Fragrance of home;
So in a long breath
Bless us unknowingly:
Bless them, the violets,
Bless me, the gardener,
Bless thee, the giver.

*   *   *   *

My business (I remind myself) behind the window is not to scribble verses: my business, or a part of it, is to criticise poetry, which involves reading poetry. But why should anyone read poetry in these days?

Well, one answer is that nobody does.

I look around my shelves and, brushing this answer aside as flippant, change the form of my question. Why do we read poetry? What do we find that it does for us? We take to it (I presume) some natural need, and it answers that need. But what is the need? And how does poetry answer it?

Clearly it is not a need of knowledge, or of what we usually understand by knowledge. We do not go to a poem as we go to a work on Chemistry or Physics, to add to our knowledge of the world about us. For example, Keats' glorious lines to the Nightingale—

> Thou wast not born for death, immortal bird...

are unchallengeable poetry; but they add nothing to our stock of information. Indeed, as Mr Bridges pointed out the other day, the information they contain is mostly in-accurate or fanciful. Man is, as a matter of fact, quite as immortal as a nightingale in every sense but that of same-ness. And as for the

> Magic casements opening on the foam
> Of perilous seas, in faëry lands forlorn,

Science tells us that no such things exist in this or any other ascertained world. So, when Tennyson tells us that birds in the high Hall garden were crying, 'Maud, Maud, Maud,' or that

> There has fallen a splendid tear
> From the passion-flower at the gate:
> She is coming, my dove, my dear;

> She is coming, my life, my fate;
> The red rose cries, 'She is near, she is near';
> And the white rose weeps, 'She is late'...

the poetry is unchallengeable, but the information by scientific standards of truth is demonstrably false, and even absurd. On the other hand (see Coleridge's *Biographia Literaria*, c. xiv.), the famous lines—

> Thirty days hath September,
> April, June, and November,...

though packed with trustworthy information, are quite as demonstrably unpoetical. The famous senior wrangler who returned a borrowed volume of *Paradise Lost* with the remark that he did not see what it proved, was right—so far as he went. And conversely (as he would have said) no sensible man would think to improve Newton's *Principia* and Darwin's *Origin of Species* by casting them into blank verse; or Euclid's *Elements* by writing them out in ballad metre—

> The King sits in Dunfermline toun,
> Drinking the blude-red wine:
> 'O wha will rear me an equilateral triangle
> Upon a given straight line?'

We may be sure that Poetry does not aim to do what Science, with other methods, can do much better. What craving, then, does it answer? And if the craving be for knowledge of a kind, then of what kind?

The question is serious. We agree—at least I assume this—that men have souls as well as intellects; that above and beyond the life we know and can describe and reduce to laws and formulas there exists a spiritual life of which our intellect is unable to render account. We have (it is believed) affinity with this spiritual world, and we hold it by virtue of something spiritual within us, which we call the soul. You may disbelieve in this spiritual region and remain, I dare say, an estimable citizen; but I cannot see what business you have with Poetry, or what satisfaction you draw from it. Nay, Poetry demands that you believe something further; which is, that in this spiritual region resides and is laid up that eternal scheme of things, that universal *order*, of which the phenomena of this world are but fragments, if indeed they are not mere shadows.

A hard matter to believe, no doubt! We see this world so clearly; the spiritual world so dimly, so rarely, if at all! We may fortify ourselves with the reminder (to be found in Blanco White's famous sonnet) that the first man who lived on earth had to wait for the darkness before he saw the stars and guessed that the Universe extended beyond this earth—

> Who could have thought such darkness lay conceal'd
> Within thy beams, O Sun! or who could find,
> Whilst fly and leaf and insect stood reveal'd,
> That to such countless orbs thou mad'st us blind?

He may, or may not, believe that the same duty governs his infinitesimal activity and the motions of the heavenly bodies—

> Awake, my soul, and *with the sun*
> Thy daily stage of duty run...

—that his duty is one with that of which Wordsworth sang—

> Thou dost preserve the stars from wrong;
> And the most ancient heavens, through thee, are
>   fresh and strong.

But in a higher order of some sort, and his duty of con-
forming with it, he does not seem able to avoid believing.

This, then, is the need which Poetry answers. It offers
to bring men knowledge of this universal order, and to help
them in rectifying and adjusting their lives to it. It is for
gleams of this spiritual country that the poets watch—

The gleam,
The light that never was on sea or land....

'I am Merlin,' sang Tennyson, its life-long watcher, in
his old age—

I am Merlin,
And I am dying;
I am Merlin,
Who follow the gleam.

They do not claim to see it always. It appears to them at
rare and happy intervals, as the Vision of the Grail to the
Knights of the Round Table. 'Poetry,' said Shelley, 'is the
record of the best and happiest moments of the happiest
and best minds.'

*   *   *   *   *   *

If this be the need, how have our poets been answering
it of late years? How, for instance, did they answer it
during the South African War, when (according to our
newspapers) there was plenty of patriotic emotion available
to inspire the great organ of national song? Well, let us
kick up what dust we will over 'Imperial ideals,' we must
admit, at least, that these ideals are not yet 'accepted of
song': they have not inspired poetry in any way adequate
to the nobility claimed for them. Mr Swinburne and
Mr Henley saluted the Boer War in verse of much
truculence, but no quality; and when Mr Swinburne and

Mr Henley lacked quality one began to inquire into causes. Mr Kipling's Absent-minded Beggars, Muddied Oafs, Goths and Huns, invited one to consider why he should so often be first-rate when neglecting or giving the lie to his pet political doctrines, and invariably below form when enforcing them. For the rest, the Warden of Glenalmond bubbled and squeaked, and Mr Alfred Austin, like the man at the piano, kept on doing his best. It all came to nothing: as poetry it never began to be more than null. Mr Hardy wrote a few mournfully memorable lines on the seamy side of war. Mr Owen Seaman (who may pass for our contemporary Aristophanes) was smart and witty at the expense of those whose philosophy goes a little deeper than surface-polish. One man alone—Mr Henry Newbolt —struck a note which even his opponents had to respect. The rest exhibited plenty of the turbulence of passion, but none of the gravity of thoughtful emotion. I don't doubt they were, one and all, honest in their way. But as poetry their utterances were negligible. As writers of real poetry the Anti-Jingoes, and especially the Celts, held and still hold the field.

I will not adduce poets of admitted eminence—Mr Watson, for instance, or Mr Yeats—to prove my case. I am content to go to a young poet who has his spurs to win, and will ask you to consider this little poem, and especially its final stanza. He calls it—

A CHARGE

If thou hast squander'd years to grave a gem
   Commissioned by thy absent Lord, and while
     'Tis incomplete,
Others would bribe thy needy skill to them—
     Dismiss them to the street!

Should'st thou at last discover Beauty's grove,
    At last be panting on the fragrant verge,
        But in the track,
Drunk with divine possession, thou meet Love—
        Turn, at her bidding, back.

When round thy ship in tempest Hell appears,
    And every spectre mutters up more dire
        To snatch control
And loose to madness thy deep-kennell'd Fears,—
        Then to the helm, O Soul!

Last, if upon the cold, green-mantling sea
    Thou cling, alone with Truth, to the last spar,
        Both castaway,
And one must perish—let it not be he
        Whom thou art sworn to obey.

The author of these lines is a Mr Herbert Trench, who
(as I say) has his spurs to win. Yet I defy you to read them
without recognising a note of high seriousness which is
common to our great poets and utterly foreign to our modern
bards of empire. The man, you will perceive, dares to talk
quite boldly about the human soul. Now you will search
long in our Jingo bards for any recognition of the human
soul: the very word is unpopular. And as men of eminence
write, so lesser wits imitate. A while ago I picked up a
popular magazine, and happened on these verses—fluently
written and, beyond a doubt, honestly meant. They are
in praise of King Henry VIII:

King Harry played at tennis, and he threw the dice a-main,
And did all things that seemed to him for his own and England's
    gain;
He would not be talked to lightly, he would not be checked
    or chid;
And he got what things he dreamed to get, and did—what
    things he did.

When Harry played at tennis it was well for this our Isle—
He cocked his nose at Interdicts; he 'stablished us the while—
He was lustful; he was vengeful; he was hot and hard and proud;
But he set his England fairly in the sight of all the crowd.

*　　*　　*　　*　　*

So Harry played at tennis, and we perfected the game
Which astonied swaggering Spaniards when the fat Armada
    came.
And possession did he give us of our souls in sturdiness;
And he gave us peace from priesthood: and he gave us English
    Bess!

When Harry played at tennis we began to know this thing—
That a mighty people prospers in a mighty-minded king.
We boasted not our righteousness—we took on us our sin,
For Bluff Hal was just an Englishman who played the game
    to win.

You will perceive that in the third stanza the word
'soul' occurs: and I invite you to compare this author's
idea of a soul with Mr Trench's. This author will have
nothing to do with the old advice about doing justice, loving
mercy, and walking humbly before God. The old notion
that to conquer self is a higher feat than to take a city he
dismisses out of hand. 'Be lustful, be vengeful,' says he,
'but play the game to win, and you have my applause. Get
what you want, set England fairly in sight of the crowd,
and you are a mighty-minded man.' Now the first and last
comment upon such a doctrine must be that, if a God
exist, it is false. It sets up a part to override the whole:
it flaunts a local success against the austere majesty of Divine
law. In brief, it foolishly derides the universal, saying that
it chooses to consider the particular as more important.
But it is not. Poetry's concern is with the universal: and
what makes the Celts (however much you may dislike

them) the most considerable force in English poetry at this moment is that they occupy themselves with that universal truth, which, before any technical accomplishment, is the guarantee of good poetry.

Now, when you tell yourself that the days of 'English Bess' were jolly fine empire-making days, and produced great poets (Shakespeare, for example) worthy of them; and when you go on to reflect that these also are jolly fine empire-making days, but that somehow Mr Austin is your laureate, and that the only poetry which counts is being written by men out of harmony with your present empire-making mood, the easiest plan (if you happen to think the difference worth considering) will be to call the Muse a traitress, and declare that every poem better than Mr Austin's is a vote given to—whatever nation your Yellow Press happens to be insulting at this moment. But, if you care to look a little deeper, you may find that some difference in your methods of empire-making is partly accountable for the change. A true poet must cling to universal truth; and by insulting it (as, for example, by importing into present-day politics the spirit which would excuse the iniquities of Henry VIII on the ground that 'he gave us English Bess'!) you are driving the true poet out of your midst. Read over the verses above quoted, and then repeat to yourself, slowly, these lines:

> Last, if upon the cold, green-mantling sea
> Thou cling, alone with Truth, to the last spar,
>   Both castaway,
> And one must perish—let it not be he
>   Whom thou art sworn to obey.

I ask no more. If a man cannot see the difference at once, I almost despair of making him perceive why poetry refuses just now even more obstinately than trade (if that be possible) to 'follow the flag.' It will not follow, because you are waving the flag over self-deception. You may be as blithe as Plato in casting out the poets from your commonwealth—though for other reasons than his. You may be as blithe as Dogberry in determining, of reading and writing, that they may appear when there is no need of such vanity. But you are certainly driving them forth to say, in place of 'O beloved city of Cecrops!' 'O beloved city of God!' There was a time, not many years ago, when an honest poet could have used both cries together and deemed that he meant the same thing by the two. But the two cries to-day have an utterly different meaning—and by your compulsion or by the compulsion of such politics as you have come to tolerate.

And therefore the young poet whom I have quoted has joined the band of those poets whom we are forcing out of the city, to leave our ideals to the fate which, since the world began, has overtaken all ideals which could not get themselves 'accepted by song.' Even as we drum these poets out we know that they are the only ones worth reckoning with, and that man cannot support himself upon assurances that he is the strongest fellow in the world, and the richest, and owns the biggest house, and pays the biggest rates, and wins whatever game he plays at, and stands so high in his clothes that while the Southern Cross rises over his hat-brim it is already broad day on the seat of his breeches. For that is what it all comes to: and the sentence upon the man who neglects the warning of these poets, while he heaps up great possessions, is still, 'Thou fool, this night thy soul shall be required of thee.' And where is the national soul you would choose, at that hasty summons, to present for inspection, having to stand your trial

upon it? Try Park Lane, or run and knock up the Laureate,
and then come and report your success!

*   *   *   *   *

Weeks ago I was greatly reproached by a correspondent
for misusing the word 'Celtic,' and informed that to call
Mr Yeats or Mr Trench a Celt is a grave abuse of ethnical
terms; that a notable percentage of the names connected
with the 'Celtic Revival'—Hyde, Sigerson, Atkinson,
Stokes—are not Celtic at all but Teutonic; that, in short,
I have been following the multitude to speak loosely. Well,
I confess it, and I will confess further that the lax use of
the word 'Celt' ill beseems one who has been irritated
often enough by the attempts of well-meaning but muddle-
headed people who get hold of this or that poet and
straightly assign this or that quality of his verse to a certain
set of corpuscles in his mixed blood. Although I believe
that my correspondent is too hasty in labelling men's
descent from their names—for the mother has usually
some share in producing a child; although I believe that
Mr Yeats, for instance, inherits Cornish blood on one
side, even if Irish be denied him on the other; yet the
rebuke contains some justice.

Still, I must maintain that these well-meaning theorists
err only in applying a broad distinction with overmuch
nicety. There is, after all, a certain quality in a poem of
Blake's, or a prose passage of Charlotte Brontë's, which a
critic is not only unable to ignore, but which—if he has
any 'comparative' sense—he finds himself accounting for
by saying, 'This man, or this woman, must be a Celt or
have some admixture of Celtic blood.' I say quite confidently that quality cannot be ignored. You open (let us

say) a volume of Blake, and your eye falls on these two
lines—

> When the stars threw down their spears
> And watered heaven with their tears,

and at once you are aware of an imagination different in
kind from the imagination you would recognise as English.
Let us, if you please, rule out all debate of superiority; let
us take Shakespeare for comparison, and Shakespeare at
his best:

> These our actors,
> As I foretold you, were all spirits, and
> Are melted into air, into thin air;
> And, like the baseless fabric of this vision,
> The cloud-capp'd towers, the gorgeous palaces,
> The solemn temples, the great globe itself,
> Yea, all which it inherit, shall dissolve
> And, like this insubstantial pageant faded,
> Leave not a rack behind. We are such stuff
> As dreams are made of, and our little life
> Is rounded with a sleep.

Finer poetry than this I can hardly find in English to
quote for you. But fine as it is, will you not observe the
matter-of-factness (call it healthy, if you will, and I shall
not gainsay you) beneath Shakespeare's noble language?
It says divinely what it has to say; and what it has to say
is full of solemn thought. But, for better or worse (or,
rather, without question of better or worse), Blake's
imagination is moving on a different plane. We may think
it an uncomfortably superhuman plane; but let us note the
difference, and note further that this plane was habitual
with Blake. Now because of his immense powers we are
accustomed to think of Shakespeare as almost superhuman:

we pay that tribute to his genius, his strength, and the
enormous impression they produce on us. But a single
couplet of Blake's will carry more of this uncanny superhuman imagination than the whole five acts of *Hamlet*.
So great is Shakespeare, that he tempts us to think him
capable of any flight of wing; but set down a line or two
of Blake's—

> A robin redbreast in a cage
> Puts all heaven in a rage...
> A skylark wounded on the wing
> Doth make a cherub cease to sing.

—and, simple as the thought is, at once you feel it to lie
outside the range of Shakespeare's philosophy. Shakespeare's men are fine, brave, companionable fellows, full
of passionate love, jealousy, ambition; of humour, gravity,
strength of mind; of laughter and rage, of the joy and stress
of living. But self-sacrifice scarcely enters into their notion
of the scheme of things, and they are by no means men to
go to death for an idea. We remember what figure Shakespeare made of Sir John Oldcastle, and I wish we could
forget what figure he made of Joan of Arc. Within the
bounds of his philosophy—the philosophy, gloriously
stated, of ordinary brave, full-blooded men—he is a great
encourager of virtue; and so such lines as—

> The expense of spirit in a waste of shame
> Is lust in action...

are thoroughly Shakespearean, while such lines as—

> A robin redbreast in a cage
> Puts all heaven in a rage...

are as little Shakespearean in thought as in phrasing. He can tell us that

> We are such stuff
> As dreams are made of, and our little life
> Is rounded with a sleep.

He can muse on that sleep to come:

> To die, to sleep;
> To sleep; perchance to dream; aye, there's the rub;
> For in that sleep of death what dreams may come
> When we have shuffled off this mortal coil,
> Must give us pause.

But that even in this life we may be more truly ourselves when dreaming than when waking—that what we dream may perchance turn out to be more real and more important than what we do—such a thought overpasses his imaginative range; or, since to dogmatise on his imaginative range is highly dangerous, let us be content with saying that it lies outside his temperament, and that he would have hit on such a thought only to dismiss it with contempt. So when we open a book of poems and come upon a monarch crying out that

> A wild and foolish labourer is a king,
> To do and do and do and never dream,

we know that we are hearkening to a note which is not Shakespearean at all, not practical, not English. And we want a name for that note.

I have followed the multitude to call it Celtic because in practice when we come upon this note we are pretty safe to discover that the poet who utters it has Celtic blood in him (Blake's poetry, for instance, told me that he must

be an Irishman before ever I reflected that his name was
Irish, or thought of looking up his descent). Since, however, the blood of most men in these islands is by this time
mixed with many strains: since also, though the note be
not native with him, nothing forbids even a pure-blooded
Anglo-Saxon from learning it and assimilating it: lastly,
since there is obvious inconvenience in using the same word
for an ethnical delimitation and a psychological, when their
boundaries do not exactly correspond—and if some Anglo-
Saxons have the 'Celtic' note it is certain that many
thousands of Celts have not; why then I shall be glad
enough to use a better and a handier and a more exact,
if only some clever person will provide it.

Meanwhile, let it be understood that in speaking of a
'Celtic' note I accuse no fellow-creature of being an Irishman, Scotsman, Welshman, Manxman, Cornishman, or
Breton. The poet will as a rule turn out to be one or other
of these, or at least to have a traceable strain of Celtic blood
in him. But to the note only is the term applied. Now
this note may be recognised by many tokens; but the first
and chiefest is its insistence upon man's brotherhood with
bird and beast, star and flower, everything, in short, which
we loosely call 'nature,' his brotherhood even with spirits
and angels, as one of an infinite number of microcosms
reflecting a common image of God. And poetry which
holds by this creed will hardly be subservient to societies
and governments and legalised doctrines and conventions;
it will hold to them by a long and loose chain, if at all.
It flies high enough, at any rate, to take a bird's-eye view
of all manner of things which in the temple, the palace,
or the market-place, have come to be taken as axiomatic.
It eyes them with an extraordinary 'dissoluteness'—if you
will give that word its literal meaning. It sees that some

accepted virtues carry no reflection of heaven; it sees that heaven, on the other hand—so infinite is its care—may shake with anger from bound to bound at the sight of a caged bird. It sees that the souls of living things, even of the least conspicuous, reach up by chains and are anchored in heaven, while 'great' events slide by on the surface of this skimming planet with empires and their ordinances.

* * * * *

And so the Emperor went in the procession under the splendid canopy. And all the people in the streets and at the windows said, 'Bless us! what matchless new clothes our Emperor has!' 'But he hasn't anything on!' cried a little child. 'Dear me, just listen to what the little innocent says,' observed his father, and the people whispered to each other what the child had said. 'He hasn't anything on!' they began to shout at last. This made the Emperor's flesh creep, because he thought that they were right; but he said to himself, 'I must keep it up through the procession, anyhow.' And he walked on still more majestically, and the Chamberlains walked behind and carried the train, though there was none to carry.

This parable of the Emperor without clothes can be matched, for simplicity and searching directness, against any parable outside of the Gospels, and it agrees with the Divine parables in exalting the wisdom of a child. I will not dare to discuss that wisdom here. I observe that when the poets preach it we tender them our applause. We applaud Vaughan's lines:

> Happy those early days, when I
> Shin'd in my angel-infancy...
> When yet I had not walk'd above
> A mile or two from my first love,

> And looking back—at that short space—
> Could see a glimpse of His bright face;
> When on some gilded cloud or flow'r
> My gazing soul would dwell an hour,
> And in those weaker glories spy
> Some shadows of eternity....

We applaud Wordsworth's glorious ode—

> Our birth is but a sleep and a forgetting:
> The Soul that rises with us, our life's Star,
> Hath had elsewhere its setting,
> And cometh from afar:
> Not in entire forgetfulness,
> And not in utter nakedness,
> But trailing clouds of glory do we come
> From God, who is our home:
> Heaven lies about us in our infancy!...

We applaud even old John Earle's prose when he tells us of a Child that—

The elder he grows, he is a stair lower from God; and, like his first father, much worse in his breeches. He is the Christian's example, and the old man's relapse; the one imitates his pureness, the other falls into his simplicity....His father hath writ him as his own little story, wherein he reads those days of his life that he cannot remember, and sighs to see what innocence he hath outlived....Could he put off his body with his little coat, he had got eternity without a burden, and exchanged but one heaven for another.

But while we applaud this pretty confident attribution of divine wisdom to children, we are much too cautious to translate it into practice. 'It is far too shadowy a notion,' says Wordsworth prudently, 'to be recommended to faith as more than an element in our instincts of immortality'; and he might have added that, while the Child may be

Father of the Man, the Man reserves the privilege of spanking. Even so I observe that, while able to agree cordially with Christ on the necessity of becoming as little children as a condition of entering the Kingdom of Heaven, we are not so injudicious as to act upon any such belief; nay, we find ourselves obliged to revise and re-interpret the wisdom of the Gospels when we find it too impracticably childish. When Christ, for instance, forbids oaths of all kinds, we feel sure He cannot be serious, or we should have to upset a settled practice of the courts. And as for resisting no evil and forgiving our enemies, why, good Heavens! what would become of our splendid armaments! The suggestion, put so down rightly, is quite too wild. In short, as a distinguished Bishop put it, society could not exist for forty-eight hours on the lines laid down in the Sermon on the Mount. (I forget the Bishop's exact words, but they amounted to a complete and thoroughly common-sense repudiation of Gospel Christianity.)

No; it is obvious that, in so far as the Divine teaching touches on conduct, we must as practical men correct it, and with a special look-out for its indulgent misunder-standing of children. Children, as a matter of experience, have no sense of the rights of property. They steal apples.

And yet—there must be something in this downright wisdom of childishness since Christ went (as we must believe) out of His way to lay such stress on it; and since our own hearts respond so readily when Vaughan or Wordsworth claim divinity for it. We cannot of course go the length of believing that the great, wise, and eminent men of our day are engaged one and all in the pursuit of shadows. 'Shadows we are and shadows we pursue' sounded an exquisitely solemn note in an election speech; but after all, we must take the world as we find it, and the world

as we find it has its own recognised rewards. No success
attended the poet who wrote that—

> Those little new-invented things—
> Cups, saddles, crowns, are childish joys,
> So ribbands are and rings,
> Which all our happiness destroys.
>> Nor God
>> In His abode,
>> Nor saints, nor little boys,
> Nor Angels made them; only foolish men,
> Grown mad with custom, on those toys
> Which more increase their wants to date....

He found no publisher, and they have been rescued by
accident after two hundred years of oblivion. (It appears,
nevertheless, that he was a happy man.)

And yet—I repeat—since we respond to it so readily,
whether in welcome or in irritation, there must be something in this claim set up for childish simplicity; and I
cannot help thinking it fortunate and salutary for us that
the Celtic poets have taken to sounding its note so boldly.
Whatever else they do, on the conventional ideals of this
generation they speak out with an uncompromising and
highly disconcerting directness. As I said just now, they
are held, if at all, by a long and loose chain to the graven
images to which we stand bound arm-to-arm and foot-to-
foot. They fly far enough aloof to take a bird's-eye view.
What they see they declare with a boldness which is the
more impressive for being unconscious. And they declare
that they see us tied to stupid material gods, and wholly
blind to ideas.

*   *   *   *   *

P.S. I made bold enough to say in the course of these
remarks that Euclid's *Elements* could hardly be improved

by writing them out in ballad metre. A friend, to whom
I happened to repeat this assertion, cast doubt on it and
challenged me to prove it. I do so with pleasure in the
following—

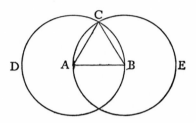

NEW BALLAD OF SIR PATRICK SPENS

The King sits in Dunfermline toun
    Drinking the blude-red wine:
'O wha will rear me an equilateral triangle
    Upon a given straight line?'

O up and spake an eldern knight,
    Sat at the King's right knee—
'Of a' the clerks by Granta side
    Sir Patrick bears the gree.

''Tis he was taught by the Tod-huntère
    Tho' not at the tod-hunting;
Yet gif that he be given a line,
    He'll do as brave a thing.'

Our King has written a braid letter
    To Cambrigge or thereby,
And there it found Sir Patrick Spens
    Evaluating π.

He hadna warked his quotient
   A point but barely three,
There stepped to him a little foot-page
   And louted on his knee.

The first word that Sir Patrick read,
   '*Plus* x' was a' he said:
The neist word that Sir Patrick read,
   'Twas '*plus* expenses paid.'

The last word that Sir Patrick read,
   The tear blinded his e'e:
'The pound I most admire is not
   In Scottish currencie.'

Stately stepped he east the wa',
   And stately stepped he north:
He fetched a compass frae his ha'
   And stood beside the Forth.

Then gurly grew the waves o' Forth,
   And gurlier by-and-by—
'O never yet was sic a storm,
   Yet it isna sic as I!'

Syne he has crost the Firth o' Forth
   Until Dunfermline toun;
And tho' he came with a kittle wame
   Fu' low he louted doun.

'A line, a line, a gude straight line,
   O King, purvey me quick!
And see it be of thilka kind
   That's neither braid nor thick.'

'Nor thick nor braid?' King Jamie said,
   'I'll eat my gude hat-band
If arra line as ye define
   Be found in our Scotland.'

'Tho' there be nane in a' thy rule,
    It sall be ruled by me';
And lichtly with his little pencil
    He's ruled the line A B.

Stately stepped he east the wa',
    And stately stepped he west;
'Ye touch the button,' Sir Patrick said,
    'And I sall do the rest.'

And he has set his compass foot
    Untill the centre A,
From A to B he's stretched it oot—
    'Ye Scottish carles, give way!'

Syne he has moved his compass foot
    Untill the centre B,
From B to A he's stretched it oot,
    And drawn it viz-a-vee.

The tane circle was B C D,
    And A C E the tither:
'I rede ye well,' Sir Patrick said,
    'They interseck ilk ither.

'See here, and where they interseck—
    To wit with yon point C—
Ye'll just obsairve that I conneck
    The twa points A and B.

'And there ye have a little triangle
    As bonny as e'er was seen;
The whilk is not isosceles,
    Nor yet it is scalene.'

'The proof! the proof!' King Jamie cried:
    'The how and eke the why!'
Sir Patrick laughed within his beard—
    ''Tis *ex hypothesi*—

'When I ligg'd in my mither's wame,
    I learn'd it frae my mither,
That things was equal to the same,
    Was equal ane to t'ither.

'Sith in the circle first I drew
    The lines B A, B C,
Be radii true, I wit to you
    The baith maun equal be.

'Likewise and in the second circle,
    Whilk I drew widdershins,
It is nae skaith the radii baith,
    A B, A C, be twins.

'And sith of three a pair agree
    That ilk suld equal ane,
By certes they maun equal be
    Ilk unto ilk by-lane.'

'Now by my faith!' King Jamie saith,
    'What *plane* geometrie!
If only Potts had written in Scots,
    How loocid Potts wad be!'

'Now wow's my life!' said Jamie the King,
    And the Scots lords said the same,
For but it was that envious knicht,
    Sir Hughie o' the Graeme.

'Flim-flam, flim-flam!' and 'Ho indeed?'
    Quod Hughie o' the Graeme;
''Tis I could better upon my heid
    This prabblin prablem-game.'

Sir Patrick Spens was nothing laith
    When as he heard 'flim-flam,'
But syne he's ta'en a silken claith
    And wiped his diagram.

 Gif my small feat may better'd be,
   Sir Hew, by thy big head,
What I hae done with an A B C
   Do thou with X Y Z.'

Then sairly sairly swore Sir Hew,
   And loudly laucht the King;
But Sir Patrick tuk the pipes and blew,
   And *played* that eldritch thing!

He's play'd it reel, he's play'd it jig,
   And the baith alternative;
And he's danced Sir Hew to the Asses' Brigg,
   That's Proposetion Five.

And there they've met, and there they've fet,
   Forenenst the Asses' Brigg,
And waefu', waefu' was the fate
   That gar'd them there to ligg.

For there Sir, Patrick's slain Sir Hew,
   And Sir Hew Sir Patrick Spens—
Now was not that a fine to-do
   For Euclid's Elemen's?

But let us sing Long live the King!
   And his foes the Deil attend 'em:
For he has gotten his little triangle,
   Quod erat faciendum!

MARCH

HOW quietly its best things steal upon the world! And in a world where a single line of Sappho's survives as a something more important than the entire political history of Lesbos, how little will the daily newspaper help us to take long views!

Whether England could better afford to lose Shakespeare or her Indian Empire is no fair question to put to an Englishman. But every Englishman knows in his heart which of these two glories of his birth and state will survive the other, and by which of them his country will earn in the end the greater honour. Though in our daily life we—perhaps wisely—make a practice of forgetting it, our literature is going to be our most perdurable claim on man's remembrance, for it is occupied with ideas which outlast all phenomena.

The other day Mr Bertram Dobell, the famous bookseller of Charing Cross Road, rediscovered (we might almost say that he discovered) a poet. Mr Dobell has in the course of his life laid the Republic of Letters under many obligations. To begin with, he loves his trade and honours the wares in which he deals, and so continues the good tradition that should knit writers, printers, vendors and purchasers of books together as partakers of an excellent mystery. He studies—and on occasion will fight for—the whims as well as the convenience of his customers. It was he who took arms against the Westminster City Council in defence of the out-of-door-stall, the 'classic sixpenny

box,' and at least brought off a drawn battle. He is at
pains to make his secondhand catalogues better reading
than half the new books printed, and they cost us nothing.
He has done, also, his pious share of service to good
literature. He has edited James Thomson, him of *The City
of Dreadful Night*. He has helped us to learn more than
we knew of Charles Lamb. He has even written poems
of his own and printed them under the title of *Rosemary
and Pansies*, in a volume marked 'Not for sale'—a warning
which I, as one of the fortunate endowed, intend strictly
to observe. On top of this he has discovered, or rediscovered,
Thomas Traherne.

Now before we contemplate the magnitude of the discovery let us rehearse the few facts known of the inconspicuous life of Thomas Traherne. He was born about
the year 1636, the son of a Hereford shoemaker, and came
in all probability (like Herbert and Vaughan) of Welsh
stock. In 1652 he entered Brasenose College, Oxford, as
a commoner. On leaving the University he took orders;
was admitted Rector of Credenhill, in Herefordshire, in
1657; took the degree of Bachelor of Divinity in 1669;
became the private chaplain of Sir Orlando Bridgman, at
Teddington; and died there a few months after his patron,
in 1674, aged but thirty-eight. He wrote a polemical tract
on *Roman Forgeries*, which had some success; a treatise
on *Christian Ethicks*, which, being full of gentle wisdom,
was utterly neglected; an exquisite work, *Centuries of
Meditations*, never published; and certain poems, which
also he left in manuscript. And there the record ends.

Next let us tell by how strange a chance this forgotten
author came to his own. In 1896 or 1897 Mr William T.
Brooke picked up two volumes of MS. on a street bookstall,
and bought them for a few pence. Mr Brooke happened

to be a man learned in sacred poetry and hymnology, and he no sooner began to examine his purchase than he knew that he had happened on a treasure. At the same time he could hardly believe that writings so admirable were the work of an unknown author. In choice of subject, in sentiment, in style, they bore a strong likeness to the poems of Henry Vaughan the Silurist, and he concluded that they must be assigned to Vaughan. He communicated his discovery to the late Dr Grosart, who became so deeply interested in it that he purchased the manuscripts and set about preparing an edition of Vaughan, in which the newly-found treasures were to be included. Dr Grosart, one may say in passing, was by no means a safe judge of characteristics in poetry. With all his learning and enthusiasm you could not trust him, having read a poem with which he was unacquainted or which perchance he had forgotten, to assign it to its true or even its probable author. But when you hear that so learned a man as Dr Grosart considered these writings worthy of Vaughan, you may be the less apt to think me extravagant in holding that man to have been Vaughan's peer who wrote the following lines:

> How like an angel came I down!
>   How bright are all things here!
> When first among His works I did appear
>   O how their Glory me did crown!
> The world resembled His Eternity,
>   In which my soul did walk;
> And everything that I did see
>   Did with me talk.

> *   *   *   *   *

> The streets were paved with golden stones,
>   The boys and girls were mine,

O how did all their lovely faces shine!
  The sons of men were holy ones;
In joy and beauty they appeared to me:
  And everything which here I found,
While like an angel I did see,
  Adorned the ground.

    *   *   *   *   *

'Proprieties'—

That is to say, 'properties,' 'estates'—

Proprieties themselves were mine,
  And hedges ornaments,
Walls, boxes, coffers, and their rich contents
  Did not divide my joys, but all combine.
Clothes, ribbons, jewels, laces, I esteemed
  My joys by others worn;
For me they all to wear them seemed
  When I was born.

Dr Grosart then set about preparing a new and elaborate edition of Vaughan, which, only just before his death, he was endeavouring to find means to publish. After his death the two manuscripts passed by purchase to Mr Charles Higham, the well-known bookseller of Farringdon Street, who in turn sold them to Mr Dobell. Later, when a part of Dr Grosart's library was sold at Sotheby's, Mr Dobell bought—and this is perhaps the strangest part of the story— a third manuscript volume, which Dr Grosart had possessed all the time without an inkling that it bore upon Mr Brooke's discovery, 'though nothing is needed but to compare it with the other volumes in order to see that all these are in the same handwriting.'

Mr Dobell examined the writings, compared them with Vaughan's, and began to have his doubts. Soon he felt convinced that Vaughan was not their author. Yet, if not Vaughan, who could the author be?

Again Mr Brooke proved helpful. To a volume of Giles Fletcher's, *Christ's Victory and Triumph*, which he had edited, Mr Brooke had appended a number of seventeenth-century poems not previously collected; and to one of these, entitled 'The Ways of Wisdom,' he drew Mr Dobell's attention as he had previously drawn Dr Grosart's. To Mr Dobell the resemblance between it and the manuscript poems was at once evident. Mr Brooke had found the poem in a little book in the British Museum entitled, *A Serious and Patheticall Contemplation of the Mercies of God, in several most Devout and Sublime Thanksgivings for the same* (a publisher's title it is likely): and this book contained other pieces in verse. These having been copied out by Mr Dobell's request, he examined them and felt no doubt at all that the author of the manuscript poem and of the *Devout and Sublime Thanksgivings* must be one and the same person. But, again, who could he be?

A sentence in an address 'To the Reader' prefixed to the *Devout and Sublime Thanksgivings* provided the clue. The editor of this work (a posthumous publication), after eulogising the unnamed author's many virtues wound up with a casual clue to his identity:

> But being removed out of the Country to the service of the late Lord Keeper Bridgman as his Chaplain, he died young and got early to those blissful mansions to which he at all times aspir'd.

But for this sentence, dropped at haphazard, the secret might never have been resolved. As it was, the clue—that the author of *Devout and Sublime Thanksgivings* was private chaplain to Sir Orlando Bridgman—had only to be fol-

lowed up; and it led to the name of Thomas Traherne.
This information was obtained from Wood's *Athenæ
Oxonienses*, which mentioned Traherne as the author of
two books, *Roman Forgeries* and *Christian Ethicks*.

The next step was to get hold of these two works and
examine them, if perchance some evidence might be found
that Traherne was also the author of the manuscripts, which
as yet remained a guess, standing on Mr Dobell's conviction that the verses in the manuscripts and those in
Devout and Sublime Thanksgivings must be by the same
hand.

By great good fortune that evidence was found in
Christian Ethicks, in a poem which, with some variations,
occurred too in the manuscript *Centuries of Meditations*.
Here then at last was proof positive, or as positive as
needs be.

* * * * *

The most of us writers hope and stake for a diuturnity
of fame; and some of us get it. *Sed ubi sunt vestimenta
eorum qui post vota nuncupata perierunt?* 'That bay leaves
were found green in the tomb of St Humbert after a
hundred and fifty years was looked upon as miraculous,'
writes Sir Thomas Browne. But Traherne's laurel has lain
green in the dust for close on two hundred and thirty years,
and his fame so cunningly buried that only by half a dozen
accidents leading up to a chance sentence in a dark preface
to a forgotten book has it come to light.

I wonder if his gentle shade takes any satisfaction in the
discovery? His was by choice a *vita fallens*. Early in life
he made, as we learn from a passage in *Centuries of
Meditations*, his election between worldly prosperity and
the life of the Spirit, between the chase of fleeting phenomena and rest upon the soul's centre:

When I came into the country and, being seated among silent trees and woods and hills, had all my time in my own hands, I resolved to spend it all, whatever it cost me, in the search of Happiness, and to satiate the burning thirst which Nature had enkindled in me from my youth; in which I was so resolute that I chose rather to live upon ten pounds a year, and to go in leather clothes, and to feed upon bread and water, so that I might have all my time clearly to myself, than to keep many thousands per annum in an estate of life where my time would be devoured in care and labour. And God was so pleased to accept of that desire that from that time to this I have had all things plentifully provided for me without any care at all, my very study of Felicity making me more to prosper than all the care in the whole world. So that through His blessing I live a free and kingly life, as if the world were turned again into Eden, or, much more, as it is at this day.

Yet Traherne is no quietist: a fervent, passionate lover, rather, of simple and holy things. He sees with the eyes of a child: the whole world shines for him 'apparell'd in celestial light,' and that light, he is well aware, shines out on it, through the eyes which observe it, from the divine soul of man. The verses which I quoted above strike a note to which he recurs again and again. Listen to the exquisite prose in which he recounts the 'pure and virgin apprehension' of his childhood:

The corn was orient and immortal wheat which never should be reaped nor was ever sown. I thought it had stood from everlasting to everlasting. The dust and stones of the street were as precious as gold; the gates were at first the end of the world. The green trees when I saw them first through one of the gates transported and ravished me; their sweetness and unusual beauty made my heart to leap and almost mad with ecstasy, they were such strange and wonderful things. The

Men! O what venerable and reverend creatures did the aged seem! Immortal Cherubim! And young men glittering and sparkling angels, and maids strange seraphic pieces of life and beauty! Boys and girls tumbling in the street were moving jewels; I knew not that they were born, or should die.... The streets were mine, the temple was mine, the people were mine, their clothes and gold and silver were mine, as much as their sparkling eyes, fair skins, and ruddy faces. The skies were mine, and so were the sun and moon and stars, and all the world was mine; and I the only spectator and enjoyer of it....

All these things he enjoyed, his life through, uncursed by the itch for 'proprietorship': he was like the Magnanimous Man in his own *Christian Ethicks*—'one that scorns the smutty way of enjoying things like a slave, because he delights in the celestial way and the Image of God.' In this creed of his all things are made for man, if only man will inherit them wisely: even God, in conferring benefits on man, is moved and rewarded by the felicity of witnessing man's grateful delight in them:

> For God enjoyed is all His end,
> Himself He then doth comprehend
> When He is blessèd, magnified,
> Extoll'd, exalted, prais'd, and glorified.

Yes, and 'undeified almost, if once denied.' A startling creed, this; but what a bold and great-hearted one! To Traherne the Soul is a sea which not only receives the rivers of God's bliss but 'all it doth receive returns again.' It is the Beloved of the old song, 'Quia Amore Langueo'; whom God pursues, as a lover. It is the crown of all things. So in one of his loveliest poems he shows it standing on the threshold to hear news of a great guest, never dreaming that itself is that great guest all the while—

ON NEWS

I

News from a foreign country came,
  As if my treasure and my wealth lay there:
So much it did my heart enflame,
  'Twas wont to call my Soul into mine ear,
        Which thither went to meet
        The approaching sweet,
    And on the threshold stood
    To entertain the unknown Good.
        It hover'd there
        As if 'twould leave mine ear,
    And was so eager to embrace
      The joyful tidings as they came,
    'Twould almost leave its dwelling-place
      To entertain that same.

II

As if the tidings were the things,
  My very joys themselves, my foreign treasure,
Or else did bear them on their wings—
  With so much joy they came, with so much pleasure—
        My Soul stood at that gate
        To recreate
    Itself with bliss, and to
    Be pleased with speed. A fuller view
        It fain would take,
        Yet journeys back again would make
    Unto my heart: as if 'twould fain
      Go out to meet, yet stay within
    To fit a place to entertain
      And bring the tidings in.

III

What sacred instinct did inspire
    My Soul in childhood with a hope so strong?
What secret force moved my desire
    To expect my joy, beyond the seas, so young?
            Felicity I knew
            Was out of view;
        And being here alone,
        I saw that happiness was gone
            From me! For this
            I thirsted absent bliss,
        And thought that sure beyond the seas,
            Or else in something near at hand
        I knew not yet (since nought did please
            I knew), my bliss did stand.

IV

But little did the infant dream
    That all the treasures of the world were by:
And that himself was so the cream
    And crown of all which round about did lie.
                Yet thus it was: The Gem,
                The Diadem,
            The Ring enclosing all
            That stood upon this earthly ball;
                The Heavenly Eye,
                Much wider than the sky,
            Wherein they all included were,
                The glorious Soul that was the King
            Made to possess them, did appear
                A small and little thing.

I must quote from another poem, if only for the pleasure
of writing down the lines:

THE SALUTATION

These little limbs,
These eyes and hands which here I find,
These rosy cheeks wherewith my life begins—
Where have ye been? behind
What curtain were ye from me hid so long?
Where was, in what abyss, my speaking tongue?
When silent I
So many thousand, thousand years
Beneath the dust did in a chaos lie,
How could I smiles or tears
Or lips or hands or eyes or ears perceive?
Welcome ye treasures which I now receive!

*   *   *   *   *

These poems waited for two hundred and thirty years
to be discovered on a street bookstall! There are lines in
them and whole passages in the unpublished *Centuries
of Meditations* which almost set one wondering with Sir
Thomas Browne 'whether the best of men be known,
or whether there be not more remarkable persons forgot
than any that stand remembered in the known account of
Time?'

*   *   *   *   *

I am tempted, but will not be drawn to discuss how
Traherne stands related to Vaughan on the one hand and
Cowley on the other. I note the discovery here, and
content myself with wondering if the reader share any of
my pleasure in it and enjoyment of the process which
brought it to pass. For me, I was born and bred a bookman. In my father's house the talk might run on divinity,
politics, the theatre; but literature was the great thing.
Other callings might do well enough, but writers were a

class apart, and to be a great writer was the choicest of ambitions. I grew up in this habit of mind, and have not entirely outgrown it yet; have not so far outgrown it but that literary discussions, problems, discoveries engage me though they lie remote from literature's service to man (who has but a short while to live, and labour and vanity if he outlast it). I could join in a hunt after Bunyan's grandmothers, and have actually spent working days in trying to discover the historical facts of which *Robinson Crusoe* may be an allegory. One half of my quarrel with those who try to prove that Bacon wrote Shakespeare rests on resentment of the time they force me to waste; and a new searcher for the secret of the Sonnets has only to whistle and I come to him—though, to be sure, that gentleman almost cured me who identified the Dark Lady with Ann Hathaway, resting his case upon—

SONNET CCXVIII

Whoever hath my wit, thou hast thy Will:
And where is Will alive but *hath a way?*
So in device thy wit is starvèd still
And as devised by Will. That is to say,
My second-best best bed, yea, and the gear withal
Thou hast; but all that capital messuage
Known as New Place goes to Susanna Hall.
Haply the disproportion may engage
The harmless all-too-wise which otherwise
Might knot themselves disknitting of a clue
That Bacon wrote me. Lastly, I devise
My wit, to whom? To wit, to-whit, to-whoo!
   And here revoke all previous testaments:
   Witness, J. SHAW and ROBERT WHATTCOAT, Gents.

After this confession you will pardon any small complacency that may happen to betray itself in the ensuing narrative.

Mr Dobell followed up his discovery of Traherne by announcing another *trouvaille*, and one which excited me not a little:

Looking recently over a parcel of pamphlets which I had purchased, I came upon some loose leaves which were headed *A Prospect of Society*. The title struck me as familiar, and I had only to read a few lines to recognise them as belonging to [Goldsmith's] *The Traveller*. But the opening lines of my fragment are not the opening lines of the poem as it was published; in fact, the first two lines of *A Prospect of Society* are lines 353–4 in the first edition of *The Traveller*.... A further examination of the fragment which I had discovered showed that it is not what is usually understood as a 'proof' of *The Traveller*, but rather the material, as yet formless and unarranged, out of which it was to be finally evolved.

Now—line for corresponding line—the text discovered by Mr Dobell often differs, and sometimes considerably, from that of the first edition of *The Traveller*, and these variations are highly interesting, and make Mr Dobell's 'find' a valuable one. But on studying the newly discovered version I very soon found myself differing from Mr Dobell's opinion that we had here the formless, unarranged material out of which Goldsmith built an exquisitely articulated poem[1]. And, doubting this, I had to doubt what Mr Dobell deduced from it—that 'it was in the manner in which a poem, remarkable for excellence of form and unity of

[1] Early editions of Goldsmith's poem bore the title, *The Traveller; or, A Prospect of Society*. Later editions dropped the sub-title.

design, was created out of a number of verses which were
at first crudely conceived and loosely connected that Goldsmith's genius was most triumphantly displayed.' For
scarcely had I lit a pipe and fallen to work on *A Prospect
of Society* before it became evident to me (1) that the lines
were not 'unarranged,' but disarranged; and (2) that whatever the reason of this disarray, Goldsmith's brain was not
responsible; that the disorder was too insane to be accepted
either as an order in which he could have written the poem,
or as one in which he could have wittingly allowed it to
circulate among his friends, unless he desired them to
believe him mad. Take, for instance, this collocation:

> Heavens! how unlike their Belgic sires of old!
> Rough, poor, content, ungovernably bold;
> Where shading elms beside the margin grew,
> And freshen'd from the waves the zephyr blew.

Or this:

> To kinder skies, where gentler manners reign,
> We turn, where France displays her bright domain.
> Thou sprightly land of mirth and social ease,
> Pleas'd with thyself, whom all the world can please,
> How often have I led thy sportive choir
> With tuneless pipe, along the sliding Loire?
> No vernal bloom their torpid rocks display,
> But Winter lingering chills the lap of May;
> No zephyr fondly sooths the mountain's breast,
> But meteors glare and frowning storms invest.

Short of lunacy, no intellectual process would account
for that sort of thing, whereas a poem more pellucidly
logical than *The Traveller* does not exist in English. So,
having lit another pipe, I took a pencil and began some
simple counting, with this result:

The first 42 lines of *The Prospect* correspond with lines 353–400 of the first edition* of *The Traveller*.

The next 42 with lines 311–352.

The next 34 with lines 277–310.

The next 36 with lines 241–276.

The next 36 with lines 205–240.

The next 36 with lines 169–204.

The next 38 with lines 131–168.

The next 28 with lines 103–130.

And the remaining fragment of 18 lines with lines 73–92.

In other words, *The Prospect* is merely an early draft of *The Traveller* printed backwards in fairly regular sections.

But how can this have happened? The explanation is at once simple and ridiculous. As Goldsmith finished writing out each page of his poem for press, he laid it aside on top of the pages preceding; and, when all was done, he forgot to sort back his pages in reverse order. That is all. Given a good stolid compositor with no thought beyond doing his duty with the manuscript as it reached him, you have what Mr Dobell has recovered—an immortal poem printed wrong-end-foremost page by page. I call the result delightful, and (when you come to think of it) the blunder just so natural to Goldsmith as to be almost postulable.

Upon this simple explanation we have to abandon the hypothesis that Goldsmith patiently built a fine poem out of a congeries of fine passages pitchforked together at haphazard—a splendid rubbish heap: and Mr Dobell's find is seen to be an imperfect set of duplicate proofs—

* Later editions of *The Traveller* contained substantial additions and variations and then umbering of the lines differs accordingly.

fellow, no doubt, to that set which Goldsmith, mildly objurgating his own or the printer's carelessness, sliced up with the scissors and rearranged before submitting it to Johnson's friendly revision.

* * * * *

The pleasantest part of the story (for me) has yet to come. We all know how easy it is to turn obstinate and defend a pet theory with acrimony. Mr Dobell did nothing of the sort. Although his enthusiasm had committed him to no little expense in publishing *The Prospect*, with a preface elaborating his theory, he did a thing which was worth a hundred discoveries. He sat down, convinced himself that my explanation was the right one, and promptly committed himself to further expense in bringing out a new edition with the friendliest acknowledgment. So do men behave who are at once generous of temper and anxious for the truth.

He himself had been close upon the explanation. In his preface he had actually guessed that the 'author's manuscript, written on loose leaves, had fallen into confusion and was then printed without any attempt at rearrangement.' In fact, he had hit upon the right solution, and only failed to follow up the clue.

His find, too, remains a valuable one; for so far as it goes we can collate it with the first edition of *The Traveller*, and exactly discover the emendations made by Johnson, or by Goldsmith after discussion with Johnson. Boswell tells us that the Doctor 'in the year 1783, at my request, marked with a pencil the lines which he had furnished, which are only line 420, "To stop too faithful, and too faint to go," and the concluding ten lines, except the last couplet but one.... He added, "These are all of which I can be sure."' We cannot test his claim to the concluding

lines, for the correspondent passage is missing from
Mr Dobell's fragment; but Johnson's word would be good
enough without the internal evidence of the verses to back
it. 'To stop too faithful, and too faint to go,' is his improvement, and an undeniable one, upon Goldsmith's 'And
faintly fainter, fainter seems to go.' I have not been at
pains to examine all the revised lines, but they are numerous,
and generally (to my thinking) betray Johnson's hand.
Also they are almost consistently improvements. There is
one alteration, however,—unmistakably due to Johnson,—
which some of us will join with Mr Dobell in regretting.
Johnson, as a fine, full-blooded Jingo, naturally showed
some restiveness at the lines—

> Yes, my lov'd brother, cursed be that hour
> When first ambition toil'd for foreign power,

and induced Goldsmith to substitute—

> Yes, brother, curse with me that baleful hour
> When first ambition struck at regal power,

which may or may not be more creditable in sentiment,
but is certainly quite irrelevant in its context, which happens
to be a denunciation of the greed for gold and foreign
conquest. It is, in that context, all but meaningless, and
must have irritated and puzzled many readers of a poem
otherwise clearly and continuously argued. In future
editions of *The Traveller*, Goldsmith's original couplet
should be restored; and I urge this (let the Tory reader
be assured) not from any ill-will towards our old friend
the Divine Right of Kings, but solely in the sacred name
of Logic.   *   *   *   *   *

Such be the bookman's trivial adventures and discoveries. They would be worse than trivial indeed if they

led him to forget or ignore that by which Goldsmith earned his immortality, or to regard Traherne merely as a freak in the history of literary reputations, and not primarily as the writer of such words as these—

A little touch of something like pride is seated in the true sense of a man's own greatness, without which his humility and modesty would be contemptible virtues.

It is a vain and insipid thing to suffer without loving God or man. Love is a transcendent excellence in every duty, and must of necessity enter into the nature of every grace and virtue. That which maketh the solid benefit of patience unknown, its taste so bitter and comfortless to men, is its *death* in the separation and absence of its soul. We suffer but love not.

> All things do first receive that give:
>   Only 'tis God above
> That from and in Himself doth live;
>   Whose all-sufficient love
> Without original can flow,
> And all the joys and glories show
> Which mortal man can take delight to know.
> He is the primitive, eternal Spring,
> The endless Ocean of each glorious thing.
>   The Soul a vessel is,
> A spacious bosom, to contain
>   All the fair treasures of His bliss,
> Which run like rivers from, into, the main,
> And all it doth receive, return again.

You never enjoy the world aright till the sea itself floweth in your veins, till you are clothed with the heavens and crowned with the stars.

APRIL

Thus, then, live I
  Till 'mid all the gloom
By Heaven! the bold sun
  Is with me in the room
    Shining, shining!

Then the clouds part,
  Swallows soaring between;
The spring is alive
  And the meadows are green!

I jump up like mad,
  Break the old pipe in twain,
And away to the meadows,
  The meadows again!

THE poem of FitzGerald's from which these verses
come was known, I believe, to very few until Mr E. V.
Lucas exhumed it from *Half-hours with the Worst Authors*,
and reprinted it in that delightful little book *The Open
Road*. I have a notion that even FitzGerald's most learned
executor was but dimly aware of its existence. For my
part, at this time of the day, I prefer it to his Omar Khayyám
—perversely, no doubt. In the year 1885 or thereabouts
Omar, known only to a few, was a wonder and a treasure
to last one's lifetime; but I confess that since a club took
him up and feasted his memory with field-marshals and
other irrelevant persons in the chair, and since his fame
has become vulgarised not only in Thames-side hotels, but
over the length and breadth of the North American continent, one at least of his admirers has suffered a not un-
natural revulsion, until now he can scarcely endure to read

the immortal quatrains. Immortal they are, no doubt, and
deserve to be by reason of their style—'fame's great
antiseptic.' But their philosophy is thin after all, and will
not bear discussion. As exercise for a grown man's thought,
I will back a lyric of Blake's or Wordsworth's, or a page
of Ibsen's *Peer Gynt* against the whole of it, any day.

This, however, is parenthetical. I caught hold of
FitzGerald's verses to express that jollity which should be
every man's who looks up from much reading or writing
and knows that Spring has come.

* * * * *

> *Solvitur acris hiems grata vice veris et favoni*
> *Trahuntque siccas machinæ carinas...*

In other words, I look out of the window and decide that
the day has arrived for launching the boat—

> This is that happy morn,
> That day, long wishèd day!

and, to my mind, the birthday of the year. Potentates and
capitalists who send down orders to Cowes or Southampton
that their yachts are to be put in commission, and anon
arrive to find everything ready (if they care to examine),
from the steam capstan to the cook's apron, have little
notion of the amusement to be found in fitting out a small
boat, say of five or six tons. I sometimes doubt if it be not
the very flower, or at least the bloom, of the whole pastime.
The serious face with which we set about it; the solemn
procession up the river to the creek where she rests, the
high tide all but lifting her; the silence in which we loose
the moorings and haul off; the first thrill of buoyant water
underfoot; the business of stepping the mast; quiet days
of sitting or pottering about on deck in the sunny harbour;

vessels passing up and down, their crews eyeing us critically
as the rigging grows and the odds and ends—block, tackle
and purchase—fall into their ordered places; and through
it all the expectation running of the summer to come, and
'blue days at sea' and unfamiliar anchorages—unfamiliar,
but where the boat is, home will be—

> Such bliss
> Beggars enjoy, when princes oft do miss.

Homer, who knew what amused men, constantly lays stress
on this business of fitting out:

> Then at length she (Athene) let drag the swift ship to the
> sea, and stored within it all such tackling as decked ships
> carry. And she moored it at the far end of the harbour.... So
> they raised the mast of pine tree, and set it in the hole of the
> cross plank, and made it fast with forestays, and hauled up the
> white sails with twisted ropes of oxhide.

And again:

> First of all they drew the ship down to the deep water,
> and fixed the oars in leathern loops all orderly, and spread
> forth the white sails. And squires, haughty of heart, bare for
> them their arms' [*but you'll observe that it was the masters
> who did the launching, etc., like wise men who knew exactly
> wherein the fun of the business consisted*]. 'And they moored
> her high out in the shore water, and themselves disembarked.
> There they supped and waited for evening to come on.

You suggest, perhaps, that our seafaring is but play:
and you are right. But in our play we catch a cupful of
the romance of the real thing. Also we have the real thing
at our doors to keep us humble. Day by day beneath this
window the statelier shipping goes by; and our twopenny
adventurings and discoveries do truly (I believe) keep the

greater wonder and interest awake in us from day to day—
the wonder and interest so memorably expressed in
Mr Bridges's poem, *A Passer By*:

Whither, O splendid ship, thy white sails crowding,
    Leaning across the bosom of the urgent West,
That fearest nor sea rising, nor sky clouding,
    Whither away, fair rover, and what thy quest?
Ah! soon when Winter has all our vales opprest,
    When skies are cold and misty, and hail is hurling,
Wilt thou glide on the blue Pacific, or rest
    In a summer haven asleep, thy white sails furling?

I there before thee, in the country so well thou knowest,
    Already arrived am inhaling the odorous air:
I watch thee enter unerringly where thou goest,
    And anchor queen of the strange shipping there,
Thy sails for awnings spread, thy masts bare....

*   *   *   *   *

And yet, O splendid ship, unhailed and nameless,
    I know not if, aiming a fancy, I rightly divine
That thou hast a purpose joyful, a courage blameless,
    Thy port assured in a happier land than mine.
But for all I have given thee, beauty enough is thine.
    As thou, aslant with trim tackle and shrouding,
From the proud nostril curve of a prow's line
    In the offing scatterest foam, thy white sails crowding.

Though in all human probability I shall never be the
first to burst into a silent sea, I can declare quite seriously
that I never steer into an unfamiliar creek or haven but, as its
recesses open, I can understand something of the awe of the
boat's crew in Andrew Marvell's 'Bermudas'; yes, and
something of the exultation of the great Columbus himself!

*   *   *   *   *

In a later paper I may have to tell of these voyages and traffickings. For the while I leave the reader to guess how and in what corner of the coast I happened on the following pendant to Mr Dobell's *trouvaille*.

It may not challenge comparison with Mr Flinders Petrie's work in Egypt or with Mr Hogarth's Cretan explorations; but I say confidently that, since Mr Pickwick unearthed the famous inscribed stone, no more fortunate or astonishing discovery has rewarded literary research upon our English soil than the two letters which with no small pride I give to the world this month.

Curiously enough, they concern Mr Pickwick.

But, perhaps, by way of preface I shall remind the reader that the final number of *Pickwick* was issued in November, 1837. The first French version—which Mr Percy Fitzgerald justly calls 'a rude adaptation rather than a translation'—appeared in 1838, and was entitled *Le Club de Pickwickistes, Roman Comique, traduit librement de l'Anglais par Mdme Eugénie Giboyet*. With equal justice Mr Fitzgerald complains (*The History of Pickwick*, p. 276) that 'the most fantastic tricks are played with the text, most of the dialogue being left out and the whole compressed into two small volumes.'

Yet, in fact, Mme Giboyet (as will appear) was more sinned against than sinning. Clearly she undertook to translate the immortal novel in collaboration with a M. Alexandre D——, and was driven by the author's disapproval to suppress M. D——'s share of the work. The dates are sufficient evidence that this was done (as it no doubt had to be done) in haste. I regret that my researches have yielded no further information respecting this M. Alexandre D——. The threat in the second letter may or may not have been carried out. I am inclined to hope that it was, feeling sure that the result, if ever discovered, will prove in the highest degree entertaining. With this I may leave the letters to speak for themselves.

(1)

'45 Doughty Street,
'*September 25th*, 1837.

'MY DEAR MADAM,—It is true that when granting the required permission to translate *Pickwick* into French, I allowed also the license you claimed for yourself and your *collaborateur*—of adapting rather than translating, and of presenting my hero under such small disguise as might commend him better to a Gallic audience. But I am bound to say that—to judge only from the first half of your version, which is all that has reached me—you have construed this permission more freely than I desired. In fact, the parent can hardly recognise his own child.

'Against your share in the work, Madame, I have little to urge, though the damages you represent Mrs Bardell as claiming—300,000 francs, or £12,000 of our money—strikes me as excessive. It is rather (I take as my guide the difference in the handwriting) to your *collaborateur* that I address, through you, my remonstrances.

'I have no radical objection to his making Messrs Snodgrass, Winkle, and Tupman members of His Majesty King Louis XIII's corps of Musketeers, if he is sincerely of opinion that French taste will applaud the departure. I even commend his slight idealisation of Snodgrass (which, by the way, is not the name of an English mountain), and the amorousness of Tupman (Aramis) gains—I candidly admit—from the touch of religiosity which he gives to the character; though I do not, as he surmises, in the course of my story, promote Tupman to a bishopric. The development—preferable as on some points the episcopal garb may be considered to the green velvet jacket with a two-inch tail worn by him at Madame Chasselion's *fête champêtre*—would jar upon our Anglican prejudices. As for Winkle (Porthos), the translation nicely hits off his love of manly exercises, while resting his pretensions on a more solid basis of fact than appears in the original. In the incident of the baldric, however, the imposture underlying Mr W.'s green shooting-coat is conveyed with sufficient neatness.

'M. D—— has been well advised again in breaking up the character of Sam Weller and making him, like Cerberus, three gentlemen at once. Buckingham (Jingle) and Fenton (a capital rendering of the Fat Boy) both please me; and in expanding the episode of the sausage and the trouser-buttons M. D—— has shown delicacy and judgment by altering the latter into diamond studs.

'Alas! madam, I wish the same could be said for his treatment of my female puppets, which not only shocks but bewilders me. In her earlier appearances Mrs Bardell (Milady) is a fairly consistent character; and why M. D—— should hazard that consistency by identifying her with the middle-aged lady at the great White Horse, Ipswich, passes my comprehension. I say, madam, that it bewilders me; but for M. D——'s subsequent development of the occurrences at that hostelry I entertain feelings of which mere astonishment is, perhaps, the mildest. I can hardly bring myself to discuss this with a lady; but you will allow me to protest in the very strongest terms that Mr Pickwick made that unfortunate mistake about the sleeping apartment in the completest innocence, that in ejaculating "ha-hum" he merely uttered a note of warning, and that "ha-hum"

is *not* (as M. D—— suspects) an English word from
which certain syllables have been discreetly removed; that
in thrusting his head through the bed-curtains he was, as
I am careful to say, "not actuated by any definite object";
and that, as a gentleman should, he withdrew at the earliest
possible moment. His intercepted duel with Mr Peter
Magnus (De Wardes) rests, as I fondly imagined I had
made clear, upon a complete misunderstanding. The whole
business of the *fleur-de-lys* on Mrs Bardell's shoulder is a
sheer interpolation and should be expunged, not only on
grounds of morality, but because when you reach the actual
trial, "Bardell *v*. Pickwick," you will find this discovery
of the defendant's impossible either to ignore or to reconcile
with the jury's verdict. Against the intervention of Richelieu
(Mr Nupkins) I have nothing to urge. M. D.—— opines
that I shall in the end deal out poetical justice to Mrs
Bardell as Milady. He is right. I have, indeed, gone so
far as to imprison her; but I own that her execution (as
suggested by him) at the hands of the Queer Client, with
Pickwick and his friends (or, alternatively, Mrs Cluppins,
Mr Perker, and Bob Sawyer) as silent spectators, seems to
me almost as inconsistent with the spirit of the tale as his
other proposal to kidnap Mr Justice Stareleigh in the boot
of Mr Weller's coach, and substitute for his lordship the
Chancery prisoner in an iron mask. I trust, madam, that
these few suggestions will, without setting any appreciable
constraint on your fancy, enable you to catch something
more of the spirit of my poor narrative than I have been
able to detect in some of the chapters submitted; and I am,
with every assurance of esteem,

'Your obliged servant,

'Boz.

'P.S.—The difference between Anjou wine and the

milk punch about which you inquire does not seem to
me to necessitate any serious alteration of the chapter in
question. M. D——'s expressed intention of making
Master Bardell in later life the executioner of King Charles I
of England must stand over for some future occasion. The
present work will hardly yield him the required opportunity for dragging in King Charles' head.'

(2)

'MADAME,—Puisque M. Boz se méfie des propositions
lui faites sans but quelconque que de concilier les gens
d'esprit, j'ai l'honneur de vous annoncer nettement que je
me retire d'une besogne aussi rude que malentendue. Il dit
que j'ai conçu son *Pickwick* tout autrement que lui. Soit!
Je l'écrirai, ce *Pickwick*, selon mon propre goût. Que
M. Boz redoute mes *Trois Pickwickistes!* Agréez, Madame,
etc., etc.   'ALEXANDRE (le Grand).'

*   *   *   *   *

I am told that literary aspirants in these days do not read
books, or read them only for purposes of review-writing.
Yet these pages may happen to fall in the way of some
literary aspirant faint on a false scent, yet pursuing; and
to him, before telling of another discovery, I will address
one earnest word of caution. Let him receive it as from an
elder brother who wishes him well.

My caution is—Avoid irony as you would the plague.

Years ago I was used to receive this warning (on an
average) once a week from my old and dear friend Sir
Wemyss Reid; and once a week I would set myself,
assailing his good nature, to cajole him into printing some

piece of youthful extravagance which he well knew—and I knew—and he knew that I knew—would infuriate a hundred staid readers of *The Speaker* and oblige him to placate in private a dozen puzzled and indignant correspondents. For those were days before the beards had stiffened on the chins of some of us who assembled to reform politics, art, literature, and the world in general from a somewhat frowsy upstairs coffee-room in C—— Street: days of old—

> When fellowship seem'd not so far to seek
> And all the world and we seem'd much less cold
> And at the rainbow's foot lay surely gold. . . .

Well, these cajoleries were not often successful, yet often enough to keep the sporting instinct alive and active, and a great deal oftener than F——'s equally disreputable endeavours: it being a tradition with the staff that F—— had sworn by all his gods to get in an article which would force the printer to flee the country. I need scarcely say that the tradition was groundless, but we worked it shamelessly.

In this way on January 9th, 1897 (a year in which the Westminster Aquarium was yet standing), and shortly after the issue of the New Year's Honours' List, the following article appeared in *The Speaker*. The reader will find it quite harmless until he comes to the sequel. It was entitled—

NOOKS OF OLD LONDON

I.—THE WESTMINSTER SCUTORIUM

LET me begin by assuring the reader that the Westminster Scutorium has absolutely no connection with the famous Aquarium across the road. I suppose that every Londoner has heard, at least, of the Aquarium, but I doubt if one in a

hundred has heard of the little Scutorium which stands removed from it by a stone's throw, or less; and I am certain
that not one in a thousand has ever stooped his head to enter
by its shy, squat, fifteenth-century doorway. It is a fact that
the very policeman at the entrance to Dean's Yard did not
know its name, and the curator assures me that the Post Office
has made frequent mistakes in delivering his letters. So my
warning is not quite impertinent.

But a reader of antiquarian tastes, who cares as little as I
do for hypnotisers and fasting men, and does not mind a trifle
of dust, so it be venerable, will not regret an hour spent in
looking over the Scutorium, or a chat with Mr Melville
Robertson, its curator, or Clerk of the Ribands (*Stemmata*)—
to give him his official title. Mr Robertson ranks, indeed, with
the four pursuivants of Heralds' College, from which the
Scutorium was originally an offshoot. He takes an innocent
delight in displaying his treasures and admitting you to the
stores of his unique information; and I am sure would welcome
more visitors.

Students of Constitutional History will remember that
strange custom, half Roman, half Medieval, in accordance
with which a baron or knight, on creation or accession to
his title and dignities, deposited in the king's keeping a waxen
effigy, or mask, of himself, together with a copy of his coat
of arms. And it has been argued—plausibly enough when we
consider the ancestral masks of the old Roman families, the
respect paid to them by the household, and the important part
they played on festival days, at funerals, etc.—that this offering
was a formal recognition of the *patria potestas* of the monarch
as father of his people. Few are aware, however, that the
custom has never been discontinued, and that the cupboards
of Westminster contain a waxen memorial of almost every man
whom the king has delighted to honour, from the Conquest
down to the very latest knight gazetted. The labour of
modelling and painting these effigies was discontinued as long

ago as 1586; and the masks are no longer likenesses, but oval
plates of copper, each bearing its name on a label. Mr Robertson
informed me that Charles I made a brief attempt to revive the
old practice. All the Stuarts, indeed, set store on the Scutorium
and its functions; and I read in an historical pamphlet, by
Mr J. Saxby Hine, the late curator, that large apartments were
allocated to the office in Inigo Jones's first designs for Whitehall.
But its rosy prospects faded with the accession of William of
Orange. Two years later the custody of the shields (from which
it obtained its name) was relegated to the Heralds' College;
and the Scutorium has now to be content with the care of its
masks and the performance of some not unimportant duties
presently to be recounted.

A reference from the Heralds' College sent me in quest of
Mr Melville Robertson. But even in Dean's Yard I found it
no easy matter to run him to earth. The policeman (as I have
said) could give me no help. At length, well within the fourth
doorway on the east side, after passing the railings, I spied a
modest brass plate with the inscription *Clerk of the Ribands.
Hours 11 to 3.* The outside of the building has a quite modern
look, but the architect has spared the portal, and the three
steps which lead down to the flagged entrance hall seem to mark
a century apiece. I call it an entrance hall, but it is
rather a small adytum, spanned by a pointed arch carrying
the legend *Stemmata Qvid Facivnt.* The modern exterior is,
in fact, but a shell. All within dates from Henry VI; and
Mr Robertson (but this is only a theory) would explain the
sunken level of the ground-floor rooms by the action of earth-
worms, which have gradually lifted the surface of Dean's Yard
outside. He contends the original level to be that of his office,
which lies on the right of the adytum. A door on the left
admits to two rooms occupied by the *nomenclator,* Mr Pender,
and two assistant clerks, who comprise the staff. Straight in
front, a staircase leads to the upper apartments.

Mr Robertson was writing when the clerk ushered me in,

but at once professed himself at my service. He is a gentleman of sixty, or thereabouts, with white hair, a complexion of a country squire, and very genial manners. For some minutes we discussed the difficulty which had brought me to him (a small point in county history), and then he anticipated my request for permission to inspect his masks.

'Would you like to see them? They are really very curious, and I often wonder that the public should evince so small an interest.'

'You get very few visitors?'

'Seldom more than two a day; a few more when the Honours' Lists appear. I thought at first that your visit might be in connection with the new List, but reflected that it was too early. In a day or two we shall be comparatively busy.'

'The Scutorium is concerned then with the Honours' Lists?'

'A little,' replied Mr Robertson, smiling. 'That is to say, we make them.' Then, observing my evident perplexity, he laughed. 'Well, perhaps that is too strong an expression. I should have said, rather, that we fill up the blanks.'

'I had always understood that the Prime Minister drew up the Lists before submitting them to Her Majesty.'

'So he does—with our help. Oh, there is no secrecy about it!' said Mr Robertson, in a tone almost rallying. 'The public is free of all information, only it will not inquire. A little curiosity on its part would even save much unfortunate misunderstanding.'

'In what way?'

'Well, the public reads of rewards (with which, by the way, I have nothing to do) conferred on really eminent men—Lord Roberts, for instance, or Sir Henry Irving, or Sir Joseph Lister. It then goes down the List and, finding a number of names of which it has never heard, complains that Her Majesty's favour has been bestowed on nonentities; whereas this is really the merit of the List, that they *are* nonentities.'

'I don't understand.'

'Well, then, *they don't exist.*'

'But surely ———'

'My dear sir,' said Mr Robertson, still smiling, and handing me his copy of *The Times*, 'cast your eye down that column; take the names of the new knights—"Blain, Clarke, Edridge, Farrant, Laing, Laird, Wardle"—what strikes you as remarkable about them?'

'Why, that I have never heard of any of them.'

'Naturally, for there are no such people. I made them up; and a good average lot they are, though perhaps the preponderance of monosyllables is a little too obvious.'

'But see here. I read that "Mr Thomas Wardle is a silk merchant of Staffordshire."'

'But I assure you that I took him out of *Pickwick.*'

'Yes, but here is "William Laird," for instance. I hear that already two actual William Lairds—one of Birkenhead, the other of Glasgow—are convinced that the honour belongs to them.'

'No doubt they will be round in a day or two. The Heralds' College will refer them to me—not simultaneously, if I may trust Sir Albert Woods's tact—and I shall tell them that it belongs to neither, but to another William Laird altogether. But, if you doubt, take the Indian promotions. Lord Salisbury sometimes adds a name or two after I send in the List, and—well, you know his lordship is not fond of the dark races and has a somewhat caustic humour. Look at the new C.I.E.'s: "Rai Bahadur Pandit Bhag Rum." Does it occur to you that a person of that name really exists? "Khan Bahadur Naoraji ('Naoraji,' mark you) Pestonji Vakil"—it's the language of extravaganza! The Marquis goes too far: it spoils all verisimilitude.'

Mr Robertson grew quite ruffled.

'Then you pride yourself on verisimilitude?' I suggested.

'As I think you may guess; and we spare no pains to attain it, whether in the names or in the descriptions supplied to the

newspapers. "William Arbuthnot Blain, Esq."—you have
heard of Balzac's scouring Paris for a name for one of his
characters. I assure you I scoured England for William
Arbuthnot Blain—"identified with the movement for improving the dwellings of the labouring classes"—or is that
Richard Farrant, Esq.? In any case, what more likely, on
the face of it? "Frederick Wills, Esq., of the well-known
tobacco firm of Bristol"—the public swallows that readily:
and yet it never buys a packet of their Westward Ho! Mixture
(which I smoke myself) without reading that the Wills's of
Bristol are W. D. and H. O.—no Frederick at all.'

'But,' I urged, 'the purpose of this——'

'I should have thought it obvious; but let me give you the
history of it. The practice began with William III. He was
justly scornful of the lax distribution of honours which had
marked all the Stuart reigns. You will hardly believe it, but
before 1688 knighthoods, and even peerages, went as often
as not to men who qualified by an opportune loan to the
Exchequer, or even by presiding at a public feast. (I say
nothing of baronetcies, for their history is notorious.) At first
William was for making a clean sweep of the Honours' List,
or limiting it to two or three well-approved recipients. But it
was argued that this seeming niggardliness might injure His
Majesty's popularity, never quite secure. The Scutorium found
a way out of the dilemma. Sir Crofton Byng, the then Clerk
of the Ribands, proposed the scheme, which has worked ever
since. I may tell you that the undue *largesse* of honours finds
in the very highest quarters as little favour as ever it did. Of
course, there are some whose services to science, literature, and
art cannot be ignored—the late Lord Leighton, for instance,
or Sir George Newnes, or Sir Joseph Lister again; and these
are honoured, while the public acclaims. But the rest are
represented only in my collection of masks—and an interesting
one it is. Let me lead the way.'

But I have left myself no space for describing the treasures of the Scutorium. The two upper stories are undoubtedly the least interesting, since they contain the modern, unpainted masks. Each mask has its place, its label, and on the shelf below it, protected by a slip of glass, a description of the imaginary recipient of the royal favour. One has only to look along the crowded shelves to be convinced that Mr Melville Robertson's office is no sinecure. The first floor is devoted to a small working library and a museum (the latter undergoing rearrangement at the time of my visit). But the cellars!—or (as I should say) the crypt! In Beaumont's words—

> Here's a world of pomp and state
> Buried in dust, once dead by fate!

Here in their native colours, by the light of Mr Robertson's duplex lantern, stare the faces of the illustrious dead, from Rinaldus FitzTurold, knighted on Senlac field, to stout old Crosby Martin, sea-rover, who received the accolade (we'll hope he deserved it) from the Virgin Queen in 1586. A few even are adorned with side-locks, which Mr Pender, the *nomenclator*, keeps scrupulously dusted. In almost every case the wax has withstood the tooth of time far better than one could have expected. Mr Robertson believes that the pigments chosen must have had some preservative virtue. If so, the secret has been lost. But Mr Pender has touched over some of the worst decayed with a mixture of copal and pure alcohol, by which he hopes at least to arrest the mischief; and certainly the masks in the Scutorium compare very favourably with the waxen effigies of our royalties preserved in the Abbey, close by. Mr Robertson has a theory that these, too, should by rights belong to his museum: but that is another story, and a long one. Suffice it to say that I took my leave with the feelings of one who has spent a profitable afternoon: and for further information concerning this most interesting nook of old London I can only refer the reader to the pamphlet already alluded to, *The Westminster Scutorium: Its History and Present Uses.* By

J. Saxby Hine, C.B., F.S.A. Theobald & Son, Skewers Alley, Chancery Lane, E.C.

*   *   *   *   *

This article appeared to my beloved editor innocent enough to pass, and to me (as doubtless to the reader) harmless enough in all conscience. Now listen to the sequel.

Long afterwards an acquaintance of mine—a barrister with antiquarian tastes—was dining with me in my Cornish home, and the talk after dinner fell upon the weekly papers and reviews. On *The Speaker* he touched with a reticence which I set down at first to dislike for his politics. By and by, however, he let slip the word 'untrustworthy.'

'Holding your view of its opinions,' I suggested, 'you might fairly say "misleading." "Untrustworthy" is surely too strong a word.'

'I am not talking,' said he, 'of its opinions, but of its mis-statements of fact. Some time ago it printed an article on a place which it called "The Westminster Scutorium," and described in detail. I happened to pick the paper up at my club and read the article. It contained a heap of historical information on the forms and ceremonies which accompany the granting of titles, and was apparently the work of a specialist. Being interested (as you know) in these matters, and having an hour to spare, I took a hansom down to Westminster. At the entrance of Dean's Yard I found a policeman, and inquired the way to the Scutorium. He eyed me for a moment, then he said, "Well, I thought I'd seen the last of 'em. You're the first to-day, so far; and yesterday there was only five. But Monday—*and* Tuesday—*and* Wednesday! There must have been thirty came as late as Wednesday; though by that time I'd found out what was the matter. All Monday they kept me hunting round and round the yard, following like a pack. Very respectable-looking old gentlemen, too, the whole of 'em, else I should have guessed they were pulling my leg. Most of 'em had copies of a paper, *The Speaker*, and read out bits from it, and insisted on my searching in this direction and that...and me being new to this beat, and seeing it all in print! We called in the postman to help. By and by they began to compare notes, and found they'd been kidded, and some of 'em used language....I really think, sir, you must be the last of 'em.'"

MAY

I WAS travelling some weeks ago by a railway line alongside of which ran a quickset hedge. It climbed to the summit of cuttings, plunged to the base of embankments, looped itself around stations, flickered on the skyline above us, raced us along the levels, dipped into pools, shot up again on their farther banks, chivvied us into tunnels, ran round and waited for us as we emerged. Its importunity drove me to the other side of the carriage, only to find another quickset hedge behaving similarly. Now I can understand that a railway company has excellent reasons for planting quickset hedges alongside its permanent way. But their unspeakable monotony set me thinking. Why do we neglect the real parks of England?—parks enormous in extent, and yet uncultivated, save here and there and in the most timid fashion. And how better could our millionaires use their wealth (since they are always confiding to us their difficulties in getting rid of it) than by seeking out these gardens and endowing them, and so, without pauperising anyone, build for themselves monuments not only delightful, but perpetual?—for, as Victor Hugo said, the flowers last always. So, you may say, do books. I doubt it; and experts, who have discussed with me the modern products of the paper trade, share my gloomy views. Anyhow, the free public library has been sufficiently exploited, if not worked out. So, you may say again, have free public gardens and parks been worked out. I think not. Admit that a fair percentage of the public

avails itself of these libraries and parks; still the mass does
not, and they were intended for the mass. Their attractive-
ness does not spread and go on spreading. The stream of
public appreciation which pours through them is not
fathomless; beyond a certain point it does not deepen,
or deepens with heart-breaking slowness; and candid
librarians and curators can sound its shallows accurately
enough. What we want is not a garden into which folk
will find their way if they have nothing better to do and
can spare the time without an effort. Or, to be accurate, we
do want such gardens for deliberate enjoyment; but what
we want more is to catch our busy man and build a garden
about him in the brief leisure which, without seeking it,
he is forced to take.

Where are these gardens? Why, beside and along our
railway lines. These are the great public parks of England;
and through them travels daily a vast population held in
enforced idleness, seeking distraction in its morning paper.
Have you ever observed how a whole carriageful of
travellers on the Great Western line will drop their papers
to gaze out on Messrs Sutton's trial-beds just outside
Reading? A garish appeal, no doubt: a few raying spokes
of colour, and the vision has gone. And I forestall the
question, 'Is that the sort of thing you wish to see extended?
—a bed of yellow tulips, for instance, or of scarlet lobelias,
or of bright-blue larkspurs, all the way from London to
Liverpool?' I suggest nothing of the sort. Our railway
lines in England, when they follow the valleys—as railway
lines must in hilly districts—are extraordinarily beautiful.
The eye, for example, could desire nothing better, in swift
flight, than the views along the Wye Valley or in the Derbyshire Peak country, and even the rich levels of Somerset
have a beauty of their own (above all in May and June,

when yellow with sheets of buttercups) which artificial planting would spoil. But—cant about Nature apart—every line has its dreary cuttings and embankments, all of which might be made beautiful at no great cost. I need not labour this: here and there by a casual bunch of rhododendrons or of gorse, or by a sheet of primroses or wild hyacinths in springtime, the thing is proved, and has been proved again and again to me by the comments of fellow-passengers.

Now I am honestly enamoured of this dream of mine, and must pause to dwell on some of its beauties. In the first place, we could start to realise it in the most modest fashion and test the appreciation of the public as we go along. Our flowers would be mainly wild flowers, and our trees, for the most part, native British plants, costing, say, from thirty shillings to three pounds the hundred. A few roods would do to begin with, if the spot were well chosen; indeed, it would be wiser in every way to begin modestly, for though England possesses several great artists in landscape gardening, their art has never to my knowledge been seriously applied to railway gardening, and the speed of the spectators introduces a new and highly-amusing condition, and one so singular and so important as to make this almost a separate art. At any rate, our gardeners would have to learn as they go, and if any man can be called enviable it is an artist learning to express art's eternal principles in a new medium, under new conditions.

Even if we miss our millionaire, we need not despond over ways and means. The beauty-spots of Great Britain are engaged just now in a fierce rivalry of advertisement. Why should not this rivalry be pressed into the service of beautifying the railway lines along which the tourist must travel to reach them? Why should we neglect the porches

(so to speak) of our temples? Would not the tourist arrive
in a better temper if met on his way with silent evidence
of our desire to please? And, again, is the advertising trades-
man quite wise in offending so many eyes with his succession of ugly hoardings standing impertinently in green
fields? Can it be that the sight of them sets up that disorder
of the liver which he promises to cure? And if not, might
he not call attention to his wares at least as effectively, if
more summarily, by making them the excuse for a vision
of delight which passengers would drop their newspapers
to gaze upon? Lastly, the railway companies themselves
have discovered the commercial value of scenery. Years
ago, and long before their discovery (and as if by a kind of
instinct they were blundering towards it) they began to offer
prizes for the best-kept station gardens—with what happy
result all who have travelled in South Wales will remember.
They should find it easy to learn that the 'development'
of watering-places and holiday resorts may be profitably
followed up by spending care upon their approaches.

But I come back to my imaginary millionaire—the
benevolent man who only wants to be instructed how to
spend his money—the 'magnificent man' of Aristotle's
Ethics, nonplussed for the moment, and in despair of
discovering an original way of scattering largesse for the
public good. For, while anxious to further my scheme by
conciliating the commercial instinct, I must insist that its
true beauty resides in the conception of our railways as
vast public parks only hindered by our sad lack of inventiveness from ministering to the daily delight of scores of
thousands and the occasional delight of almost everyone.
The millionaire I want is one who can rise to this conception of it, and say with Blake—

        I will not cease from mental fight,

(nor from pecuniary contribution, for that matter)

> Nor shall my sword sleep in my hand
> Till we have built Jerusalem
> In England's green and pleasant land.

For these millionaires are bediamonded all over with good intentions. The mischief with them is their lack of inventiveness. Most of my readers will agree that there is no easier game of solitaire than to suppose yourself suddenly endowed with a million of money, and to invent modes of dispensing it for the good of your kind. As a past master of that game I offer the above suggestion gratis to those poor brothers of mine who have more money than they know how to use.

*   *   *   *   *

The railway—not that of the quickset hedges, but the Great Western, on to which I changed after a tramp across Dartmoor—took me to pay a pious visit to my old school: a visit which I never pay without thinking—especially in the chapel where we used to sing 'Lord, dismiss us with Thy blessing' on the evening before holidays—of a passage in Izaak Walton's *Life of Sir Henry Wotton*:

He yearly went also to Oxford. But the summer before his death he changed that for a journey to Winchester College, to which school he was first removed from Bocton. And as he returned from Winchester towards Eton College, said to a friend, his companion in that journey, 'How useful was that advice of a holy monk who persuaded his friend to perform his customary devotions in a constant place, because in that place we usually meet with those very thoughts which possessed us at our last being there! And I find it thus far experimentally true that at my now being in that school, and seeing the very place where I sat when I was a boy, occasioned me to remember those very thoughts of my youth which then possessed me: sweet thoughts indeed, that promised my growing years numerous pleasures without mixtures of cares: and those to be enjoyed when time—which I therefore thought slow-paced —had changed my youth into manhood. But age and experience have taught me that those were but empty hopes: for I have always found it true, as my Saviour did foretell, "Sufficient for the day is the evil thereof." Nevertheless, I saw there a succession of boys using the same recreations and, questionless, possessed with the same thoughts that then possessed me. Thus one generation succeeds another, both in their lives, recreations, hopes, fears, and death.'

But my visit on this occasion was filled with thought less of myself than of a poet I had known in that chapel, those cloisters, that green close; not intimately enough to call him friend, yet so intimately that his lately-departed shade still haunted the place for me—a small boy whom he had once, for a day or two, treated with splendid kindness and thereafter (I dare say) had forgotten.

*   *   *   *   *

'T. E. B.'

Thomas Edward Brown was born on May 5th, 1830, at Douglas, in the Isle of Man, where his father held the living of St Matthew's. Sixty-five years later he wrote his last verses to aid a fund raised for a new St Matthew's Church, and characteristically had to excuse himself in a letter penetrated with affection for the old plain edifice and its memories.

I was baptised there; almost all whom I loved and revered were associated with its history... 'The only church in Douglas where the poor go'—I dare say that is literally true. But I believe it will continue to be so.... I postulate the continuity....

I quote these words (and so leave them for a while) with a purpose, aware how trivial they may seem to the reader. But to those who had the privilege of knowing Brown that cannot be trivial which they feel to be characteristic and in some degree explicative of the man; and with this 'I postulate the continuity' we touch accurately and simply for once a note which sang in many chords of the most vocal, not to say orchestral, nature it has ever been my lot to meet.

Let me record, and have done with, the few necessary incidents of what was by choice a *vita fallens* and 'curiously devoid of incident.' The boy was but two years old when the family removed to Kirk Braddan Vicarage, near Douglas; the sixth of ten children of a witty and sensible Scots mother and a father whose nobly humble idiosyncrasies continued in his son and are worthy to live longer in his description of them:

> To think of a *Pazon* respecting men's vices even; not as vices, God forbid! but as parts of *them*, very likely all but inseparable from them; at any rate, *theirs!* Pitying with an eternal pity, but not exposing, not rebuking. My father would have considered he was 'taking a liberty' if he had confronted the sinner with his sin. Doubtless he carried this too far. But don't suppose for a moment that the 'weak brethren' thought he was conniving at their weakness. Not they: they saw the delicacy of his conduct. You don't think, do you, that these poor souls are incapable of appreciating delicacy? God only knows how far down into their depths of misery the sweetness of that delicacy descends.... He loved sincerity, truth and modesty. It seemed as if he felt that, with these virtues, the others could not fail to be present.

Add to this that the Vicar of Kirk Braddan, though of no University, was a scholar in grain; was, for example, so fastidious about composition that he would make his son read some fragment of an English classic to him before answering an invitation! 'To my father style was like the instinct of personal cleanliness.' Again we touch notes which echoed through the life of his son—who worshipped continuity.

From a course of tuition divided between his father and the parish schoolmaster, Brown went, at fifteen or over, to King William's College, and became its show scholar; thence, by the efforts of well-meaning friends (but at the cost of much subsequent pain), to Christ Church, Oxford, as a servitor. He won his double first; but he has left on record an account of a servitor's position at Christ Church in the early fifties, and to Brown the spiritual humiliation can have been little less than one long dragging anguish. He had, of course, his intervals of high spirits; but (says Mr Irwin, his friend and biographer) 'there is no doubt he did not exaggerate what the position was to him. I have heard him refer to it over and over again with a dispassionate bitterness there was no mistaking.' Dean Gaisford absolutely refused to nominate him, after his two first classes, to a fellowship, though all the resident dons wished it. 'A servitor never has been elected student—*ergo*, he never shall be.' Brown admired Gaisford, and always spoke kindly of him 'in all his dealings with me.' Yet the night after he won his double first was 'one of the most intensely miserable I was ever called to endure.' Relief, and of the right kind, came with his election as Fellow of Oriel in April, 1854. In those days an Oriel Fellowship still kept and conveyed its peculiar distinction, and the brilliant young scholar had at length the ball at his feet.

'This is none of your empty honours,' he wrote to his mother; 'it gives me an income of about £300 per annum as long as I choose to reside at Oxford, and about £220 in cash if I reside elsewhere. In addition to this it puts me in a highly commanding position for pupils, so that on the whole I have every reason to expect that (except perhaps the first year) I shall make between £500 and £600 altogether per annum. So you see, my dear mother, that your prayers have not been unanswered, and that God will bless the generation of those who humbly strive to serve Him.... I have not omitted to remark that the election took place on April 21st, the anniversary of your birth and marriage.'

How did he use his opportunity? 'He never took kindly to the life of an Oxford fellow,' thought the late Dr Fowler (an old schoolfellow of Brown's, afterwards President of Corpus and Vice-Chancellor of the University). Mr Irwin quotes another old friend, Archdeacon Moore, to much the same effect. Their explanations lack something of definiteness. After a few terms of private pupils Brown returned to the Island, and there accepted the office of Vice-principal of his old school. We can only be sure that his reasons were honourable, and sufficed for him; we may include among them, if we choose, that *nostalgia* which haunted him all his days, until fate finally granted his wish and sent him back to his beloved Argos 'for good.'

In the following year (1857) he married his cousin, Miss Stowell, daughter of Dr Stowell, of Ramsay; and soon after left King William's College to become 'by some strange mischance' Head Master of the Crypt School, Gloucester. Of this 'Gloucester episode,' as he called it, nothing needs to be recorded except that he hated the whole business and, incidentally, that one of his pupils was Mr W. E. Henley—destined to gather into his *National Observer*, many years later, many blooms of Brown's last and not least memorable efflorescence in poesy.

From Gloucester he was summoned, on a fortunate day, by Mr Percival (now Bishop of Hereford), who had recently been appointed to Clifton College, then a struggling new foundation, soon to be lifted by him into the ranks of the great Public Schools. Mr Percival wanted a man to take the Modern Side; and, as fate orders these things, consulted the friend reserved by fate to be his own successor at Clifton—Mr Wilson (now Canon of Worcester). Mr Wilson was an old King William's boy; knew Brown, and named him.

'Mr Wilson having told me about him,' writes the bishop, 'I made an appointment to see him in Oxford, and there, as chance would have it, I met him standing at the corner of St Mary's Entry, in a somewhat Johnsonian attitude, four-square, his hands deep in his pockets to keep himself still, and looking decidedly *volcanic*. We very soon came to terms, and I left him there under promise to come to Clifton as my colleague at the beginning of the following Term; and, needless to say, St Mary's Entry has had an additional interest to me ever since. Sometimes I have wondered, and it would be worth a good deal to know, what thoughts were crossing through that richly-furnished, teeming brain as he stood there by St Mary's Church, with Oriel College in front of him, thoughts of his own struggles and triumphs, and of all the great souls that had passed to and fro over the pavement around him; and all set in the lurid background of the undergraduate life to which he had been condemned as a servitor at Christ Church.'

Was he happy in his many years' work at Clifton? On the whole, and with some reservation, we may say 'yes'— 'yes,' although in the end he escaped from it gladly and enjoyed his escape. One side of him, no doubt, loathed formality and routine; he was, as he often proclaimed

himself, a nature-loving, somewhat intractable Celt; and
if one may hint at a fault in him, it was that now and then
he soon *tired*. A man so spendthrift of emotion is bound
at times to knock on the bottom of his emotional coffers;
and no doubt he was true *to a mood* when he wrote—

> I'm here at Clifton, grinding at the mill
>> My feet for thrice nine barren years have trod,
> But there are rocks and waves at Scarlett still,
>> And gorse runs riot in Glen Chass—thank God!
> Alert, I seek exactitude of rule,
>> I step and square my shoulders with the squad,
> But there are blaeberries on old Barrule,
>> And Langness has its heather still—thank God!

—with the rest of the rebellious stanzas. We may go farther
and allow that he played with the mood until he sometimes
forgot. on which side lay seriousness and on which side
humour. Still it *was* a mood; and it was Brown, after all,
who wrote 'Planting':

> Who would be planted chooseth not the soil
>> Or here or there,
>> Or loam or peat,
>> Wherein he best may grow
> And bring forth guerdon of the planter's toil—
>> The lily is most fair,
>> But says not 'I will only blow
> Upon a southern land'; the cedar makes no coil
>> What rock shall owe
>> The springs that wash his feet;
> The crocus cannot arbitrate the foil
>> That for his purple radiance is most meet—
>> Lord, even so
>> I ask one prayer,
>>> The which if it be granted,
>> It skills not where
>>> Thou plantest me, only I would be planted.

'You don't care for school-work,' he writes to an Old
Cliftonian....'I demur to your statement that when you take
up schoolmastering your leisure for this kind of thing will be
practically gone. Not at all. If you have the root of the matter
in you the school-work will insist upon this kind of thing as
a relief. My plan always was to recognise two lives as necessary
—the one the outer Kapelistic life of drudgery, the other the
inner and cherished life of the spirit. It is true that the one
has a tendency to kill the other, but it must not, and you must
see that it does not.... The pedagogic is needful for bread
and butter, also for a certain form of joy; of the inner life you
know what I think.'

These are wise words, and I believe they represent Brown
more truly than utterances which only seem more genuine
because less deliberate. He was as a house master excellent,
with an excellence not achievable by men whose hearts
are removed from their work: he awoke and enjoyed
fervent friendships and the enthusiastic admiration of many
youngsters; he must have known of these enthusiasms, and
was not the man to condemn them; he had the abiding
assurance of assisting in a kind of success which he certainly
respected. He longed for the day of emancipation, to
return to his Island; he was impatient; but I must decline
to believe he was unhappy.

Indeed, his presence sufficiently denied it. How shall
I describe him? A sturdy, thick-set figure, inclining to
rotundity, yet athletic; a face extraordinarily mobile; bushy,
grey eyebrows; eyes at once deeply and radiantly human, yet
holding the primitive faun in their coverts; a broad mouth
made for broad, natural laughter, hearty without lewdness.
'There are nice Rabelaisians, and there are nasty; but the
latter are not Rabelaisians.' 'I have an idea,' he claimed,
'that my judgment within this area is infallible.' And it
was. All honest laughter he welcomed as a Godlike function.

> God sits upon His hill,
> And sees the shadows fly;
> And if He laughs at fools, why should He not?

And for that matter, why should not we? Though at
this point his fine manners intervened, correcting, counsel-
ling moderation. 'I am certain God made fools for us to
enjoy, but there must be *an economy of joy* in the presence
of a fool; you must not betray your enjoyment.' Imagine
all this overlaid with a certain portliness of bearing, suggestive of the high-and-dry Oxford scholar. Add something
of the parsonic (he was ordained deacon before leaving
Oxford, but did not proceed to priest's orders till near the
end of his time at Clifton); add a simple natural piety which
purged the parsonic of all 'churchiness.'

'This silence and solitude are to me absolute food,' he writes
from the Clifton College Library on the morning of Christmas
Day, 1875, 'especially after all the row and worry at the end
of Term....Where are the men and women? Well, now look
here, you'll not mention it again. They're all in church. See
how good God is! See how He has placed these leitourgic
traps in which people, especially disagreeable people, get
caught—and lo! the universe for me!!! me—me....'

I have mentioned his fine manners, and with a certain right,
since it once fell to me—a blundering innocent in the hands
of fate—to put them to severest proof. A candidate for a
scholarship at Clifton—awkward, and abominably conscious of it, and sensitive—I had been billeted on Brown's
hospitality without his knowledge. The mistake (I cannot
tell who was responsible) could not be covered out of sight;
it was past all aid of kindly dissimulation by the time Brown
returned to the house to find the unwelcome guest bathing
in shame upon his doorstep. Can I say more than that he

took me into the family circle—by no means an expansive one, or accustomed, as some are, to open gleefully to intruders—and for the inside of a week treated me with a consideration so quiet and pleasant, so easy yet attentive, that his dearest friend or most distinguished visitor could not have demanded more? A boy notes these things, and remembers.... 'If I lose my manners,' Mr Irwin quotes him as saying once over some trivial forgetfulness, 'what is to become of me?' He was shy, too, like the most of his countrymen—'jus' the shy'—but with a proud reserve as far removed as possible from sham humility—being all too sensible and far too little of a fool to blink his own eminence of mind, though willing on all right occasions to forget it. 'Once,' records Mr Irwin, 'when I remarked on the omission of his name in an article on "Minor Poets" in one of the magazines, he said, with a smile, "Perhaps I am among the major!"' That smile had just sufficient irony—no more.

To this we may add a passion for music and a passion for external nature—external to the most of us, but so closely knit with his own that to be present at his ecstasies was like assisting a high priest of elemental mysteries reserved for him and beyond his power to impart. And yet we are beating about the bush and missing the essential man, for he was imprehensible—'Volcanic,' the Bishop of Hereford calls him, and must go to the Bay of Naples to fetch home a simile:

We can find plenty of beauty in the familiar northern scenes; but we miss the pent-up forces, the volcanic outbursts, the tropic glow, and all the surprising manifold and tender and sweet-scented outpourings of soil and sunshine, so spontaneous, so inexhaustibly rich, and with the heat of a great fire burning and palpitating underneath all the time.

Natures more masterfully commanding I have known: never one more remarkable. In the mere possession of him, rather than in his direct influence, all Cliftonians felt themselves rich. We were at least as proud of him as Etonians of the author of 'Ionica.' But no comparisons will serve. Falstaffian—with a bent of homely piety; Johnsonian —with a fiery Celtic heat and a passionate adoration of Nature: all such epithets fail as soon as they are uttered. The man was at once absolute and Protean: entirely sincere, and yet a different being to each separate friend. 'There was no getting to the end of Brown.'

I have said that we—those of us, at any rate, who were not of Brown's House—were conscious of a rich and honourable possession in him, rather than of an active influence. Yet that influence must not be underrated. Clifton, as I first knew it, was already a great school, although less than twenty years old. But, to a new-comer, even more impressive than its success among schools, or its aspirations, was a firmness of tradition which (I dare to say) would have been remarkable in a foundation of five times its age. It had already its type of boy; and having discovered it and how to produce it, fell something short of tolerance towards other types. For the very reason which allows me with decency to call the type an admirable one, I may be excused for adding that the tradition demanded some patience of those who could not easily manage to conform with it. But there the tradition stood, permanently rooted in a school not twenty years old. Is it fanciful to hold that Brown's passion for 'continuity' had much to do with planting and confirming it? Mr Irwin quotes for us a passage from one of his sermons to the school: 'Suffer no chasm to interrupt this glorious tradition.... Continuous life...that is what we want—to feel the pulses of hearts

that are now dust.' Did this passage occur, I wonder, in
the sermon of which I rather remember a fierce, hopeless,
human protest against 'change and decay'?—the voice
ringing down on each plea, 'What do the change-and-
decay people say to *that*?'

'I postulate the continuity.' Vain postulate it often
seems, yet of all life Brown demanded it. Hear him as
he speaks of his wife's death in a letter to a friend:

> My dear fellow-sufferer, what is it after all? Why this
> sinking of the heart, this fainting, sorrowing of the spirit?
> There is no separation: life is continuous. All that was stable
> and good, good and therefore stable, in our union with the
> loved one, is unquestionably permanent, will endure for ever.
> It cannot be otherwise....When love has done its full work,
> has wrought soul into soul so that every fibre has become part
> of the common life—*quis separabit?* Can you conceive your-
> self as existing at all without *her*? No, you can't; well, then,
> it follows that you don't, and never will.

I believe it to have been this passion for continuity that
bound and kept him so absolute a Manxman, drawing his
heart so persistently back to the Island that there were times
(one may almost fancy) when the prospect of living his
life out to the end elsewhere seemed to him a treachery to
his parents' dust. I believe this same passion drew him—
master as he was of varied and vocal English—to clothe
the bulk of his poetry in the Manx dialect, and thereby to
miss his mark with the public, which inevitably mistook
him for a rustic singer, a man of the people, imperfectly
educated.

I would not be forgotten in this land—

This line of another true poet of curiously similar tempera-

ment[1] has haunted me through the reading of Brown's
published letters. But Brown's was no merely selfish
craving for continuity—to be remembered. By a fallacy
of thought, perhaps, but by a very noble one, he transferred
the ambition to those for whom he laboured. His own
terror that Time might obliterate the moment,

> And all this personal dream be fled,

became for his countrymen a very spring of helpfulness.
Antiquam exquirite matrem—he would do that which they,
in poverty and the stress of earning daily bread, were
careless to do—would explore for them the ancient springs
of faith and custom.

> Dear countrymen, whate'er is left to us
>> Of ancient heritage—
>> Of manners, speech, of humours, polity,
>> The limited horizon of our stage—
>> Old love, hope, fear,
>> All this I fain would fix upon the page;
>> That so the coming age,
>> Lost in the empire's mass,
>> Yet haply longing for their fathers, here
>> May see, as in a glass,
>> What they held dear—
> May say, "'Twas thus and thus
>> They lived'; and as the time-flood onward rolls
>> Secure an anchor for their Keltic souls.

This was his task, and the public of course set him down
for a rustic. 'What ought I to do?' he demands. 'Shall
I put on my next title-page, "Late Fellow of Oriel, etc.".?
or am I always to abide under this ironic cloak of rusticity?'
To be sure, on consideration (if the public ever found time

[1] 'The Quest of the Sangraal,' R. S. Hawker.

to consider), the language and feeling of the poems were penetrated with scholarship. He entered his countrymen's hearts; but he also could, and did, stand outside and observe them with affectionate, comprehending humour. Scholarship saved him, too—not always, but as a rule—from that emotional excess to which he knew himself most dangerously prone. He assigns it confidently to his Manx blood; but his mother was Scottish by descent, and from my experience of what the Lowland Scot can do in the way of pathos when he lets himself go, I take leave to doubt that the Manxman was wholly to blame. There can, however, be no doubt that the author of 'The Doctor,' of 'Catherine Kinrade,' of 'Mater Dolorosa,' described himself accurately as a 'born sobber,' or that an acquired self-restraint saved him from a form of intemperance by which of late our literature has been somewhat too copiously afflicted.

To scholarship, too, imposed upon and penetrating a taste naturally catholic, we owe the rare flavour of the many literary judgments scattered about his letters. They have a taste of native earth, beautifully rarefied: to change the metaphor, they illuminate the page with a kind of lambent common sense. For a few examples:

I have also read a causerie on Virgil and one on Theocritus. So many French *littérateurs* give me the idea that they don't go nearer the Greek authors than the Latin translations.... Sainte Beuve [*Nouveaux Lundis*, vii. 1–52, on 'The Greek Anthology'] is an enthusiastic champion for our side, but, oddly enough, he never strikes me as knowing much about the matter!

Your Latin verses [translating Cowley] I greatly enjoy. The dear old Abraham goes straight off into your beautiful lines. Of course he has not a scrap of modern *impedimenta*. You go through the customs at the frontier with a whistle and a smile. You have *nothing to declare*. The blessed old man by your side is himself a Roman to begin with, and you pass together as cheerfully as possible....

I have also been reading Karl Elze's *Essays on Shakespeare*. He is not bad, but don't you resent the imperturbable confidence of men who, after attributing a play of Shakespeare's to two authors, proceed to suggest a third, urged thereto by some fatuous and self-sought exigency?

Did you ever try to write a Burns song? I mean the equivalent in ordinary English of his Scotch. Can it be done? A Yorkshireman—could he do it? A Lancashire man (Waugh)? I hardly think so. The Ayrshire dialect has a *Schwung* and a confidence that no English county can pretend to. Our dialects are apologetic things, half-ashamed, half-insolent. Burns has no doubts, and for his audience unhesitatingly demands the universe....

There is an ἦθος in Fitzgerald's letters which is so exquisitely idyllic as to be almost heavenly. He takes you with him, exactly accommodating his pace to yours, walks through meadows so tranquil, and yet abounding in the most delicate surprises. And these surprises seem so familiar, just as if they had originated with yourself. What delicious blending! What a perfect interweft of thought and diction! What a *sweet* companion!

Lastly, let me quote a passage in which his thoughts return to Clifton, where it had been suggested that Greek should be omitted from the ordinary form-routine and taught in 'sets,' or separate classes:

This is disturbing about Greek, 'set' Greek. Yes, you would fill your school to overflowing, of course you would, so long as other places did not abandon the old lines. But it would be detestable treachery to the cause of education, of

humanity. To me the *learning* of any blessed thing is a matter
of little moment. Greek is not learned by nineteen-twentieths
of our Public School boys. But it is a baptism into a cult,
a faith, not more irrational than other faiths or cults; the
baptism of a regeneration which releases us from I know not
what original sin. And if a man does not see that, he is a fool,
such a fool that I shouldn't wonder if he gravely asked me
to explain what I meant by original sin in such a connection....

So his thoughts reverted to the school he had left in 1892.
In October, 1897, he returned to it on a visit. He was the
guest of one of the house masters, Mr Tait, and on Friday
evening, October 29th, gave an address to the boys of the
house. He had spoken for some minutes with brightness
and vigour, when his voice grew thick and he was seen to
stagger. He died in less than two hours.

His letters have been collected and piously given to the
world by Mr Irwin, one of his closest friends. By far the
greatest number of them belong to those last five years in
the Island—the happiest, perhaps, of his life, certainly the
happiest temperamentally. 'Never the time and the place...'
but at least Brown was more fortunate than most men. He
realised his dream, and it did not disappoint him. He could
not carry off his friends to share it (and it belongs to criticism
of these volumes to say that he was exceptionally happy in
his friends), but he could return and visit them or stay at
home and write to them concerning the realisation, and
be sure they understood. Therefore, although we desire
more letters of the Clifton period—although twenty years
are omitted, left blank to us—those that survive confirm
a fame which, although never wide, was always unques-
tioned within its range. There could be no possibility of
doubt concerning Brown. He was absolute. He lived a
fierce, shy, spiritual life; a wise man, keeping the child

in his heart: he loved much and desired permanence in
the love of his kind. 'Diuturnity,' says his great seventeenth-
century namesake, 'is a dream and folly of expectation.
There is nothing strictly immortal but immortality.' And
yet, *prosit amâsse!*

*   *   *   *   *

The railway took me on to Oxford—

> Like faithful hound returning
> For old sake's sake to each loved track
> With heart and memory burning.

'I well remember,' writes Mrs Green of her husband,
the late John Richard Green, 'the passionate enthusiasm
with which he watched from the train for the first sight
of the Oxford towers against the sky': and although our
enthusiasm nowadays has to feed on a far tamer view than
that which saluted our forefathers when the stage-coach
topped the rise of Shotover and its passengers beheld the
city spread at their feet, yet what faithful son of Oxford
can see her towers rise above the water-meadows and re-
greet them without a thrill?

In the year 1688, and in a book entitled *The Guardian's
Instruction*, a Mr Stephen Penton gave the world a pleasing
and lifelike little narrative—superior, in my opinion, to
anything in *Verdant Green*—telling us how a reluctant
father was persuaded to send his son to Oxford; what
doubts, misgivings, hesitations he had, and how they were
overcome. I take the story to be fictitious. It is written
in the first person, professedly by the hesitating parent:
but the parent can hardly have been Penton, for the story
will not square with what we know of his life. The actual
Penton was born, it seems, in 1640, and educated at

Winchester and New College; proceeded to his fellowship, resided from 1659 to 1670, and was Principal of St Edmund's Hall from 1675 to 1683. He appears to have been chaplain to the Earl of Aylesbury, and, according to Antony à Wood, possessed a 'rambling head.' He died in 1706.

The writer in *The Guardian's Instruction* is portrayed for us—or is allowed to portray himself—rather as an honest country squire, who had himself spent a year or so of his youth at the University, but had withdrawn when Oxford was invaded by the Court and the trouble between King Charles and Parliament came to a head: and 'God's grace, the Good example of my parents, and a natural love of virtue secured me so far as to leave Oxford, though not much more learned, yet not much worse than I came thither.' A chill testimonial! In short, the old squire (as I will take leave to call him) nursed a somewhat crotchety detestation of the place, insomuch 'that when I came to have children, I did almost *swear* them in their childhood never to be friends with Oxford.'

He tried his eldest son with a course of foreign travel as a substitute for University training; but this turned out a failure, and he had the good sense to acknowledge his mistake. So for his second boy he cast about to find a profession; 'but what course to take I was at a loss: Cambridge was so far off, I could not have an eye upon him; Oxford I was angry with.'

In this fix he consulted with a neighbour, 'an old grave learned divine,' and rigid Churchman, who confessed that many of the charges against Oxford were well grounded, but averred that the place was mending. The truth was, the University had been loyal to the monarchy all through the Commonwealth times; and when Oliver Cromwell was dead, and Richard dismounted, its members perceived,

through the maze of changes and intrigues, that in a little
time the heart of the nation would revert to the government which twenty years before it had hated. And their
impatient hopes of this 'made the scholars talk aloud, drink
healths, and curse Meroz in the very streets; insomuch
that when the King came in, they were not only like them
that dream, but like them who are out of their wits, mad,
stark, staring mad.' This unholy 'rag' (to modernise the
old gentleman's language) continued for a twelvemonth:
that is to say, until the Vice-Chancellor—holding that the
demonstration, like Miss Mary Bennet's pianoforte playing
in *Pride and Prejudice*, had delighted the company long
enough—put his foot down. And from that time the University became sober, modest, and studious as perhaps any
in Europe. The old gentleman wound up with some
practical advice, and a promise to furnish the squire with
a letter of recommendation to one of the best tutors in
Oxford.

Thus armed, the squire (though still with misgivings)
was not long in getting on horseback with his wife, his
daughters, and his young hopeful, and riding off to Oxford,
where at first it seemed that his worst suspicions would be
confirmed; 'for at ten o'clock in the inn, there arose such
a roaring and singing that my hair stood on end, and my
former prejudices were so heightened that I resolved to
lose the journey and carry back my son again, presuming
that no noise in Oxford could be made but *scholars* must
do it'—a hoary misconception still cherished, or until
recently, by the Metropolitan Police and the Oxford City
Bench. In this instance a proctor intervened, and quelled
the disturbance by sending 'two young pert townsmen' to
prison; 'and quickly came to my chamber, and perceiving
my boy designed for a gown, told me that it was for the

preservation of such fine youths as he that the proctors made so bold with gentlemen's lodgings.' The squire had some talk with this dignitary, who was a man of presence and suitable address, and of sufficient independence to deny—not for the first time in history—that dons were overpaid.

Next morning the whole family trooped off to call upon the tutor whom their old neighbour had recommended. Oddly enough, the tutor seemed by no means overwhelmed by the honour. 'I thought to have found him mightily pleased with the opinion we had of his conduct, and the credit of having a gentleman's son under his charge, and the father with cap in hand. Instead of all this he talked at a rate as if the gentry were *obliged* to tutors more than tutors to them.' The tutor, in short, was decidedly tart in his admonitions to this honest family—he did not forget, either, to assure them that (*generally*) a college tutor was worse paid than a dancing-master. Here is a specimen of his advice—sound and practical enough in its way:

I understand by one of your daughters that you have brought him up a *fine padd* to keep here for his health's sake. Now I will tell you the use of an horse in Oxford, and then do as you think fit. The horse must be kept at an *ale-house* or an *inn*, and he must have leave to go once *every day* to see him eat oats, because the master's eye makes him fat; and it will not be genteel to go often to an house and spend nothing; and then there may be some danger of the horse growing *resty* if he be not used often, so you must give him leave to go to *Abingdon* once every week, to look out of the tavern window and see the maids sell turnips; and in one month or two come home with a surfeit of poisoned wine, and save any *farther trouble* by dying, and then you will be troubled to send for your horse *again....*

The humour of college tutors has not greatly altered in

two hundred years. I have known one or two capable of
the sardonic touch in those concluding words. But conceive its effect upon the squire's lady and daughters! No:
you need not trouble to do so, for the squire describes it:
'When the tutor was gone out of the room, I asked how
they liked the person and his converse. My boy clung
about his mother and cry'd to go home again, and she had
no more wit than to be of the same mind; she thought him
too weakly to undergo so much hardship as she foresaw
was to be expected. My daughter, who (instead of
catechism and *Lady's Calling*) had been used to read
nothing but speeches in romances, and hearing nothing of
Love and *Honour* in all the talk, fell into downright *scolding*
at him; call'd him the *merest* scholar; and if this were your
Oxford breeding, they had rather he should go to *Con-
stantinople* to learn manners! But I, who was older and
understood the language, call'd them all great fools. . . .'

On the tutor's return they begged to have his company
at dinner, at their inn: but he declined, kept the young
man to dine with him, and next day invited the family to
luncheon. They accepted, fully expecting (after the austerity
of his discourse) to be starved: 'and the girles drank choco-
lette at no rate in the morning, for fear of the *worst*.' But
they were by no means starved. 'It was very pleasant,' the
squire confesses, 'to see, when we came, the *constrain'd*
artifice of an unaccustomed complement.' There were silver
tankards 'heaped upon one another,' 'napkins some twenty
years younger than the rest,' and glasses 'fit for a *Dutchman*
at an *East-India Return*.' The dinner was full enough for
ten. 'I was asham'd, but would not disoblige him, considering with myself that I should put this man to such a
charge of forty shillings at least, to entertain me; when for
all his honest care and pains he is to have but forty or fifty

shillings a quarter; so that for one whole quarter he must doe the drudgery to my son for nothing.' After dinner, our good squire strolled off to a public bowling-green, 'that being the onely recreation I can affect.' And 'coming in, I saw half a score of the finest youths the sun, I think, ever shined upon. They walked to and fro, with their hands in their pockets, to see a match played by some scholars and some gentlemen fam'd for their skill. I gaped also and stared as a man in his way would doe; but a country ruff gentleman, being like to *lose*, did swear at such a rate that my heart did grieve that those fine young men should *hear* it, and know there was such a thing as swearing in the kingdom. Coming to my lodging, I charged my son never to go to such publick places unless he resolved to quarrel with me.'

And so, having settled the lad and fitted him up with good advice, the father, mother, and sisters returned home. But the squire, being summoned to Oxford shortly after to 'sit in *parliament*' (presumably in the last Parliament held at Oxford, in March, 1681), took that opportunity to walk the streets and study the demeanour of the 'scholars.' And this experiment would seem to have finally satisfied him. 'I walk'd the streets as late as most people, and never in ten days ever saw any scholar rude or disordered: so that as I grow old, and more engaged to speak the *truth*, I do repent of the *ill-opinion* I have had of that place, and hope to be farther obliged by a very good *account* of my son.'

Old Stephen Penton may have had a rambling head; but unless I have thumbed the bloom off his narrative in my attempt to summarise it, the reader will allow that he knew how to write. He gives us the whole scene in the fewest possible touches: he wastes no words in describing

the personages in his small comedy—comic idyll I had
rather call it, for after a fashion it reminds me of the immortal chatter between Gorgo and Praxinoë in the fifteenth
idyll of Theocritus. There the picture is: the honest
opinionated country squire; the acidulous tutor; the coltish
son; the fond, foolish, fussing mother; the prinking young
ladies with their curls and romantic notions; the colours
of all as fresh as if laid on yesterday, the humour quite
untarnished after two hundred years. And I wonder the
more at the vivacity of this little sketch because, as many
writers have pointed out, no one has yet built upon University life a novel of anything like first-class merit, and the
conclusion has been drawn that the elements of profound
human interest are wanting in that life. 'Is this so?' asks
the editor of Stephen Penton's reminiscences in a volume
published by the Oxford Historical Society—

> In spite of the character given to Oxford of being a city
> of short memories and abruptly-ended friendships, in spite of
> the inchoative qualities of youths of eighteen or twenty,
> especially in respect to the 'ruling passion' so dear to novelists,
> yet surely in the three or four years spent at Oxford by an
> incredible company of young students 'fresh from public
> schools, and not yet tossed about and hardened in the storms
> of life'—some of them Penton's 'finest youths,' some obviously
> otherwise—there must be, one would think, abundance of
> romantic incident awaiting its Thackeray or Meredith. For
> how many have these years been the turning point of a
> life . . .!

There at any rate is the fact: *the* novel of University
life has not been written yet, and perhaps never will be.
I am not at all sure that *The Adventures of Mr Verdant
Green* does not mark the nearest approach to it—save the
mark! And I am not at all sure that *The Adventures of*

Mr Verdant Green can be called a novel at all, while I am
quite certain it cannot be called a novel of first-class merit.
Tom Brown at Oxford still counts its admirers, and has,
I hear, attained the dignity of translation into French; but
Tom Brown, though robust enough, never seemed to get
over his transplantation from Rugby—possibly because his
author's heart remained at Rugby. *Loss and Gain* is
not a book for the many; and the many never did justice
to Mr Hermann Merivale's *Faucit of Balliol* or Mr St
John Tyrwhitt's *Hugh Heron of Christ Church*. Neither
of these two novels obtained the hearing it deserved—and
Faucit of Balliol was a really remarkable book: but neither
of them aimed at giving a full picture of Oxford life. And
the interest of Miss Broughton's *Belinda* and Mr Hardy's
Jude the Obscure lies outside the proctor's rounds. Yes
(and humiliating as the confession may be), with all its
crudities and absurdities, *Verdant Green* does mark the
nearest approach yet made to a representative Oxford
novel.

How comes this? Well, to begin with, *Verdant Green*,
with all his faults, did contrive to be exceedingly youthful
and high-spirited. And in the second place, with all its
faults, it did convey some sense of what I may call the
'glamour' of Oxford. Now the University, on its part, being
fed with a constant supply of young men between the ages
of eighteen and twenty, does contrive, with all its faults,
to keep up a fair show of youth and high spirits; and even
their worst enemies will admit that Oxford and Cambridge
wear, in the eyes of their sons at any rate, a certain glamour.
You may argue that glamour is glamour, an illusion which
will wear off in time; an illusion, at all events, and to be
treated as such by the wise author intent on getting at
truth. To this I answer that, while it lasts, this glamour

is just as much a fact as *The Times* newspaper, or St Paul's
Cathedral, just as real a feature of Oxford as Balliol College,
or the river, or the Vice-Chancellor's poker: and until you
recognise it for a fact and a feature of the place, and allow
for it, you have not the faintest prospect of realising Oxford.
Each succeeding generation finds that glamour, or brings
it; and each generation, as it passes, deems that its successor
has either found or brought less of it. But the glamour is
there all the while. In turning over a book the other day,
written in 1870 by the Rev. Robert Stephen Hawker, I
come on this passage:

> When I recall my own undergraduate life of thirty years
> and upwards agone, I feel, notwithstanding modern vaunt, the
> *laudator temporis acti* earnest within me yet, and strong. Nowa-
> days, as it seems to me, there is but little originality of character
> in the still famous University; a dread of eccentric reputation
> appears to pervade College and Hall: every 'Oxford man,' to
> adopt the well-known name, is subdued into sameness within
> and without, controlled as it were into copyism and mediocrity
> by the smoothing-iron of the nineteenth century. Whereas *in*
> my time and before it there were distinguished names, famous
> in every mouth for original achievements and 'deeds of
> daring-do.' There were giants in those days—men of varied
> renown—and they arose and won for themselves in strange
> fields of fame, record and place. Each became in his day a
> hero of the Iliad or Odyssey of Oxford life—a kind of Homeric
> man.

To which I am constrained to reply, 'Mere stuff and
nonsense!' Mr Hawker—and more credit to him—carried
away Homeric memories of his own seniors and contemporaries. But was it in nature that Mr Hawker should
discover Homeric proportions in the feats of men thirty
years his juniors? How many of us, I ask, are under any

flattering illusion about the performances of our juniors?
We cling to the old fond falsehood that there were giants
in *our* days. We honestly believed they were giants; it
would hurt us to abandon that belief. It does not hurt
us in the least to close the magnifying-glass upon the feats
of those who follow us. But this generation, too, will have
its magnifying-glass. 'There were giants in our days?' To
be sure there were; and there are giants, too, in these, but
others, not we, have the eyes to see them.

Say that the scales have fallen from our eyes. Very well,
we must e'en put them on again if we would write a novel
of University life. And, be pleased to note, it does not
follow, because we see the place differently now, that we
see it more truly. Also, it does not follow, because Oxford
during the last twenty years has, to the eye of the visitor,
altered very considerably, that the characteristics of Oxford
have altered to anything like the same extent. Undoubtedly
they have been modified by the relaxation and suspension
of the laws forbidding Fellows to marry. Undoubtedly
the brisk growth of red-brick houses along the north of
the city, the domestic hearths, afternoon teas and peram-
bulators, and all things covered by the opprobrious name
of 'Parks-system,' have done something to efface the difference between Oxford and other towns. But on the whole
I think they have done surprisingly little.

*   *   *   *   *

Speaking as a writer of novels, then, I should say that
to write a good novel entirely concerned with Oxford lies
close upon impossibility, and will prophesy that, if ever
it comes to be achieved, it will be a story of friendship.
But her glamour is for him to catch who can, whether in
prose or rhyme.

ALMA MATER

Know you her secret none can utter?
　Hers of the Book, the tripled Crown?
Still on the spire the pigeons flutter;
　Still by the gateway flits the gown;
Still on the street, from corbel and gutter,
　Faces of stone look down.

Faces of stone, and other faces—
　Some from library windows wan
Forth on her gardens, her green spaces
　Peer and turn to their books anon.
Hence, my Muse, from the green oases
　Gather the tent, begone!

Nay, should she by the pavement linger
　Under the rooms where once she played,
Who from the feast would rise and fling her
　One poor *sou* for her serenade?
One poor laugh from the antic finger
　Thrumming a lute string frayed?

Once, my dear—but the world was young then—
　Magdalen elms and Trinity limes—
Lissom the blades and the backs that swung then,
　Eight good men in the good old times—
Careless we, and the chorus flung then
　Under St Mary's chimes!

Reins lay loose and the ways led random—
　Christ Church meadow and Iffley track—
'Idleness horrid and dogcart' (tandem)—
　Aylesbury grind and Bicester pack—
Pleasant our lines, and faith! we scanned 'em:
　Having that artless knack.

Come, old limmer, the times grow colder:
  Leaves of the creeper redden and fall.
Was it a hand then clapped my shoulder?
  —Only the wind by the chapel wall.
Dead leaves drift on the lute; so...fold her
  Under the faded shawl.

Never we wince, though none deplore us,
  We, who go reaping that we sowed;
Cities at cock-crow wake before us—
  Hey, for the lilt of the London road!
One look back, and a rousing chorus!
  Never a palinode!

Still on her spire the pigeons hover;
  Still by her gateway haunts the gown
Ah, but her secret? You, young lover,
  Drumming her old ones forth from town,
Know you the secret none discover?
  Tell it—when *you* go down.

Yet if at length you seek her, prove her,
  Lean to her whispers never so nigh;
Yet if at last not less her lover
  You in your hansom leave the High;
Down from her towers a ray shall hover—
  Touch you, a passer-by!

JUNE

THE following verses made their appearance some years ago in the pages of *The Pall Mall Magazine*. Since then (I am assured) they have put a girdle round the world, and threaten, if not to keep pace with the banjo hymned by Mr Kipling, at least to become the most widely-diffused of their author's works. I take it to be of a piece with his usual perversity that until now they have never been re-published except for private amusement.

They belong to a mood, a moment, and I cannot be at pains to rewrite a single stanza, even though an allusion to 'Oom Paul' cries out to be altered or suppressed. But, after all, the allusion is not likely to trouble President Kruger's massive shade as it slouches across the Elysian fields; and after all, though he became our enemy, he remained a sportsman. So I hope we may glance at his name in jest without a suspicion of mocking at the tragedy of his fate.

THE FAMOUS BALLAD OF THE
JUBILEE CUP

You may lift me up in your arms, lad, and turn my face to
    the sun,
For a last look back at the dear old track where the Jubilee
    Cup was won;
And draw your chair to my side, lad—no, thank ye, I feel
    no pain—
For I'm going out with the tide, lad, but I'll tell you the tale
    again.

I'm seventy-nine, or nearly, and my head it has long turned
grey,
But it all comes back as clearly as though it was yesterday—
The dust, and the bookies shouting around the clerk of the
scales,
And the clerk of the course, and the nobs in force, and 'Is
'Ighness, the Pr*nce of W*les.

'Twas a nine-hole thresh to wind'ard, but none of us cared for
that,
With a straight run home to the service tee, and a finish along
the flat.
'Stiff?' Ah, well you may say it! Spot-barred, and at five-
stone-ten!
But at two and a bisque I'd ha' run the risk; for I was a green-
horn then.

So we stripped to the B. Race signal, the old red swallow-tail—
There was young Ben Bolt, and the Portland colt, and Aston
Villa, and Yale;
And W. G., and Steinitz, Leander, and The Saint,
And the German Emperor's Meteor, a-looking as fresh as paint;

John Roberts (scratch), and Safety Match, The Lascar, and
Lorna Doone,
Oom Paul (a bye), and Romany Rye, and me upon Wooden
Spoon;
And some of us cut for partners, and some of us strung to baulk,
And some of us tossed for stations—But there, what use to talk?

Three-quarter-back on the Kingsclere crack was station enough
for me,
With a fresh jackyarder blowing and the Vicarage goal a-lee!
And I leaned and patted her centre-bit, and eased the quid in
her cheek,
With a 'Soh, my lass!' and a 'Woa, you brute!'—for she could
do all but speak.

She was geared a thought too high, perhaps; she was trained
a trifle fine;

But she had the grand reach forward! *I* never saw such a line!

Smooth-bored, clean-run, from her fiddle head with its dainty
ear half-cock,

Hard-bit, *pur sang*, from her overhang to the heel of her off
hind sock.

Sir Robert he walked beside me as I worked her down to the
mark;

'There's money on this, my lad,' said he, 'and most of 'em's
running dark;

But ease the sheet if you're bunkered, and pack the scrimmages
tight,

And use your slide at the distance, and we'll drink to your
health to-night!'

But I bent and tightened my stretcher. Said I to myself,
said I,—

'John Jones, this here is the Jubilee Cup, and you have to do
or die.'

And the words weren't hardly spoken when the umpire
shouted 'Play!'

And we all kicked off from the Gasworks end with a 'Yoicks!'
and a 'Gone away!'

And at first I thought of nothing, as the clay flew by in lumps,

But stuck to the old Ruy Lopez, and wondered who'd call for
trumps,

And luffed her close to the cushion, and watched each one as
it broke,

And in triple file up the Rowley mile we went like a trail of
smoke.

The Lascar made the running: but he didn't amount to much,

For old Oom Paul was quick on the ball, and headed it back
to touch;

And the whole first flight led off with the right, as The Saint
took up the pace,
And drove it clean to the putting green and trumped it there
with an ace.

John Roberts had given a miss in baulk, but Villa cleared with
a punt;
And keeping her service hard and low, The Meteor forged to
the front,
With Romany Rye to windward at dormy and two to play,
And Yale close up—but a Jubilee Cup isn't run for every day.

We laid our course for the Warner—I tell you the pace was hot!
And again off Tattenham Corner a blanket covered the lot.
Check side! Check side! Now steer her wide! and barely an
inch of room,
With The Lascar's tail over our lee rail, and brushing Leander's
boom!

We were running as strong as ever—eight knots—but it
couldn't last;
For the spray and the bails were flying, the whole field tailing
fast;
And the Portland colt had shot his bolt, and Yale was bumped
at the Doves,
And The Lascar resigned to Steinitz, stale-mated in fifteen
moves.

It was bellows to mend with Roberts—starred three for a
penalty kick:
But he chalked his cue and gave 'em the butt, and Oom Paul
scored the trick—
'Off-side—no-ball—and at fourteen all! Mark cock! and two
for his nob!'—
When W. G. ran clean through his lee, and yorked him twice
with a lob.

He yorked him twice on a crumbling pitch, and wiped his eye
    with a brace,
But his guy-rope split with the strain of it, and he dropped
    back out of the race;
And I drew a bead on The Meteor's lead, and challenging
    none too soon,
Bent over and patted her garboard strake, and called upon
    Wooden Spoon.

She was all of a shiver forward, the spoondrift thick on her
    flanks,
But I'd brought her an easy gambit, and nursed her over the
    banks;
She answered her helm—the darling!—and woke up now with
    a rush,
While The Meteor's jock he sat like a rock—he knew we rode
    for his brush!

There was no one else left in it. The Saint was using his whip,
And Safety Match, with a lofting catch, was pocketed deep
    at slip;
And young Ben Bolt with his niblick took miss at Leander's
    lunge,
But topped the net with the ricochet, and Steinitz threw up
    the sponge.

But none of the lot could stop the rot—nay, don't ask *me* to
    stop!—
The Villa had called for lemons, Oom Paul had taken his drop,
And both were kicking the referee. Poor fellow! he done his
    best;
But, being in doubt, he'd ruled them out—which he always
    did when pressed.

So, inch by inch, I tightened the winch, and chucked the
    sandbags out—
I heard the nursery cannons pop, I heard the bookies shout:

'The Meteor wins!' 'No, Wooden Spoon!' 'Check!'
'Vantage!' 'Leg before!'
'Last lap!' 'Pass Nap!' At his saddle-flap I put up the helm
and wore.

You may overlap at the saddle-flap, and yet be loo'd on the tape:
And it all depends upon changing ends, how a seven-year-old
will shape;
It was tack and tack to the Lepe and back—a fair ding-dong
to the Ridge,
And he led by his forward canvas yet as we shot 'neath
Hammersmith Bridge.

He led by his forward canvas—he led from his strongest suit—
But along we went on a roaring scent, and at Fawley I gained
a foot.
He fisted off with his jigger, and gave me his wash—too late!
Deuce—vantage—check! By neck and neck, we rounded into
the straight.

I could hear the 'Conquering 'Ero' a-crashing on Godfrey's
band,
And my hopes fell sudden to zero, just there with the race in
hand—
In sight of the Turf's Blue Ribbon, in sight of the umpire's
tape,
As I felt the tack of her spinnaker crack, as I heard the steam
escape!

Had I lost at that awful juncture my presence of mind?...
but no!
I leaned and felt for the puncture, and plugged it there with
my toe...
Hand over hand by the Members' Stand I lifted and eased
her up,
Shot—clean and fair—to the crossbar there, and landed the
Jubilee Cup!

'The odd by a head, and leg before,' so the Judge he gave
 the word:
And the Umpire shouted 'Over!' but I neither spoke nor
 stirred.
They crowded round: for there on the ground I lay in a
 dead-cold swoon,
Pitched neck and crop on the turf atop of my beautiful
 Wooden Spoon.

Her dewlap tire was punctured, her bearings all red-hot;
She'd a lolling tongue, and her bowsprit sprung, and her
 running gear in a knot;
And amid the sobs of her backers, Sir Robert loosened her girth
And led her away to the knacker's. She had raced her last on
 earth!

But I mind me well of the tear that fell from the eye of our
 noble Pr*nce,
And the things he said as he tucked me in bed—and I've lain
 there ever since;
Tho' it all gets mixed up queerly that happened before my
 spill,—
But I draw my thousand yearly: it'll pay for the doctor's bill.

I'm going out with the tide, lad.—You'll dig me a humble
 grave,
And whiles you will bring your bride, lad, and your sons (if
 sons you have),
And there, when the dews are weeping, and the echoes murmur
 'Peace!'
And the salt, salt tide comes creeping and covers the popping-
 crease,

In the hour when the ducks deposit their eggs with a boasted
 force,
They'll look and whisper 'How was it?' and you'll take them
 over the course,

And your voice will break as you try to speak of the glorious
first of June,
When the Jubilee Cup, with John Jones up, was won upon
Wooden Spoon.

*　　*　　*　　*　　*

'To me,' said a well-known authority upon education,
'these athletics are the devil.' To me no form of athletics
is the devil but that of paying other people to be athletic
for you; and this, unhappily—and partly, I believe, through
our neglect to provide our elementary schools with decent
playgrounds—is the form affected nowadays by large and
increasing crowds of Englishmen. The youth of our urban
populations would seem to be absorbed in this vicarious
sport. It throngs the reading-rooms of free public libraries
and working men's institutes in numbers which delight the
reformer until he discovers that all this avidity is for racing
tips and cricket or football 'items.' I am not, as a rule,
a croaker; but I do not think the young Briton concerns
himself as he did in the fifties, sixties, and seventies of the
last century with poetry, history, politics, or indeed anything that asks for serious thought. I believe all this
professional sport likely to be as demoralising for us as a
nation as were the gladiatorial shows for Rome; and I
cannot help attributing to it some measure of that com-
bativeness at second-hand—that itch to fight anyone and
every one by proxy—which, abetted by a cheap press, has
for twenty years been our curse.

Curse or no curse, it is spreading; and something of its
progress may be marked in the two following dialogues,
the first of which was written in 1897. Many of the names
in it have already passed some way toward oblivion; but
the moral, if I mistake not, survives them, and the warning
has become more urgent than ever.

THE FIRST DIALOGUE ON CRICKET
1897

Some time in the summer of 1897—I think towards the
end of August—I was whiling away the close of an afternoon in the agreeable twilight of Mr D——'s bookshop
in the Strand, when I heard my name uttered by some one
who had just entered; and, turning about, saw my friend
Verinder, in company with Grayson and a strapping youth
of twenty or thereabouts, a stranger to me. Verinder and
Grayson share chambers in the Temple, on the strength
(it is understood) of a common passion for cricket. Longer
ago than we care to remember—but Cambridge bowlers
remember—Grayson was captain of the Oxford eleven.
His contemporary, Verinder, never won his way into the
team: he was a comparatively poor man and obliged to
read, and reading spoiled his cricket. Therefore he had to
content himself with knocking up centuries in college
matches, and an annual performance among the Seniors.
It was rumoured that Grayson—always a just youth, too—
would have given him his blue, had not Verinder's con-
scientiousness been more than Roman. My own belief is
that the distinction was never offered, and that Verinder
liked his friend all the better for it. At the same time the
disappointment of what at that time of life was a serious
ambition may account for a trace of acidity which began,
before he left college, to flavour his comments on human
affairs, and has since become habitual to him.

Verinder explained that he and his companions were on
their way home from Lord's, where they had been
'assisting'—he laid an ironical stress on the word—in an
encounter between Kent and Middlesex. 'And, as we were

passing, I dragged these fellows in, just to see if old D——
had anything.' Verinder is a book-collector. 'By the way,
do you know Sammy Dawkins? You may call him the
Boy when you make his better acquaintance and can forgive
him for having chosen to go to Cambridge. Thebes did
his green, unknowing youth engage, and—as *The Oxford
Magazine* gloomily prophesied—he bowls out Athens in
his later age.' The Boy laughed cheerfully and blushed.
I felt a natural awe in holding out an exceedingly dusty
hand to an athlete whose fame had already shaken the
Antipodes. But it is the way of young giants to be amiable;
and indeed this one saluted me with a respect which he
afterwards accounted for ingenuously enough—'He always
felt like that towards a man who had written a book: it
seemed to him a tremendous thing to have done, don't
you know?'

I thought to myself that half an hour in Mr D——'s
shop (which contains new books as well as old) would
correct his sense of the impressiveness of the feat. Indeed,
I read a dawning trouble in the glance he cast around the
shelves. 'It takes a fellow's breath away,' he confessed.
'Such a heap of them! But then I've never been to the
British Museum.'

'Then,' said I, 'you must be employing researchers for
the book you are writing.'

'What?' he protested. '*Me* writing a book? Not likely!'

'An article for some magazine, then?'

'Not a line.'

'Well, at least you have been standing for your photograph, to illustrate some book on Cricket that another fellow
is writing.'

He laughed.

'You have me there. Yes, I've been photographed in

the act of bowling—"Before" and "After": quite like Somebody's Hair Restorer.'

'Well,' said I, 'and I wish you had contributed to the letterpress, too. For the wonder to me is, not that you cricketers write books (for all the world wants to read them), but that you do it so prodigiously well.'

'Oh,' said he, 'you mean Ranji! But he's a terror.'

'I was thinking of him, of course; but of others as well. Here, for instance, is a book I have just bought, or rather an instalment of one: *The Encyclopædia of Sport*, edited by the Earl of Suffolk and Berkshire, Mr Hedley Peek, and Mr Aflalo, published by Messrs Lawrence and Bullen: Part IV, CHA to CRO. I turn to the article on Cricket, and am referred "for all questions connected with fast bowling, and for many questions associated with medium and slow" to "the following paper by TOM RICHARDSON."'

'Tom Richardson ought to know,' put in Grayson.

'Good Heavens!' said I, 'I am not disputing that! But I remember Ruskin's insisting—I think in *Sesame and Lilies*—that no true artist ever talks much of his art. The greatest are silent. "The moment," says Ruskin, "a man can really do his work he becomes speechless about it. All words become idle to him—all theories." And he goes on to ask, in his vivacious way, "Does a bird theorise about building its nest?" Well, as to that one cannot be sure. But I take it we may call Richardson a true artist?'

'Certainly we may.'

'And allow that he can really do his work?'

'Rather!'

'Then it seems to me that Ruskin's rule may apply to other arts, but not to Cricket. For here is Richardson not only talking about fast bowling, but expressing himself with signal ease and precision. Listen to this, for instance:

A ball is said to *break* when, on touching the ground, it deviates sharply from its original line of flight.

And again:

A ball is said to have *spin* on it when it gains an acceleration of pace, not necessarily a variation of direction, on touching the ground.

'It would be hard, I think, to improve upon these definitions. But let me satisfy you that I was not exaggerating when I spoke of the dignity of Mr Richardson's English style:

The bowler, whether born or made, should cultivate and acquire a high action and a good swing of arm and body, as such a delivery will make the ball rise quickly and perpendicularly from the pitch; but the action must at all costs be easy and free, qualities which neither imitation nor education must allow to disappear.

'We often hear complaints—and reasonable ones for the most part—that the wage given to first-class professional cricketers is no longer adequate. But one of the pet arguments for increasing it is that their employment begins and ends with the summer. Now, I certainly think that, while bowlers write in this fashion, they can have little or nothing to dread from the winter months.'

'I declare,' said Grayson, 'I believe you are jealous!'

'Well, and why not? For, mark you, Mr Richardson's is no singular case, of which we might say—to comfort ourselves—that the Goddess of Cricket, whom he serves so mightily, has touched his lips and inspired him for a moment. Turn over these pages. We poor novelists, critics, men of letters, have no such paper, such type, as are lavished on the experts who write here upon their various branches of sport. *Our* efforts are not illustrated by the Swan Engraving Company. And the rub for us is that these gentlemen deserve it all! I am not going to admit—to you, at any rate—that their subjects are of higher interest than ours, or of more importance to the world. But I confess that, as a rule, they make theirs more interesting. When Mr C. B. Fry discourses about Long Jumping, or Mr W. Ellis about Coursing, or Mr F. C. J. Ford upon Australian Cricket, there are very few novelists to whom I had rather be listening. It cannot be mere chance that makes them all so eloquent; nor is it that they have all risen together to the height of a single great occasion; for though each must have felt it a great occasion when he was invited to assist in this sumptuous work, I remarked a similar eloquence in those who contributed, the other day, to Messrs Longmans' "Badminton Library." When sportsmen take to writing admirable English, and peers of the realm to editing it, I hardly see where we poor men of letters can expect to come in.'

'The only cure that I can see,' said Verinder, 'is for Her Majesty to turn you into peers of the realm. Some of you suggest this from time to time, and hitherto it has puzzled me to discover why. But if it would qualify you to edit the writings of sportsmen——'

'And why not? These books sell: and if aristocracy have its roots in commerce, shall not the sale of books count as high as the sale of beer? The principle has been granted. Already the purveyors of cheap and wholesome literature are invited to kneel before the Queen, and receive the *accolade*.'

'She must want to cut Tit-bits out of them,' put in the Boy.

'Of course we must look at the proportion of profit.

Hitherto the profits of beer and literature have not been comparable; but this wonderful boom in books of sport may redress the balance. Every one buys them. When you entered I was glancing through a volume of new verse, but without the smallest intention of buying it. My purchases, you see, are all sporting works, including, of course, Prince Ranjitsinhji's *Jubilee Book of Cricket.*'

'Just so,' snapped Verinder. 'You buy books about sport: we spend an afternoon in looking on at sport. And so, in one way or another, we assist at the damnation of the sporting spirit in England.'

When Verinder begins in this style an oration is never far distant. I walked back with the three to the Temple. On our way he hissed and sputtered like a kettle, and we had scarcely reached his chamber before he boiled over in real earnest.

'We ought never to have been there! It's well enough for the Boy: he has been playing steadily all the summer, first for Cambridge and afterwards for his county. Now he has three days off and is taking his holiday. But Grayson and I—What the deuce have we to do in that galley? Far better we joined a club down at Dulwich or Tooting and put in a little honest play, of a week-end, on our own account. We should be crocks, of course: our cricketing is done. But we should be honest crocks. At least it is better to take a back row in the performance, and find out our own weakness, than pay for a good seat at Lord's or the Oval, and be connoisseurs of what Abel and Hearne and Brockwell can and cannot do. If a man wants to sing the praises of cricket as a national game, let him go down to one of the Public Schools and watch its close or cricket-ground on a half-holiday: fifteen acres of turf, and a dozen games going on together, from Big Side down to the lowest form

match: from three to four hundred boys in white flannels—
all keen as mustard, and each occupied with his own game,
and playing it to the best of his powers. *Playing it*—mark
you: not looking on. That's the point: and that's what
Wellington meant by saying—if he ever said it—that
Waterloo was won upon the playing-fields at Eton. In
my old school if a boy shirked the game he had a poor
time. Say that he shirked it for an afternoon's lawn-tennis:
it was lucky for him if he didn't find his racquet, next day,
nailed up on the pavilion door like a stoat on a gamekeeper's
tree. That was the sporting spirit, sir, if the sporting spirit
means something that is to save England: and we shall not
win another Waterloo by enclosing twenty-two gladiators
in a ring of twenty-two thousand loafers, whose only
exercise is to cheer when somebody makes a stroke, howl
when some other body drops a catch, and argue that a
batsman was not out when the umpire has given him
"leg-before." Even at football matches the crowd has *some*
chance of taking physical exercise on its own account—by
manhandling the referee when the game is over. Sport?
The average subscriber to Lord's is just as much of a
sportsman as the Spaniard who watches a bull-fight, and
just a trifle more of a sportsman than the bar-loafer who
backs a horse he has never clapped eyes on. You may call
it Cricket if you like: I call it assisting at a Gladiatorial
Show. True cricket is left to the village greens.'

'Steady, old man!' protested the Boy.

'I repeat it. For the spirit of the game you might have
gone, a few years ago, to the Public Schools; but even they
are infected now with the gladiatorial ideal. As it is you
must go to the village green; for the spirit, you understand
—not the letter——'

'I believe you!' chuckled young Dawkins. 'Last season

I put in an off day with the villagers at home. We played
the nearest market town, and I put myself on to bowl slows.
Second wicket down, in came the fattest man I ever saw.
He was a nurseryman and seedsman in private life, and
he fairly hid the wicket-keep. In the first over a ball of
mine got up a bit and took him in the ab-do-men. "How's
that?" I asked. "Well," said the umpire, "I wasn't azackly
looking, so I leave it to you. If it hit en in the paunch, it's
'not out'; and the fella must have suffered. But if it took
en in the rear, I reckon it didn't hurt much, and it's 'leg-
before.'" I suppose that is what you would call the "spirit"
of cricket. But, I say, if you have such a down on Lord's
and what you call the gladiatorial business, why on earth
do you go?'

'Isn't that the very question I've been asking myself?'
replied Verinder testily.

'Perhaps we have an explanation here,' I suggested;
for during Verinder's harangue I had settled myself in the
window-seat, and was turning over the pages of Prince
Ranjitsinhji's book.

It is a grand thing for people who have to work most of
their time to have an interest in something or other outside
their particular groove. Cricket is a first-rate interest. The game
has developed to such a pitch that it is worth taking interest·
in. Go to Lord's and analyse the crowd. There are all sorts
and conditions of men there round the ropes—bricklayers,
bank-clerks, soldiers, postmen, and stockbrokers. And in the
pavilion are Q.C.'s, artists, archdeacons, and leader-writers....

'Oh, come!' Grayson puts in. 'Isn't that rather hard
on the stockbroker?'

'It is what the book says.'

Bad men, good men, workers and idlers, all are there, and
all at one in their keenness over the game.....Anything that

puts very many different kinds of people on a common ground must promote sympathy and kindly feelings. The workman does not come away from seeing Middlesex beating Lancashire, or vice versa, with evil in his heart against the upper ten; nor the Mayfair *homme de plaisir* with a feeling of contempt for the street-bred masses. Both alike are thinking how well Mold bowled, and how cleanly Stoddart despatched Briggs's high-tossed slow ball over the awning. Even that cynical *nil admirari* lawyer——

I pointed a finger at Verinder.

Even that cynical *nil admirari* lawyer caught himself cheering loudly when Sir Timothy planted Hallam's would-be yorker into the press-box. True, he caught himself being enthusiastic, and broke off at once——

'When I found it hadn't killed a reporter,' Verinder explained. 'But I hope Ranjitsinhji has some better arguments than these if he wants to defend gladiatorial cricket. At least he allows that a change has come over the game of late years, and that this change has to be defended?'

'Yes, he admits the change, and explains how it came about. In the beginning we had local club cricket pure and simple—the game of your Village Green, in fact. Out of this grew representative local cricket—that is, district or county cricket which flourished along with local club cricket. Out of county cricket, which in those days was only local cricket glorified, sprang exhibition or spectacular or gladiatorial cricket, which lived side by side with, but distinct from, the other. Finally, exhibition and county cricket merged and became one. And that is where we are now.'

'Does he explain how exhibition and county cricket came, as he puts it, to be merged into one?'

'Yes. The introduction of spectacular cricket (he says) changed the basis of county cricket considerably. For many years the exhibition elevens and the counties played side by side; but gradually the former died out, and the new elements they had introduced into the game were absorbed into county cricket. The process was gradual, but in the end complete. The old county clubs and the new ones that from time to time sprang up added the exhibition side of cricket to the old local basis. The county clubs were no longer merely glorified local clubs, but in addition business concerns. They provided popular amusement and good cricket; in fact, they became what they are now—local in name, and partly local in reality, but also run upon exhibition or spectacular lines.'

'A truly British compromise! Good business at the bottom of it, and a touch of local sentiment by way of varnish. For of course the final excuse for calling an eleven after Loamshire (let us say), and for any pride a Loamshire man may take in its doings, is that its members have been bred and trained in Loamshire. But, because any such limitation would sorely affect the gate-money, we import players from Australia or Timbuctoo, stick a Loamshire cap with the county arms on the head of each, and confidently expect our public to swallow the fiction and provide the local enthusiasm undismayed.'

'My dear Verinder, if you propose to preach rank Chauvinism, I have done. But I don't believe you are in earnest.'

'In a sense, I am not. My argument would exclude Ranjitsinhji himself from all matches but a few unimportant ones. I vote for Greater Britain, as you know: and in any case my best arguments would go down before the sheer delight of watching him at the wicket. Let the

territorial fiction stand, by all means. Nay, let us value it
as the one relic of genuine county cricket. It is the other
side of the business that I quarrel with.'

'Be good enough to define the quarrel.'

'Why, then, I quarrel with the spectacular side of the
New Cricket; which, when you come to look into it, is
the gate-money side. How does Ranjitsinhji defend it?'

'Let me see. "Its justification is the pleasure it provides
for large numbers of the public."'

'Quite so: the bricklayer and the stockbroker by the
ropes, and the cynical lawyer in the pavilion! But I prefer
to consider the interests of the game.'

'"From a purely cricket point of view," he goes on,
"not much can be said against it."'

'Let us inquire into that. The New Cricket is a business
concern: it caters for the bricklayer, the stockbroker, and
the whole crowd of spectators. Its prosperity depends on
the attraction it offers them. To attract them it must provide
first-class players, and the county that cannot breed first-
class players is forced to hire them. This is costly; but again
the cash comes out of the spectators' pockets, in subscrip-
tions and gate-money. Now are you going to tell me that
those who pay the piper will refrain from calling the tune?
Most certainly they will not. More and more frequently
in newspaper reports of cricket-matches you find discussions
of what is "due to the public." If stumps, for some reason
or other, are drawn early, it is hinted that the spectators
have a grievance; a captain's orders are canvassed and
challenged, and so is the choice of his team; a dispute
between a club and its servants becomes an affair of the
streets, and is taken up by the press, with threats and counter-
threats. In short, the interest of the game and the interest
of the crowd may not be identical; and whereas a captain

used to consider only the interest of the game, he is now
obliged to consider both. Does Ranjitsinhji point this out?'

'He seems, at any rate, to admit it; for I find this on
page 232, in his chapter upon "Captaincy":

The duties of a captain vary somewhat according to the
kind of match in which his side is engaged, and to the kind of
club which has elected him. To begin with, first-class cricket,
including representative M.C.C., county and university
matches, is quite different from any other—partly because the
results are universally regarded as more important, partly
*because certain obligations towards the spectators have to be
taken into consideration. The last point applies equally to any
match which people pay to come to see....*With regard to gate-
money matches. The captains of the two sides engaged are,
during the match, responsible for everything in connection
with it. *They are under an obligation to the public to see that
the match is played in such a way as the public has a reasonable
right to expect.'*

'And pray,' demanded Verinder, 'what are these "obligations towards the spectators," and "reasonable rights" of
the public?'

'Well, I suppose the public can reasonably demand
punctuality in starting play; a moderate interval for luncheon
and between innings; and that stumps shall not be drawn,
nor the match abandoned, before the time arranged, unless
circumstances make it absolutely necessary.'

'And who is to be judge of these circumstances?'

'The captain, I suppose.'

'In theory, yes; but he has to satisfy the crowd. It is
the crowd's "reasonable right" to be satisfied; and by
virtue of it the crowd becomes the final judge. It allows
the captain to decide, but will barrack him if displeased

with his decision. Moreover, you have given me examples
to illustrate this "reasonable right," but you have not
defined it. Now I want to know precisely how far it
extends, and where it ceases. Does Ranjitsinhji provide
this definition?'

'No,' said I; 'I cannot find that he does.'

'To be sure he does not; and for the simple reason that
these claims on the side of the public are growing year by
year. Already no one can say how much they cover, and
assuredly no one can say where they are likely to stop. You
observe that our author includes even University matches
under the head of exhibition cricket, in which obligations
towards the spectators have to be taken into account. You
remember the scene at Lord's in 1893 when Wells pur-
posely bowled no-balls; and again in 1896 when Shine
bowled two no-balls to the boundary and then a ball which
went for four byes, the object in each case being to deprive
Oxford of the follow-on. This policy was hotly discussed;
and luckily the discussion spent itself on the question
whether play could be at the same time within the laws
and clean contrary to the ethics of cricket. But there was
also a deal of talk about what was "due to the public";
talk which would have been altogether wide of the mark
in the old days, when Oxford and Cambridge met to play
a mere friendly match and the result concerned them
alone.'

'And is this,' I asked, 'the sum of your indictment?'

'Yes, I think that is all. And surely it is enough.'

'Then, as I make out, your chief objections to spectacular
cricket are two. You hold that it gives vast numbers of
people a false idea that they are joining in a sport when in
truth they are doing no more than look on. And you contend that as the whole institution resolves itself more and

more into a paid exhibition, the spectators will tend more and more to direct the development of the game; whereas cricket in your opinion should be uninfluenced by those who are outside the ropes?'

'That is my case.'

'And I think, my dear Verinder, it is a strong one. But there is just one little point which you do not appear to have considered. And I was coming to it just now—or rather Prince Ranjitsinhji was coming to it—when you interrupted us. "From a purely cricket point of view," he was saying, "not much can be said against exhibition cricket." And in the next sentence he goes on: "At any rate it promotes skill in the game and keeps up the standard of excellence."'

'To be sure it does that.'

'And cricket is played by the best players to-day with more skill than it was by the best players of twenty or forty years ago?'

'Yes, I believe that; in spite of all we hear about the great Alfred Mynn and other bygone heroes.'

'Come then,' said I, 'tell me, Is Cricket an art?'

'Decidedly it is.'

'Then Cricket, like other arts, should aim at perfection?'

'I suppose so.'

'And that will be the highest aim of Cricket—its own perfection? And its true lovers should welcome whatever helps to make it perfect?'

'I see what you are driving at,' said he. 'But Cricket is a social art, and must be judged by the good it does to boys and men. You, I perceive, make it an art-in-itself, and would treat it as the gardeners treat a fine chrysanthemum, nipping off a hundred buds to feed and develop a single perfect bloom.'

'True: we must consider it also as a social art. But, my dear fellow, are you not exaggerating the destruction necessary to produce the perfect bloom? You talk of the crowd at Lord's or the Oval as if all these thousands were diverted from honest practice of the game to the ignoble occupation of looking on; whereas two out of three of them, were this spectacle not provided, would far more likely be attending a horse-race, or betting in clubs and public-houses. The bricklayer, the stockbroker, the archdeacon, by going to see Lockwood bowl, depopulate no village green. You judge these persons by yourself, and tell yourself reproachfully that but for this attraction *you*, John Verinder, would be creditably perspiring at a practice-net in Tooting or Dulwich; whereas, the truth is——'

'Why are you hesitating?'

'Because it is not a very pleasant thing to say. But the truth is, your heart and your conscience in this matter of athletics are a little younger than your body.'

'You mean that I am getting on for middle age.'

'I mean that, though you talk of it, you will never subscribe to that suburban club. You will marry; you will be made a judge: you will attend cricket matches, and watch from the pavilion while your son takes block for his first score against the M.C.C.

> And when with envy Time transported,
>   Shall think to rob us of our joys,
> I, with my girls (if I ever have any), will sit on the top
>   of a drag (if I ever acquire one) and teach them at
>   what to applaud,
>   While you go a-batting with your boys.'

Verinder pulled a wry face, and the Boy smacked him on the back and exhorted him to 'buck up.'

'And the round world will go on as before, and the sun will patrol Her Majesty's dominions, and still where the Union Jack floats he will pass the wickets pitched and white-flannelled Britons playing for all they are worth, while men of subject races keep the score-sheet. And still when he arrives at this island he will look down on green closes and approve what we all allow to be one of the most absolutely gracious sights on earth—the ordered and moving regiments of schoolboys at cricket. Grayson, reach round to that shelf against which your chair is tilted; take down poor Lefroy's poems, and read us that sonnet of his, "The Bowler."'

Grayson found the book and the place, and read:

> Two minutes' rest till the next man goes in!
> The tired arms lie with every sinew slack
> On the mown grass. Unbent the supple back,
> And elbows apt to make the leather spin
> Up the slow bat and round the unwary shin,—
> In knavish hands a most unkindly knack;
> But no guile shelters under the boy's black
> Crisp hair, frank eyes, and honest English skin.
> Two minutes only! Conscious of a name,
> The new man plants his weapon with profound
> Long-practised skill that no mere trick may scare.
> Not loth, the rested lad resumes the game:
> The flung ball takes one maddening, tortuous bound,
> And the mid-stump three somersaults in air!

'Topping!' the Boy ejaculated. 'Who wrote it?'

'His name was Lefroy. He died young. He left Oxford a few years before we went up. And I think,' continued Verinder, musing, 'that I, who detest making acquaintances, would give at this moment a considerable sum to have known him. Well,' he continued, turning to me and puffing at his pipe, 'so you warn Grayson and me that we must prepare to relinquish these and all the other delights sung by Lefroy and Norman Gale and that other poet—anonymous, but you know the man—in his incomparable parody of Whitman: "the perfect feel of a fourer"—

> The thousand melodious cracks, delicious cracks, the responsive echoes of my comrades and the hundred thence resulting runs, passionately yearned for, never, never again to be forgotten.
>
> Overhead meanwhile the splendid silent sun, blending all, fusing all, bathing all in floods of soft ecstatic perspiration.

—to all this we must say good-bye. And what do you offer us in exchange?'

'Merely the old consolation that life is short, art is long; that while you grow old, cricket in other hands will be working out its perfection, and your son, when you have one, will start with higher ideals than you ever dreamed of.'

'And this perfection—will it ever be attained?'

'I dare say never. For perhaps we may say after Plato, and without irreverence, that the pattern of perfect cricket is laid up somewhere in the skies, and out of man's reach. But between it and ordinary cricket we may set up a copy of perfection, as close as man can make it, and, by little and little, closer every year. This copy will be preserved, and cared for, and advanced, by those professional cricketers against whom the unthinking have so much to say; by these and by the few amateurs who, as time goes on, will be found able to bear the strain. For the search after perfection is no light one, and will admit of no half-hearted service. I say nothing here of material rewards, beyond reminding you that your professional cricketer is poorly paid in comparison with an inferior singer of the music-halls, although he gives twice as much pleasure as your *lion comique*, and of a more innocent kind. But he does more than this. He feeds and guards the flame of art; and when his joints are stiff and his vogue is past, he goes down as groundman and instructor to a public school, and imparts to a young generation what knowledge he can of the high mysteries whose servant he has been: quite like the philosopher in the *Republic*——'

'Steady on!' interposed Grayson. 'How on earth will the Boy stand up to Briggs' bowling if you put these notions in his head? He'll be awe-struck, and begin to fidget with his right foot.'

'Oh, fire ahead!' said that cheerful youth. He had possessed himself of Prince Ranjitsinhji's book and coiled himself comfortably into a wicker chair.—'You're only rotting, I know. And you've passed over the most important sentence in the whole book. Listen to this: "There are very few newspaper readers who do not turn to the cricket column first when the morning journal comes; who do not buy a halfpenny evening paper to find out how many runs W.G. or Bobby Abel has made." That's the long and short of the matter. Verinder, which do you read first in your morning paper—the Foreign Intelligence or the Cricket News?'

THE SECOND DIALOGUE

1905

A few days ago—to be precise, on Saturday the 24th of this month—my friend Verinder reminded me of the long-past conversation. We had met by appointment at Paddington to travel down to Windsor for the second day of the Eton and Winchester match, taking with us (or rather,

being taken by) a youngster whom we call The Infant.
The Infant, who talks little save in the bosom of his
family, and even so preserves beneath his talk that fine
reticence of judgment which most adorns the age of fifteen,
not unfrequently surprises me by his experiments in the
art of living. On this occasion, while I was engaged in the
booking-office and Verinder in scanning the shelves of
Messrs Smith's bookstall, he had found our train, chosen
our compartment, and laid out twopence in four halfpenny
papers, which he spread on the cushions by way of reserving
our seats.

'But why four,' I asked, 'seeing there are but three of
us?'

'It will give us more room,' he answered simply.

He had hoped, I doubt not, by this devise to retain the
whole compartment; but the hope was soon and abruptly
frustrated by a tall, well-dressed and pompous man who
came striding down the platform while we idled by the
door, and thrusting past us almost before we could give
way, entered the compartment, dropped into a corner seat,
tossed his copy of *The Times* on to the seat opposite, took
off his top-hat, examined it, replaced it when satisfied of
its shine, drew out a spare handkerchief, opened it, flicked
a few specks of dust from his patent-leather boots, looked
up while reaching across for *The Times*, recognised me
with a nod and a 'Good morning!' and buried himself in
his paper.

I on my part, almost before glancing at his face, had
recognised him by his manner for a personage next to
whom it has been my lot to sit at one or two public banquets.
I will call him Sir John Crang. He is a K.C.M.G., a
Colonial by birth and breeding, a Member of Parliament,
and a person of the sort we treat in these days with con-

sideration. Since the second year of Jubilee (in which he
was knighted) he and his kind have found themselves at
ease in Sion, and of his kind he has been perhaps the most
fortunate. In his public speeches he alludes to himself
humorously as a hustler. He has married a wealthy lady,
in every other respect too good for him, entertains largely
at dinners which should be private but are reported in the
press, and advocates conscription for the youth of Great
Britain. Upon conscription for his native colony, as upon
any other of its duties towards Imperial defence, if you
question him, you will find him sonorously evasive.

The Infant, accustomed to surprise at the extent of my
acquaintance, gazed at him politely for a moment as we
took our seats and the train moved out of the station. I noted
a veiled disapproval in his eye as he picked up a newspaper,
and at that moment Verinder, who had picked up another,
emitted a noise not unlike the snort of the engine as it
gathered speed. I glanced at him in some apprehension.
Verinder's bearing toward strangers is apt to be brutal, and
by an instinct acquired as his companion on old reading-
parties I was prepared to be apologetic.

His ill-humour, however, had nothing to do with Sir
John Crang. He had laid the newspaper across his knee,
and was pointing to it with a scornful forefinger.

'Look here,' he said. 'Do you remember a talk we had
some years ago—you and I and Grayson? It started in
D——'s shop one afternoon after a Kent and Middlesex
match. You ought to remember, for I picked up *The Pall
Mall Magazine* a month later and found you had made
copy out of it.'

'To be sure,' said I. 'We discussed cricket, and a number
of reputations then well known, about which the public
troubles itself no longer. Let us try their names upon

The Infant here, and discover with how many of them
he is acquainted.'

'We discussed,' said Verinder, 'the vulgarisation of
cricket. You made me say some hard things about it, but
be hanged to me if anything I prophesied then came near
to *this*! Listen—

I suppose I may say that, after some luck at starting, I
played a pretty good innings: but a total of 240 is poor enough
for first knock on such a wicket as Hove, and, as things stand,
the omens are against us. However, as I write this wire the
clouds are gathering, and there's no denying that a downfall
during the night may help our chances.'

'What on earth are you reading?' I asked.

'Stay a moment. Here's another—

With Jones's wicket down, the opposition declared, somewhat to the annoyance of the crowd: and indeed, with Robinson
set and playing the prettiest strokes all around the wicket, I
must admit that they voiced a natural disappointment. They
had paid their money, and, after the long period of stone-
walling which preceded the tea interval, a crowded hour of
glorious life would have been exhilarating, and perhaps was
no more than their due. Dickson, however, took his barracking
good-humouredly. Towards the end Jones had twice appealed
against the light.'

'I suppose,' said I, 'that is how cricket strikes the Yellow
Press. Who are the reporters?'

'The reporters are the captains of two county teams—
two first-class county teams; and they are writing of a
match actually in progress at this moment. Observe A.'s
fine sense of loyalty to a captain's duty in his published
opinion that his side is in a bad way. Remark his chivalrous
hope for a sodden wicket to-morrow.'

'It is pretty dirty,' I agreed.

Verinder snorted. 'I once tried to kill a man at mid-on for wearing a pink shirt. But these fellows! They ought to wear yellow flannels.'

'What, by the way, is the tea interval?' I asked.

'It is an interval,' answered Verinder seriously, 'in which the opposing captains adjourn to the post office and send telegrams about themselves and one another.'

'Excuse me,' put in Sir John Crang, looking up from his *Times* and addressing me, 'but I quite agree with what you and your friend are saying. Interest in the Australian tour, for instance, I can understand; it promotes good feeling, and anything that draws closer the bonds of interest between ourselves and the colonies is an imperial asset.'

'Good Lord!' murmured Verinder.

Sir John fortunately did not hear him. 'But I agree with you,' he continued, 'in condemning this popular craze for cricket *per se*, which is after all but a game with a ball and some sticks. I will not go the length of our imperial poet and dub its votaries "flannelled fools." That was poetical license, eh? though pardonable under the circumstances. But, as he has said elsewhere, "How little they know of England who only England know."' (At this point I reached out a foot and trod hard on Verinder's toe.) 'And to the broader outlook—I speak as a pretty wide traveller—this insular absorption in a mere game is bewildering.'

'Infant!' said Verinder suddenly, still under repression of my foot, 'What are you reading?'

The Infant looked up sweetly, withdrawing himself from his paper, however, by an effort.

'There's a Johnny here who tells you how Bosanquet bowls with what he calls his "over-spin." He has a whole column about it with figures, just like Euclid; and the funny thing is, Bosanquet writes just after to say that the Johnny knows nothing about it.'

'Abandoned child,' commanded Verinder, 'pass me the paper. You are within measurable distance of studying cricket for its own sake, and will come to a bad end.'

Within twenty seconds he and The Infant were intently studying the diagrams, which Verinder demonstrated to be absurd, while Sir John, a little huffed by his manner, favoured me with a vision of England as she should be, with her ploughshares beaten into Morris Tubes.

In the midst of this discourse Verinder looked up.

'Let us not despair of cricket,' says he. 'She has her victories, but as yet no prizes to be presented with public speeches.'

'Curious fellow that friend of yours,' said Sir John, as he took leave of me on Windsor platform. 'Yes, yes, I saw how you humoured him: but why should he object to a man's playing cricket in a pink shirt?'

He went on his way toward the Castle, while we turned our faces for Agar's Plough and the best game in the world.

JULY

OUR Parliamentary Candidate—or Prospective Candidate, as we cautiously call him—has been visiting
us, and invited me to sit on the platform and give the
speeches my moral support. I like our candidate, who
is young, ardent, good-natured, and keeps his temper when
he is heckled; seems, indeed, to enjoy being heckled, and
conciliates his opponents by that bright pugnacity which
a true Briton loves better than anything else in politics.
I appreciate, too, the compliment he pays me. But I wish
he would not choose to put his ardour in competition with
Sirius and the dog-days; and I heartily wish he had not
brought down Mr Blank, M.P., to address us in his support.

Mr Blank and I have political opinions which pass, for
convenience, under a common label. Yet there are few
men in England whose attitude of mind towards his alleged
principles I more cordially loathe. Not to put too fine a
point upon it, I think him a hypocrite. But he has chosen
the side which is mine, and I cannot prevent his saying a
hundred things which I believe.

We will suppose that Mr Blank is a far honester fellow
than I am able to think him. Still, and at the best, he is a
sort of composite photograph of your average Member of
Parliament—the type of man to whom Great Britain com-
mits the direction of her affairs and, by consequence, her
well-doing and her well-being and her honour. Liberal
or Conservative, are not the features pretty much the same?
a solid man, well past fifty, who has spent the prime of his

life in business and withdrawn from it with a good reputation and a credit balance equally satisfactory to himself and his bankers. Or it may be that he has not actually retired but has turned to politics to fill up those leisure hours which are the reward or vexation (as he chooses to look at them) of a prosperous man of business; for, as Bagehot pointed out, the life of a man of business who employs his own capital, and employs it nearly always in the same way, is by no means fully employed. 'If such a man is very busy, it is a sign of something wrong. Either he is working at detail, which subordinates would do better, or he is engaged in too many speculations.' In consequence our commerce abounds with men of great business ability and experience who, being short of occupation, are glad enough to fill up their time with work in Parliament, as well as proud to write M.P. after their names. For my part I can think of nothing better calculated to reassure anyone whose dreams are haunted by apprehensions of wild-cat legislative schemes, or the imminence of a Radical millennium, than five minutes' contemplation of our champions of progress as they recline together, dignified and whiskered and bland, upon the benches of St Stephen's.

But let us proceed with our portrait, which I vow is a most pleasing one. Our typical legislator is of decent birth, or at least hopeful of acquiring what he rightly protests to be but 'the guinea stamp' by judiciously munificent contributions to his party's purse; honest and scrupulous in dealing; neither so honest nor so scrupulous in thinking; addicted to phrases and a trifle too impatient of their meaning, yet of proved carefulness in drawing the line between phrase and practice; a first-rate committeeman (and only those who have sat long in committee can sound the depths of this praise); locally admired; with much *bonhomie* of manner, backed by a reputation for standing no nonsense; good-tempered, honestly anxious to reconcile conflicting interests and do the best for the unconflicting ones of himself and his country; but above all a man who knows where to stop. I vow (I repeat) he makes a dignified and amiable figure. One can easily understand why people like to be represented by such a man. It gives a feeling of security—a somewhat illusory one, I believe; and security is the first instinct of a state. One can understand why the exhortations, dehortations, precepts, and instructions of parents, preachers, schoolmasters tend explicitly and implicitly to the reproduction of this admired bloom.

Yet one may whisper that it has—shall we say?—its failings; and its failings are just those which are least to be commended to the emulation of youth. It is, for instance, constitutionally timid. Violent action of any kind will stampede it in a panic, and, like the Countess in *Evan Harrington*, it 'does not ruffle well.' It betrays (I think) ill-breeding in its disproportionate terror whenever an anarchist bomb explodes, and in the ferocity of its terror it can be crueller than the assailant. 'My good people,' it provokes one to say, 'by all means stamp out these dangers, but composedly, as becomes men conscious of their strength. Even allowing for the unscrupulousness of your assailant, you have still nine hundred and ninety-nine out of a thousand of the odds in your favour; and so long as you answer the explosions of weak anarchy by cries suggestive of the rage of the sheep, you merely raise the uncomfortable suspicion that, after all, there must be something amiss with a civilisation which counts you among its most expensive products.'

But in the untroubled hour of prosperity this weakness of breeding is scarcely less apparent. Our admired bloom is admired rather for not doing certain things than for doing others. His precepts are cautious and mainly negative. He does not get drunk (in public at any rate), and he expends much time and energy in preventing men from getting drunk. But he does not lead or heartily incite to noble actions, although at times—when he has been badly frightened—he is ready to pay men handsomely to do them. He wins and loses elections on questions of veto. He had rather inculcate the passive than the active virtues. He prefers temperance and restraint to energy and resolve. He thinks more of the organisation than the practice of charity, esteems a penny saved as three halfpence gained, had liefer detect an impostor than help a deserving man. He is apt to label all generous emotions as hysterical, and in this he errs; for when a man calls the generous emotions hysterical he usually means that he would confuse them with hysterics if they happened to him.

Now the passive virtues—continence, frugality, and the like—are desirable, but shade off into mere want of pluck; while the active virtues—courage, charity, clemency, cheerfulness, helpfulness—are ever those upon which the elect and noble souls in history have laid the greater stress. I frankly detest Blank, M.P., because I believe him to be a venal person, a colourable (and no doubt self-deceiving) imitation of the type. But, supposing him to be the real thing, I still think that, if you want a model for your son, you will do better with Sir Philip Sidney. If ever a man illustrated the beauty of the active virtues in his life and in his death, that man was Sidney; but he also gave utterance in noble speech to his belief in them. In the *Apologie for Poetrie* you will find none of your art-for-art's-sake chatter: Sidney boldly takes the line that poetry helps men, and helps them not to well-being only, but to well-doing, and again helps them to well-doing not merely by teaching (as moral philosophy does) but by inciting. For an instance—

Who readeth Æneas carrying old Anchises on his back that wisheth not it were his fortune to perform so excellent an act?

There speaks, anticipating Zutphen, the most perfect knight in our history. Again—

Truly I have known men that even with reading *Amadis de Gaule* (which, God knoweth, wanteth much of a perfect poesy) have found their hearts moved to the exercise of courtesy, liberality, and especially courage—

all active virtues be it noted. 'We are not damned for doing wrong,' writes Stevenson, 'but for not doing right. Christ will never hear of negative morality: *Thou shalt* was ever His word, with which He superseded *Thou shalt not*. To make our morality centre on forbidden acts is to defile the imagination and to introduce into our judgments of our fellow-men a secret element of gusto....In order that a man may be kind and honest it may be needful that he should become a total abstainer: let him become so then, and the next day let him forget the circumstance. Trying to be kind and honest will require all his thoughts.' Yet how many times a day will we say 'don't' to our children for once that we say 'do'? But here I seem to be within reasonable distance of discussing original sin, and so I return to Mr Blank.

* * * * *

I do not like Mr Blank; and I disliked his speech the other night so heartily that it drove me to sit down when I reached home and put my reflections into verse; into a form of verse, moreover, which (I was scornfully aware) Mr Blank would understand as little as the matter of it. He would think them both impractical. Heaven help the creature!

CHANT ROYAL OF HIGH VIRTUE

Who lives in suit of armour pent,
  And hides himself behind a wall,
For him is not the great event,
  The garland, nor the Capitol.
And is God's guerdon less than they?
Nay, moral man, I tell thee Nay:
Nor shall the flaming forts be won
By sneaking negatives alone,
  By Lenten fast or Ramazàn,
But by the challenge proudly thrown—
  Virtue is that beseems a Man!

God, in His Palace resident
  Of Bliss, beheld our sinful ball,
And charged His own Son innocent
  Us to redeem from Adam's fall.
—'Yet must it be that men Thee slay.'
—'Yea, tho' it must must I obey,'
Said Christ,—and came, His royal Son,
To die, and dying to atone
  For harlot and for publican.
Read on that rood He died upon—
  Virtue is that beseems a Man!

And by that rood where He was bent
  I saw the world's great captains all
Go riding to the tournament—
  Cyrus the Great and Hannibal,
Cæsar of Rome and Attila,
Lord Charlemagne with his array,
Lord Alisaundre of Macedon—
With flaming lance and habergeon
  They passed, and to the rataplan
Of drums gave salutation—
  Virtue is that beseems a Man!

Had tall Achilles lounged in tent
  For aye, and Xanthus neigh'd in stall,
The towers of Troy had ne'er been shent,
  Nor stay'd the dance in Priam's hall
Bend o'er thy book till thou be grey,
Read, mark, perpend, digest, survey—
Instruct thee deep as Solomon—
One only chapter thou shalt con,
  One lesson learn, one sentence scan,
One title and one colophon—
    Virtue is that beseems a Man!

High Virtue's hest is eloquent
  With spur and not with martingall:
Sufficeth not thou'rt continent:
  BE COURTEOUS, BRAVE, AND LIBERAL.
God fashion'd thee of chosen clay
For service, nor did ever say
'Deny thee this,' 'Abstain from yon,'
Save to inure thee, thew and bone,
  To be confirmèd of the clan
That made immortal Marathon—
    Virtue is that beseems a Man!

ENVOY.

Young Knight, the lists are set to-day:
Hereafter shall be long to pray
In sepulture with hands of stone.
Ride, then! outride the bugle blown
  And gaily dinging down the van
Charge with a cheer—Set on! Set on!
    Virtue is that beseems a Man!

*   *   *   *   *

A friend to whom I showed these verses remarked that Mr Blank was indeed a person who fed his soul upon negatives; but that I possibly did him some injustice in charging so much of this to timidity, whereas the scent lay rather in the gusto with which he judged his fellow-men. 'And, by the way,' said he, 'is there not some gusto in the scorn with which you are judging Mr Blank at this moment?' 'Do you remember,' I answered, 'how that man, after voting for war the other day, went straight off to a meeting of the Peace Society and put up a florid appeal to the Prince of Peace for a time when wars should be no more? Let him be, however: I do wrong to lose my temper with him. But on this matter of national timidity I have something to say....'

I have been reading John Holland's two *Discourses of the Navy*, written in 1638 and 1659, and published the other day by the Navy Records Society. The object of Mr Holland's discourses was to reform the Navy, purge it of abuses, and strengthen it for the defence of this realm; and I have been curious to compare his methods with those of our own Navy League, which has been making such a noise for ten years or so. The first thing I observe is the attitude of mind in which he approaches his subject:

If either the honour of a nation, commerce or trust with all nations, peace at home, grounded upon our enemies' fear or love of us abroad, and attended with plenty of all things necessary either for the preservation of the public weal or thy private welfare, be things worthy thy esteem (though it may be beyond thy shoal conceit) then next to God and thy King give thy thanks for the same to the Navy. As for honour, who knows not (that knows anything) that in all records of late times of actions, chronicled to the everlasting fame and renown of this nation, still the naval part is the thread that runs through the whole wooft, the burden of the song, the scope of the text?...

He proceeds to enumerate some particular commercial advantages due to our mastery of the sea, and sums up in these words:

Suffice it thus far, nothing under God, who doth all, hath brought so much, so great commerce to this Kingdom as the rightly noble employments of our navy; a wheel, if truly turned, that sets to work all Christendom by its motion; a mill, if well extended, that in a sweet yet sovereign composure contracts the grist of all nations to its own dominions, and requires only the tribute of its own people, not for, but towards, its maintenance.

The eloquence may be turgid, but the attitude is dignified. The man does not scold; does not terrify. He lays his stress on the benefits of a strong navy—on the renown it has won for England in the past. He assumes his readers to be intelligent men, amenable to advice which will help them to perpetuate this renown and secure these benefits in time to come. His exordium over, he settles down to an exposition of the abuses which are impairing our naval efficiency, and suggests reforms, some wisely conceived, others not so wisely, with the business-like, confident air of one who knows what he is talking about.

Now I open the prospectus in which our Navy League started out to make everyone's flesh creep, and come plump upon language of this sort:

It is the close, let us suppose, of our second month of war. The fleet has been neglected, and has been overwhelmed, unready and unprepared. We have been beaten twice at sea, and our enemies have established no accidental superiority, but a permanent and overwhelming one. The telegraph cables have been severed, one and all; these islands are in darkness—

for presumably the gas-mains, as well as the cables, have
been 'severed' (imposing word!)—

—under a heavy cloud of woe. Invasion is in the air; our
armies are mustering in the south. We are cut off from the
world, and can only fitfully perceive what is happening. Our
liners have been captured or sunk on the high seas; our ocean
tramps are in our enemies' hands; British trade is dead, killed
by the wholesale ravages of the hostile cruisers. Our ports are
insulted or held up to ransom; when news reaches us from
India it is to the effect that the enemy is before our troops,
a native insurrection behind. Malta has fallen, and our out-
lying positions are passing from our hands. Food is contra-
band, and may not be imported. Amid the jeers of Europe
'the nation of shopkeepers' is writhing in its death agony.

Pretty, is it not? But let us have just a little more.

COMMERCIAL COLLAPSE

And what of the internal, of the social position? Consols have
fallen to nearly 30; our vast investments in India have been
lost; trade no longer exists....The railways have no traffic to
carry....Banks and companies are failing daily....The East
End of London is clamouring for bread and peace at any
price. If we fall, we fall for ever....The working man has
to choose whether he will have lighter taxation for the moment,
starvation and irretrievable ruin for the future...

—and so on, till Z stands for Zero, or nothing at all. Or,
as the late Mr Lear preferred to write:

Z said, 'Here is a box of Zinc. Get in, my little master!
We'll shut you up: we'll nail you down: we will, my little
    master!
We think we've all heard quite enough of this your sad disaster!'

To speak as seriously as may be, the language is no longer hortatory, like Holland's, but minatory, even comminatory. It is (as its author would not deny) the language of panic deliberately employed, a calculated attempt to strengthen the *matériel* of the navy at the cost of Englishmen's fears. Now let me define my feeling towards the Navy League. As an ordinary British citizen, I must heartily approve its aim of strengthening the navy and keeping it efficient. As an ordinary reasonable man, I must admit that its efforts, if rightly directed, may be of great national service. But language such as I have quoted must (so far as it is not merely contemptible) be merely demoralising, and anyone who works on the fears of a nation—and especially of a nation which declines conscription and its one undoubted advantage of teaching men what war means—does a harm which is none the less wicked for being incalculable. These Navy Leaguers cry incessantly for more *material* strength. They tell us that in material strength we should at least be equal to any two other countries. A few months pass, and then, their appetite growing with the terror it feeds upon, they insist that we must be equal to any three other countries. Also 'it does not appear,' they sagely remark, 'that Nelson and his contemporaries left any record as to what the proportion of the blockading should bear (*sic*) to one blockaded'—a curious omission of Nelson's, to be sure! He may perhaps have held that it depended on the quality of the antagonists.

To this a few ordinary stupid Britons like myself have always answered that no amount of *matériel* can ever replace *morale;* and that all such panic-making is a mischievous attempt to lower the breed, and the more mischievous because its mischief may for a while be imperceptible. We can see our warships growing: we cannot see the

stamina decaying; yet it is our stamina on which we must
rely finally in the fatal hour of trial. We said this, and we
were laughed at; insulted as unpatriotic—a word of which
one may say in kindness that it would not so readily leap
to the lips of professional patriots if they were able to understand what it means and, by consequence, how much it
hurts.

Yes, and behold, along comes Admiral Togo, and at
one stroke proves that we were simply, absolutely and hence-
forward incontestably right! What were our little three-
power experts doing on the morrow of Togo's victory?
They are making irrelevant noises in the halfpenny press,
explaining how Admiral Togo did it with an inferior force,
and in a fashion that belies all their axioms. But I turn to
The Times and I read:

> The event shows that mere material equality is but as dust
> in the balance when weighed in the day of battle against
> superiority of moral equipment.

—which, when you come to think of it, is precisely what
Bacon meant when he wrote:

> Walled Townes, stored Arcenalls and Armouries, Goodly
> Races of Horse, Chariots of Warre, Elephants, Ordnance,
> Artillery and the like: all this is but a Sheep in a Lion's skin
> except the Breed and disposition of the People be stout and
> warlike. Nay, Number (it selfe) in Armies importeth not
> much where the People is of weake Courage: For (as *Virgil* saith)
> *it never troubles a Wolfe how many the Sheepe be.*

Do our friends of the Navy League seriously believe
that a principle as old as humankind can be suddenly
upset by the invention of a submarine or of some novelty
in guns? Even in their notions of what material strength

means I hold them to be mistaken. The last resource which a nation ought to neglect is its financial credit. It was Walpole's long policy of peace which made possible Pitt's conquests. But I hold with far stronger conviction that he does wickedly who trades on a nation's cowardice to raise money for its protection. An old text, my masters! It seems a long while that some of us were preaching it in vain until Admiral Togo came along and proved it.

*   *   *   *   *

I observe that a Member of Parliament for a West of England constituency (a better fellow than Mr Blank, too) has been using one of the arguments with which these precious experts attacked me; that because I sometimes write novels I cannot be supposed to think seriously on public affairs. My only wonder is that those who hold this cloistral view of the province of a man of letters consider him worthy to pay income-tax.

I pass over some tempting reflections on the queer anomaly that this prohibition should be addressed (as it so often is) by writers to writers, by newspaper writers to men who write books, and (so far as a distinction can be drawn) by men who write in a hurry to men who write deliberately. I wish to look quietly into the belief on which it rests and to inquire how that belief was come by.

There certainly was a time when such a belief would have been laughed at as scarcely reasonable enough to be worth discussing. And that time, oddly enough, was almost conterminous with the greatest era of the world's literature, the greatest era of political discovery, and the greatest era of Empire-making. The men who made Athens and the men who made Rome would have disputed (I fear somewhat contemptuously) the axiom on which my friend the West Country member builds his case. They held it for axiomatic that the artist and man of letters ought not to work in cloistral isolation, removed from public affairs, and indifferent to them; that on the contrary they are direct servants of their State, and have a peculiar call to express themselves on matters of public moment. To convince you that I am not advancing any pet theory of my own let me present it in the words of a grave and judicious student, Mr W. J. Courthope, late Professor of Poetry at Oxford:

> The idea of the State lay at the root of every Greek conception of art and morals. For though, in the view of the philosopher, the virtue of the good citizen was not always necessarily identical with the virtue of the individual man, and though, in the city of Athens at all events, a large amount of life was possible to the individual apart from public interests, yet it is none the less true that the life of the individual in every Greek city was in reality moulded by the customary life, tradition and character, in one intranslatable word, by the $\mathring{\eta}\theta os$ of the State. Out of this native soil grew that recognised, though not necessarily public, system of education ($\pi o\lambda\iota\tau\iota\kappa\mathring{\eta}$ $\pi a\iota\delta\epsilon\acute{\iota}a$), consisting of reading and writing, music and gymnastic, which Plato and Aristotle themselves accepted as the basis of the constitution of the State. But this preliminary education was only the threshold to a subsequent system of political training, of which, in Athens at least, every citizen had an opportunity of availing himself by his right to participate in public affairs; so that, in the view of Pericles, politics themselves were an instrument of individual refinement. 'The magistrates,' said he, in his great funeral oration, 'who discharge public trusts, fulfil their domestic duties also; the private citizen, while engaged in professional business, has competent knowledge of public affairs; for we stand alone in regarding the man who keeps aloof from these latter not as

harmless, but as useless. Moreover, we always hear and pronounce on public matters when discussed by our leaders, or
perhaps strike out for ourselves correct reasonings upon them;
far from accounting discussion an impediment to action, we
complain only if we are not told what is to be done before it
becomes our duty to do it.'

The strenuous exertion of the faculties of the individual in
the service of the State, described in these eloquent words,
reflects itself in the highest productions of Greek art and
literature, and is the source of that 'political' spirit which
every one can detect, alike in the poems of Homer and the
sculpture of the Parthenon, as the inspiring cause of the noblest
efforts of imitation. It prevailed most strongly through the
period between the battle of Marathon and the battle of
Chaeronea, and has left its monuments in such plays as the
Persae and *Eumenides* of Æschylus, the *Antigone* of Sophocles,
the *Clouds* of Aristophanes, the History of Thucydides and
the Orations of Demosthenes, its last embodiment being perhaps the famous oath of that orator on the souls of those who
risked their lives at Marathon.—*History of English Poetry*,
vol. I, c. 2.

In the most brilliant age of Greece, then, and of Greek
art and letters, the civic spirit was the inspiring spirit.
But as the Greek cities sank one by one before the Mace-
donian power and forfeited their liberties, this civic spirit
died for lack of nourishment and exercise, and literature
was driven to feed on itself—which is about the worst
thing that can ever happen to it, and one of the worst
things that can happen to a nation. The old political education gave place to an 'encyclopædic' education. The language fell into the hands of grammarians and teachers of
rhetoric, whose inventions may have a certain interest of
their own, but—to quote Mr Courthope again—no longer
reflect the feelings and energies of free political life.

Roman literature drives home the same, or a similar, moral. 'The greatness of Rome was as entirely civic in its origin as that of any Greek city, and, like the Greek cities, Rome in the days of her freedom, and while she was still fighting for the mastery, preserved a system of political education, both in the hearth and the Senate, which was suited to her character. Cato, the Censor, according to Plutarch, "wrote histories for his son, with his own hand, in large characters; so that without leaving his father's house he might gain a knowledge of the illustrious actions of the ancient Romans and the customs of his country": and what is of importance to observe,' adds Mr Courthope, 'is that, even after the introduction of Greek culture, Cato's educational ideal was felt to be the foundation of Roman greatness by the orators and poets who adorned the golden age of Latin literature.' The civic spirit was at once the motive and vitalising force of Cicero's eloquence, and still acts as its antiseptic. It breaks through the conventional forms of Virgil's Eclogues and Georgics, and declares itself exultantly in such passages as the famous eulogy—

> Sed neque Medorum silvae, ditissima terra,
> Nec pulcher Ganges atque auro turbidus Hermus
> Laudibus Italiæ certent....

It closes the last Georgic on a high political note. Avowedly it inspires the *Æneid*. It permeates all that Horace wrote. These two poets never tire of calling on their countrymen to venerate the Roman virtues, to hold fast by the old Sabine simplicity and

> Pure religion breathing household laws.

Again, when the mischief was done, and Rome had accepted the Alexandrine model of education and literary

culture, Juvenal reinvoked the old spirit in his denunciation
of the hundred and more trivialities which the new spirit
engendered. It was a belated, despairing echo. You cannot
expect quite the same shout from a man who leads a forlorn
sortie, and a man who defends a proud citadel while yet
it is merely threatened. But, allowing for changed circumstances, you will find that Juvenal's is just the old civic
spirit turned to fierceness by despair. And he strikes out
unerringly enough at the ministers of Rome's decline—at
the poets who chatter and the rhetoricians who declaim on
merely 'literary' topics; the rich who fritter away life on
private luxuries and the pursuit of trivial aims; the debased
Greek with his 'smattering of encyclopædic knowledge,'
but no devotion to the city in which he only hopes to make
money.

Now is this civic spirit in literature (however humble
its practitioners) one which England can easily afford to
despise? So far as I know, it has been reserved for an age
of newspapers to declare explicitly that such a spirit is
merely mischievous; that a poet ought to be a man of the
study, isolated amid the stir of passing events, serenely
indifferent to his country's fortunes, or at least withholding
his gift (allowed, with magnificent but unconscious irony,
to be 'divine') from that general contribution to the public
wisdom in which journalists make so brave a show. He
may, if he have the singular luck to be a Laureate, be
allowed to strike his lyre and sing of an *accouchement;* this
being about the only event on which politicians and
journalists have not yet claimed the monopoly of offering
practical advice. But farther he may hardly go: and all
because a silly assertion has been repeated until second-
rate minds confuse it with an axiom. People of a certain
class of mind seem capable of believing anything they see

in print, provided they see it often. For these, the announcement that somebody's lung tonic possesses a peculiar virtue has only to be repeated at intervals along a railway line, and with each repetition the assurance becomes more convincing, until towards the journey's end it wears the imperativeness almost of a revealed truth. And yet no reasonable inducement to belief has been added by any one of these repetitions. The whole thing is a psychological trick. The moral impressiveness of the first placard beyond Westbourne Park Station depends entirely on whether you are travelling from London to Birmingham, or from Birmingham to London. A mind which yields itself to this illusion could probably, with perseverance, be convinced that pale pills are worth a guinea a box for pink people, were anyone interested in enforcing such a harmless proposition: and I have no doubt that the Man in the Street has long since accepted the reiterated axiom that a poet should hold aloof from public affairs, having no more capacity than a child for understanding their drift.

Yet, as a matter of fact, the cry is just a cant party trick, used by each party in its turn. Mr Kipling writes 'Cleared,' Mr Alfred Austin hymns 'Jameson's Ride,' and forthwith the Liberals lift hands and voices in horror. Mr Watson denounces the Armenian massacres or the Boer War, and the Unionists can hardly find words to express their pained surprise. Mr Swinburne inveighed against Irishmen, and delighted a party; inveighed against the Czar, and divided a whole Front Bench between shocked displeasure and half-humorous astonishment that a poet should have any opinions about Russia, or, having some, should find anybody to take them seriously. It is all cant, my friends—nothing but cant; and at its base lies the old dispute between principle and casuistry. If politics and statecraft rest ulti-

mately on principles of right and wrong, then a poet has
as clear a right as any man to speak upon them: as clear
a right now as when Tennyson lifted his voice on behalf
of the Fleet, or Wordsworth penned his 'Two Voices'
sonnet, or Milton denounced the massacres at Piedmont.
While this nation retains a conscience, its poets have a
clear right and a clear call to be the voice of that conscience.
They may err, of course; they may mistake the voice of
party for the voice of conscience: 'Jameson's Ride' and
'The Year of Shame'—one or both—may misread that
voice. Judge them as severely as you will by their rightness
or wrongness, and again judge them by their merits or
defects as literature. Only do not forbid the poet to speak
and enforce the moral conviction that is in him.

If, on the other hand, politics be a mere affair of casuistry;
or worse—a mere game of opportunism in which he excels
who hits on the cleverest expedient for each several crisis
as it occurs; then indeed you may bid the poet hush the
voice of principle, and listen only to the sufficiently dissonant
instruction of those specialists at the game who make play
in Parliament and the press. If politics be indeed that base
thing connoted by the term '*drift* of public affairs,' then
the axiom rests on wisdom after all. The poet cannot be
expected to understand the 'drift,' and had better leave it
to these specialists in drifting.

But if you search, you will find that poetry—rare gift
as it is, and understood by so few—has really been exerting
an immense influence on public opinion all the while that
we have been deluged with assertions of this unhappy
axiom. Why, I dare to say that one-half of the sense of
Empire which now dominates political thought in Great
Britain has been the creation of her poets. The public, if it
will but clear its mind of cant, is grateful enough for such

poetry as Mr Kipling's 'Flag of England' and Mr Henley's 'England, my England'; and gratefully recognises that the spirit of these songs has passed on to thousands of men, women, and children, who have never read a line of Mr Henley's or Mr Kipling's composition.

As for the axiom, it is merely the complement of that 'Art-for-Art's-sake' chatter which died a dishonoured death but a short while ago, and which it is still one of the joys of life to have outlived. You will remember how loftily we were assured that Art had nothing to do with morality: that the novelist, *e.g.* who composed tales of human conduct, had no concern with ethics—that is to say with the principles of human conduct: that 'Art's only business was to satisfy Art,' and so forth. Well, it is all over now, and packed away in the rag-bag of out-worn paradoxes; and we are left to enjoy the revived freshness of the simple truth that an artist exists to serve his art, and his art to serve men and women.

AUGUST

AS it was reported to me, the story went that one Sunday morning in August a family stood in a window not far from this window of mine—the window of an hotel coffee-room—and debated where to go for divine worship. They were three: father, mother, and daughter, arrived the night before from the Midlands, to spend their holiday. 'The fisher-folk down here are very religious,' said the father, contemplating the anchored craft—yachts, trading-steamers, merchantmen of various rigs and nationalities—in which he supposed the native population to go a-fishing on week-days: for he had been told in the Midlands that we were fisher-folk. 'Plymouth Brethren mostly, I suppose,' said the wife: 'we changed at Plymouth.' 'Bristol.' 'Was it Bristol? Well, Plymouth was the last big town we stopped at: I am sure of *that*. And this is on the same coast, isn't it?' 'What *are* Plymouth Brethren?' the daughter asked. 'Oh, well, my dear, I expect they are very decent, earnest people. It won't do us any harm to attend their service, if they have one. What I say is, when you're away on holiday, do as the Romans do.' The father had been listening with an unprejudiced air, as who should say, 'I am here by the seaside for rest and enjoyment.' He called to the waiter, 'What places of worship have you?' The waiter with professional readiness hinted that he had some to suit all tastes, 'Church of England, Wesleyan, Con-gregational, Bible Christian——' 'Plymouth Brethren?' The waiter had never heard of them: they had not, at any rate, been asked for within his recollection. He retired crestfallen. 'That's the worst of these waiters,' the father explained: 'they get 'em down for the season from Lord knows where, Germany perhaps, and they can tell you nothing of the place.' 'But this one is not a German, and he told me last night he'd been here for years.' 'Well, the question is, Where we are to go? Here, Ethel'—as a second daughter entered, buttoning her gloves—'your mother can't make up her mind what place of worship to try.' 'Why, father, how can you *ask*? We must go to the Church, of course—I saw it from the 'bus—and hear the service in the fine old Cornish language.'

Now, I suspect that the friend to whom I am indebted for this story introduced a few grace-notes into his report. But it is a moral story in many respects, and I give it for the sake of the one or two morals which may be drawn from it. In the first place, absurd as these people appear, their ignorance but differs by a shade or two from the knowledge of certain very learned people of my acquaintance. That is to say, they know about as much concerning the religion of this corner of England to-day as the archæologists, for all their industry, know concerning the religion of Cornwall before it became subject to the See of Canterbury in the reign of Athelstan, A.D. 925–40; and their hypotheses were constructed on much the same lines. Nay, the resemblance in method and in the general muddle of conclusions obtained would have been even more striking had these good persons mixed up Plymouth Brethren (founded in 1830) with the Pilgrim Fathers who sailed out of Plymouth in 1620, and are already undergoing the process of my-thopœic conversion into Deucalions and Pyrrhas of the United States of America. Add a slight confusion of their tenets with those of Mormonism, or at least a disposition to lay stress on all discoverable points of similarity between

Puritans and Mormons, and really you have a not unfair
picture of the hopeless mess into which our researchers in
the ancient religions of Cornwall have honestly contrived
to plunge themselves and us. It was better in the happy
old days when we all believed in the Druids; when the
Druids explained everything, and my excellent father
grafted mistletoe upon his apple-trees—in vain, because
nothing will persuade the mistletoe to grow down here.
But nobody believes in the Druids just now: and the old
question of the Cassiterides has never been solved to general
satisfaction: and the Indian cowrie found in a barrow at
Land's End, the tiny shell which raised such a host of
romantic conjectures and inspired Mr Canton to write his
touching verses:

> What year was it that blew
> The Aryan's wicker-work canoe
> Which brought the shell to English land?
> What prehistoric man or woman's hand,
> With what intent, consigned it to this grave—
> This barrow set in sound of the Ancient World's last wave?
>
> Beside it in the mound
> A charmèd bead of flint was found.
> Some woman surely in this place
> Covered with flowers a little baby-face,
> And laid the cowrie on the cold dead breast;
> And, weeping, turned for comfort to the landless West?
>
> *　　*　　*　　*　　*
>
> No man shall ever know.
> It happened all so long ago
> That this same childless woman may
> Have stood upon the cliffs around the bay
> And watched for tin-ships that no longer came,
> Nor knew that Carthage had gone down in Roman flame.

This cowrie—are we even certain that it was Indian?—
that it differed so unmistakably from the cowries discoverable by twos and threes at times on a little beach off
which I cast anchor half a dozen times every summer?
I speak as a man anxious to get at a little plain knowledge
concerning the land of his birth, and the researchers seem
honestly unable to give me any that does not tumble to
pieces even in their own hands. For—and this seems the
one advance made—the researchers themselves are honest
nowadays. Their results may be disappointing, but at least
they no longer bemuse themselves and us with the fanciful
and even mystical speculations their predecessors indulged
in. Take the case of our inscribed stones and wayside crosses.
Cornwall is peculiarly rich in these: of crosses alone it
possesses more than three hundred. But when we make inquiry into their age we find ourselves in almost complete
fog. The merit of the modern inquirer (of Mr Langdon,
for instance) is that he acknowledges the fog, and does not
pretend to guide us out of it by haphazard hypotheses
propounded with pontifical gravity and assurance—which
was the way of that erratic genius, the Rev. R. S. Hawker:

Wheel-tracks in old Cornwall there were none, but there
were strange and narrow paths across the moorlands, which,
the forefathers said, in their simplicity, were first traced by
Angels' feet. These, in truth, were trodden and worn by
religious men: by the Pilgrim as he paced his way towards
his chosen and votive bourne; or by the Palmer, whose listless
footsteps had neither a fixed Kebla nor future abode. Dimly
visible, by the darker hue of the crushed grass, these strait and
narrow roads led the traveller along from one Hermitage to
another Chapelry, or distant and inhabited cave; or the bye-
ways turned aside to reach some legendary spring, until at
last, far, far away, the winding track stood still upon the shore,

where St Michael of the Mount rebuked the dragon from his throne of rock above the seething sea. But what was the wanderer's guide along the bleak unpeopled surface of the Cornish moor? The Wayside Cross!...

Very pretty, no doubt! but, unlike the Wayside Cross, this kind of writing leads nowhere. We want Mr Hawker's authority for what 'the forefathers said, in their simplicity'; without that, what the forefathers said resembles what the soldier said in being inadmissible as evidence. We want Mr Hawker's authority for saying that these paths '*in truth*, were trodden and worn by religious men.' Nay we want his authority for saying that there were any paths at all! The hypotheses of symbolism are even worse; for these may lead to anything. Mr Langdon was seriously told on one occasion that the four holes of a cross represented the four evangelists. 'This,' says he plaintively, 'it will be admitted, is going a little too far, as nothing else but four holes could be the result of a ring and cross combined.' At Phillack, in the west of Cornwall, there is *part* of a coped stone having a rude cable mounting along the top of the ridge. Two sapient young archæologists counted the remaining notches of this cable, and, finding they came to *thirty-two*, decided at once that they represented our Lord's age! They were quite certain, having counted them twice. In fact, there seems to be nothing that symbolism will not prove. Do you meet with a pentacle? Its five points are the fingers of Omnipotence. With a six-pointed star? Then Omnipotence has taken an extra finger, to include the human nature of the Messiah: and so on. It reminds one of the Dilly Song:

'I will sing you Five, O!'
'What is your Five, O?'
'Five it is the Dilly Bird that's never seen but heard, O!'
'I will sing you Six, O!...'

And six is 'The Cherubim Watchers,' or 'The Crucifix,'
or 'The Cheerful Waiters,' or 'The Ploughboys under the
Bowl,' or whatever local fancy may have hit on and made
traditional.

The modern researcher is honest and sticks to facts; but
there are next to no facts. And when he comes to a tentative
conclusion, he must hedge it about with so many 'ifs,' that
practically he leaves us in total indecision. Nothing, for
instance, can exceed the patient industry displayed in the
late Mr William Copeland Borlase's *Age of the Saints*—a
monograph on Early Christianity in Cornwall: but, in a
way, no more hopeless book was ever penned. The author
confessed it, indeed, on his last page. 'There seems to be
little ground for hope that we shall be ever able to gain a
perfectly true insight into the history of the epoch with
which we have attempted to deal, or to unravel the meshes
of so tangled a web.' He felt his task, as he put it, to be not
unlike that of gathering up the broken pieces of pottery
from some ancient tomb, with the hope of fitting them
together so as to make one large and perfect vase, but
finding during the process that they belong to several vessels,
not one of which is capable of restoration as a whole, though
some faint notion of the pristine shape of each may be
gained from the general pattern and contour of its shards.
All that can be gained from the materials at hand is a
reasonable probability that Cornwall, before it bent its
neck to the See of Canterbury, had been invaded by three
distinct streams of missionary effort—from Ireland, from
Wales, and from Brittany. But even in what order they
came no man can say for certain.

The young lady in my friend's story wished to hear the
service of the Church of England in 'the fine old Cornish
language.' Alas! if Edward VI and his advisers had been

as wise, the religious history of Cornwall, during two centuries at least, had been a happier one. It was liberal to give Englishmen a Liturgy in their own tongue; but it was neither liberal nor conspicuously intelligent to impose the same upon the Cornishmen, who neither knew nor cared about the English language. It may be easy to lay too much stress upon this grievance; since Cornishmen of this period had a knack of being 'agin the government, anyway,' and had contrived two considerable rebellions less than sixty years before, one because they did not see their way to subscribing £2500 towards fighting King James IV of Scotland for protecting Perkin Warbeck, and the other under Perkin's own leadership. But it was at least a serious grievance; and the trouble began in the first year of Edward VI's reign. The King began by issuing several Injunctions about religion; and among them, this one: That all images found in churches, for divine worship or otherwise, should be pulled down and cast forth out of those churches; and that all preachers should persuade the people from praying to saints, or for the dead, and from the use of beads, ashes, processions, masses, dirges, and praying to God publicly in an unknown tongue. A Mr Body, one of the commissioners appointed to carry out this Injunction, was pulling down images in Helston church, near the Lizard, when a priest stabbed him with a knife: 'of which wound he instantly fell dead in that place. And though the murderer was taken and sent up to London, tried, found guilty of murder in Westminster Hall, and executed in Smithfield, yet the Cornish people flocked together in a tumultuous and rebellious manner, by the instigation of their priests in divers parts of the shire or county, and committed many barbarities and outrages in the same.' These disturbances ended in Arundel's rebellion,

the purpose of which was to demand the restoration of the
old Liturgy; and, in truth, the Seven Articles under which
they formulated this demand must have seemed very
moderate indeed to their conservative minds. The rebellion
failed, of course, after a five weeks' siege of Exeter; and
was bloodily revenged, with something of the savage
humour displayed by Jeffreys in punishing a later Western
rebellion. This part of the business was committed to
Sir Anthony (*alias* William) Kingston, Knight, a Glou-
cestershire man, as Provost Marshal; and 'it is memorable
what sport he made, by virtue of his office, upon men in
misery.' Here are one or two of his merry conceits, which
read strangely like the jests reported by Herodotus:

(1) One Boyer, Mayor of Bodmin in Cornwall, had been
amongst the rebels, not willingly, but enforced: to him the
Provost sent word he would come and dine with him: for
whom the Mayor made great provision. A little before dinner,
the Provost took the Mayor aside, and whispered him in the
ear, that an execution must that day be done in the town, and
therefore required to have a pair of gallows set up against
dinner should be done. The Mayor failed not of the charge.
Presently after dinner the Provost, taking the Mayor by the
hand, intreated him to lead him where the gallows was, which,
when he beheld, he asked the Mayor if he thought them to be
strong enough. 'Yes' (said the Mayor), 'doubtless they are.'
'Well, then' (said the Provost), 'get you up speedily, for they
are provided for you.' 'I hope' (answered the Mayor), 'you
mean not as you speak.' 'In faith' (said the Provost), 'there
is no remedy, for you have been a busie rebel.' And so without
respite or defence he was hanged to death; a most uncourteous
part for a guest to offer his host.—Sir Rich. Baker, 1641.

(2) Near the same place dwelt a Miller, who had been a
busie actor in that rebellion; who, fearing the approach of

the Marshal, told a sturdy fellow, his servant, that he had occasion to go from home, and therefore bid him, that if any man came to inquire after the miller, he should not speak of him, but say that himself was the miller, and had been so for three years before. So the Provost came and called for the miller, when out comes the servant and saith he was the man. The Provost demanded how long he had kept the mill? 'These three years' (answered the servant). Then the Provost commanded his men to lay hold on him and hang him on the next tree. At this the fellow cried out that he was not the miller, but the miller's man. 'Nay, sir' (said the Provost), 'I will take you at your word, and if thou beest the miller, thou art a busie knave; if thou beest not, thou art a false lying knave; and howsoever, thou canst never do thy master better service than to hang for him'; and so, without more ado, he was dispatched.—*Ibid.*

The story of one Mayow, whom Kingston hanged at a tavern signpost in the town of St Columb, has a human touch. 'Tradition saith that his crime was not capital; and therefore his wife was advised by her friends to hasten to the town after the Marshal and his men, who had him in custody, and beg his life. Which accordingly she prepared to do; and to render herself the more amiable petitioner before the Marshal's eyes, this dame spent so much time in attiring herself and putting on her French hood, then in fashion, that her husband was put to death before her arrival.'

Such was the revenge wreaked on a population which the English of the day took so little pains to understand that (as I am informed) in an old geography book of the days of Elizabeth, Cornwall is described as 'a foreign country on that side of England next to Spain.'

*   *   *   *   *

And now that the holiday season is upon us, and the
visitor stalks our narrow streets, perhaps he will not resent
a word or two of counsel in exchange for the unreserved
criticism he lavishes upon us. We are flattered by his
frequent announcement that on the whole he finds us clean
and civil and fairly honest; and respond with the assurance
that we are always pleased to see him so long as he behaves
himself. We, too, have found him clean and fairly honest;
and if we have anything left to desire, it is only that he
will realise, a little more constantly, the extent of his knowledge of us, and the extent to which his position as a visitor
should qualify his bearing towards us. I address this hint
particularly to those who make copy out of their wanderings
in our midst; and I believe it has only to be suggested,
and it will be at once recognised for true, that the proper
attitude for a visitor in a strange land is one of modesty.
He may be a person of quite considerable importance in
his own home, even if that home be London; but when
he finds himself on strange soil he may still have a deal to
learn from the people who have lived on that soil for
generations, adapted themselves to its conditions and sown
it with memories in which he cannot have a share.

In truth, many of our visitors would seem to suffer from
a confusion of thought. Possibly the Visitors' Books at
hotels and places of public resort may have fostered this.
Our guest makes a stay of a few weeks in some spot to which
he has been attracted by its natural beauty: he idles and
watches the inhabitants as they go about their daily business;
and at the end he deems it not unbecoming to record his
opinion that they are intelligent, civil, honest, and sober—
or the reverse. He mistakes. It is *he* who has been on
probation during these weeks—*his* intelligence, *his* civility,
his honesty, *his* sobriety. For my part, I look forward to

a time when Visitors' Books shall record the impressions
which visitors leave behind them, rather than those which
they bear away. For an instance or two:

(1) The Rev. and Mrs ——, of——, arrived here in August,
1897, and spent six weeks. We found them clean, and invariably
sober and polite. We hope they will come often.

(2) Mr X and his friend Y, from Z, came over here, attired
in flannels and the well-known blazer of the Tooting Bec
Cricket Club. They shot gulls in the harbour, and made themselves a public nuisance by constant repetition of a tag from
a music-hall song, with an indecent sub-intention. Their
behaviour towards the young women of this town was offensive.
Seen in juxtaposition with the natural beauties of this coast,
they helped one to realise how small a thing (under certain
conditions) is man.

(3) Mr and Mrs So-and-so and family spent a fortnight
here. The lady complained that the town was dull, which we
(who would have the best reason to complain of such a defect)
do not admit. She announced her opinion in the street, at
the top of her voice; and expressed annoyance that there should
be no band, to play of an evening. She should have brought
one. Her husband carried about a note-book and asked us
questions about our private concerns. He brought no letters
of introduction, and we do not know his business. The children
behaved better.

(4) Mr Blank arrived here on a bicycle, and charmed us
with the geniality of his address. We hope to see him again,
as he left without discharging a number of small debts.

It is, I take it, because the Briton has grown accustomed
to invading other people's countries, that he expects, when
travelling, to find a polite consideration which he does not
import. But the tourist pushes the expectation altogether

too far. When he arrives at a town which lays itself out to attract visitors for the sake of the custom they bring, he has a right to criticise, *if he feel quite sure he is a visitor of the sort which the town desires.* This is important: for a town may seek to attract visitors, and yet be exceedingly unwilling to attract some kinds of visitors. But should he choose to plant himself upon a spot where the inhabitants ask only to go about the ordinary occupations of life in quietness, it is the height of impertinence to proclaim that the life of the place does not satisfy his needs. Most intolerable of all is the conduct of the uninvited stranger who settles for a year or two in some quiet town—we suffer a deal from such persons along the south-western littoral—and starts with the intention of 'putting a little "go" into it,' or, in another of his favourite phrases, of 'putting the place to rights.' Men of this mind are not to be reasoned with; nor is it necessary that they should be reasoned with. Only, when the inevitable reaction is felt, and they begin to lose their temper, I would beg them not to assume too hastily that the 'natives' have no sense of humour. All localities have a sense of humour, but it works diversely with them. A man may even go on for twenty years, despising his neighbours for the lack of it. But when the discovery comes, he will be lucky if the remembrance of it do not wake him up of nights, and keep him writhing in his bed —that is, if we suppose *him* to have a sense of humour too.

An aëronaut who had lost his bearings, descending upon some farm labourers in Suffolk, demanded anxiously where he was. 'Why, don't you know? You be up in a balloon, bo.' A pedestrian in Cornwall stopped a labourer returning from work, and asked the way to St ——. 'And where might you come from?' the labourer demanded. 'I don't see what affair that is of yours. I asked you the way to

St ———.' 'Well then, if you don't tell us where you be
come from, we bain't goin' to tell you the way to St ———.'
It seems to me that both of these replies contain humour,
and the second a deal of practical wisdom.

The foregoing remarks apply, with very little modifica-
tion, to those strangers who take up their residence in
Cornwall and, having sojourned among us for a while
without ever penetrating to the confidence of the people,
pass judgment on matters of which, because they were
above learning, knowledge has been denied to them.
A clergyman, dwelling in a country parish where perhaps
he finds himself the one man of education (as he understands it), is prone enough to make the mistake; yet not
more fatally prone than your Gigadibs, the literary man,
who sees his unliterary (even illiterate) neighbours not as
they are, but as a clever novelist would present them to
amuse an upper or middle class reader. Stevenson (a
greater man than Gigadibs) frankly confessed that he could
make nothing of us:

There were no emigrants direct from Europe—save one
German family and a knot of Cornish miners who kept grimly
by themselves, one reading the New Testament all day long
through steel spectacles, the rest discussing privately the secrets
of their old-world mysterious race. Lady Hester Stanhope
believed she could make something great of the Cornish: for
my part, I can make nothing of them at all. A division of
races, older and more original than that of Babel, keeps this
close esoteric family apart from neighbouring Englishmen.
Not even a Red Indian seems more foreign in my eyes. This
is one of the lessons of travel—that some of the strangest races
dwell next door to you at home.

This straightforward admission is worth (to my mind)
any half-dozen of novels written about us by 'foreigners'

who, starting with the Mudie-convention and a general sense that we are picturesque, write commentaries upon what is a sealed book and deal out judgments which are not only wrong, but wrong with a thoroughness only possible to entire self-complacency.

*   *   *   *   *

And yet. . . It seems to a Cornishman so easy to get at Cornish hearts—so easy even for a stranger if he will approach them, as they will at once respond, with that modesty which is the first secret of fine manners. Some years ago I was privileged to edit a periodical—though short-lived not wholly unsuccessful—*The Cornish Magazine*. At the end of each number we printed a page of 'Cornish Diamonds,' as we called them—scraps of humour picked up here and there in the Duchy by Cornish correspondents; and in almost all of them the Cornishman was found gently laughing at himself; in not one of them (so far as I remember) at the stranger. Over and over again the jest depended on our small difficulties in making our own distinctions of thought understood in English. Here are a few examples:

(1) 'Please God,' said Aunt Mary Bunny, 'if I live till this evenin' and all's well I'll send for the doctor.'

(2) 'I don't name no names,' said Uncle Billy, 'but Jack Tremenheere's the man.'

(3) 'I shan't go there nor nowhere else,' said old Jane Caddy, 'I shall go 'long up Redruth.'

(4) 'I thought 'twere she, an' she thought 'twere I,' said Gracey Temby, 'but when we come close 'twadn't narry wan o' us.'

(5) A crowd stood on the cliff watching a stranded
vessel and the lifeboat going out to her.
'What vessel is it?' asked a late arrival.
'The *Dennis Lane.*'
'How many be they aboord?'
'Aw, love and bless 'ee, there's three poor dear sawls
and wan old Irishman.'

(6) Complainant (cross-examining defendant's witness):
'What colour was the horse?'
'Black.'
'Well, I'm not allowed to contradict you, and I
wouldn' for worlds: but I say he wasn't.'

(7) A covey of partridges rose out of shot, flew over the
hedge, and was lost to view.
'Where do you think they've gone?' said the sportsman to his keeper. 'There's a man digging potatoes
in the next field. Ask if he saw them.'
'Aw, that's old Sam Petherick: he hasna seed 'em,
he's hard o' hearin'.'

(8) *Schoolmaster.*—'I'm sorry to tell you, Mr Minards,
that your son Zebedee is little better than a fool.'
Parent. 'Naw, naw, schoolmaster; my Zebedee's
no fule; only a bit easy to teach.'

[I myself know a farmer who approached the head
master of a Grammar School and begged for a reduction
in terms: 'because,' he pleaded, 'I know my son: he's that
thick you can get very little into en, and I believe in
payment by results.']

Here we pass from confusion of language into mere
confusion of thought, the classical instance of which is the
Mevagissey man who, having been asked the old question,

'If a herring and a half cost three-halfpence, how many
can you buy for a shilling?' and having given it up and
been told the answer, responded brightly, 'Why, o' course!
Darn me if I wasn' thinkin' of pilchards!' I met with a
fair Devon rival to this story the other day in the reported
conversation of two farmers discussing the electric light at
Chagford (run by Chagford's lavish water-power). 'It do
seem out of reason,' said the one, 'to make vire out o'
watter.' 'No,' agreed the other, 'it don't seem possible:
but there'—after a slow pause—''tis bütiful water to
Chaggyford!'

It was pleasant, while the Magazine lasted, to record
these and like simplicities: and though the voyage was not
long, one may recall without regret its send-off, brave
enough in its way:

'WISH 'EE WELL!'

The ensign's dipped; the captain takes the wheel.
  'So long!' the pilot waves, and 'Wish 'ee well!'
Go little craft, and with a home-made keel
'Mid loftier ships, but with a heart as leal,
    Learn of blue waters and the long sea swell!

Through the spring days we built and tackled thee,
  Tested thy timbers, saw thy rigging sound,
Bent sail, and now put forth unto the sea
Where those leviathans, the critics, be,
    And other monsters diversely profound.

Some bronzed Phœnician with his pigmy freight
  Haply thy herald was, who drave of yore
Deep-laden from Bolerium by the Strait
Of Gades, and beside his city's gate
    Chaffered in ingots cast of Cornish ore.

So be thou fortunate as thou art bold;
  Fare, little craft, and make the world thy friend:
And, it may be—when all thy journey's told
With anchor dropped and tattered canvas rolled,
  And some good won for Cornwall in the end—

Thou wilt recall, as best, a lonely beach,
  And a few exiles, to the barter come,
Who recognised the old West-country speech,
And touched thee, reverent, whispering each to each—
  'She comes from far—from very far—from home.'

*   *   *   *   *

I have a special reason for remembering *The Cornish
Magazine*, because it so happened that the first number
(containing these hopeful verses) was put into my hands
with the morning's letters as I paced the garden below this
Cornish Window, careless of it or of anything but a doctor's
verdict of life or death in the house above. The verdict
was for life....

Years ago as a child I used to devour in that wonderful
book *Good Words for the Young*, the *Lilliput Levee* and
Lilliput Lyrics of the late William Brighty Rands: and
among Rands' lyrics was one upon 'The Girl that Garibaldi
kissed.' Of late years Rands has been coming to something
like his own. His verses have been republished, and that
excellent artist Mr Charles Robinson has illustrated them.
But I must tell Mr Robinson that his portrait of the Girl
that Garibaldi kissed does not in the least resemble her.
I speak with knowledge—I the child who have lived to
meet and know the child whom Garibaldi kissed and
blessed as the sailors were weighing anchor to carry him
out of this harbour and away from England. Wild horses
shall not drag from me the name of that young person;

because it happened—well, at an easily discoverable date—
and she may not care for me to proclaim her age (as
certainly she does not look it).

> He bowed to my own daughter,
>   And Polly is her name;
> She wore a shirt of slaughter,
>   Of Garibaldi flame—
>
> Of course I mean of scarlet;
>   But the girl he kissed—who knows?—
> May be named Selina Charlotte,
>   And dressed in yellow clothes!

But she isn't; and she wasn't; for she wore a scarlet
pelisse as they handed her up the yacht's side, and the
hero took her in his arms.

> It would be a happy plan
>   For everything that's human,
> If the pet of such a man
>   Should grow to such a woman!
>
> If she does as much in her way
>   As he has done in his—
> Turns bad things topsy-turvy,
>   And sad things into bliss—
>
> O we shall not need a survey
>   To find that little miss,
> Grown to a woman worthy
>   Of Garibaldi's kiss!

Doggrel? Yes, doggrel no doubt! Let us pass on.

*   *   *   *   *

In the early numbers of our *Cornish Magazine* a host
of contributors (some of them highly distinguished) discussed the question, 'How to develop Cornwall as a holiday

resort.' 'How to bedevil it' was, I fear, our name in the editorial office for this correspondence. More and more as the debate went on I found myself out of sympathy with it, and more and more in sympathy with a lady who raised an indignant protest—

Unless Cornishmen look to it, their country will be spoilt before they know it. Already there are signs of it—pitiable signs. Not many months ago I visited Tintagel, which is justly one of the prides of the Duchy. The 'swinging seas' are breaking against the great cliffs as they broke there centuries ago when Arthur and Launcelot and the Knights of the Round Table peopled the place. The castle is mostly crumbled away now, but some fraction of its old strength still stands to face the Atlantic gales, and to show us how walls were built in the grand old days. In the valley the grass is green and the gorse is yellow, and overhead the skies are blue and delightful: but facing Arthur's Castle—grinning down, as it were, in derision—there is being erected a modern hotel—'built in imitation of Arthur's Castle,' as one is told!...There is not yet a rubbish shoot over the edge of the cliff, but I do not think I am wrong in stating that the drainage is brought down into that cove where long ago (the story runs) the naked baby Arthur came ashore on the great wave!

In summing up the discussion I confess with shame that I temporised. It was hard to see one's native country impoverished by the evil days in which mining (and to a lesser degree, agriculture) had fallen; to see her population diminishing and her able-bodied sons emigrating by the thousand. It is all very pretty for a visitor to tell us that the charm of Cornwall is its primæval calm, that it seems to sleep an enchanted sleep, and so on; but we who inhabit her wish (and not altogether from mercenary motives) to see her something better than a museum of a dead past.

I temporised therefore with those who suggested that Cornwall might yet enrich herself by turning her natural beauty to account: yet even so I had the sense to add that—

Jealous as I am for the beauty of our Duchy, and delighted when strangers admire her, I am, if possible, more jealous for the character of her sons, and more eager that strangers should respect *them*. And I do see (and hope to be forgiven for seeing it) that a people which lays itself out to exploit the stranger and the tourist runs an appreciable risk of deterioration in manliness and independence. It may seem a brutal thing to say, but as I had rather be poor myself than subservient, so would I liefer see my countrymen poor than subservient. It is not our own boast—we have it on the fairly unanimous evidence of all who have visited us—that hitherto Cornishmen have been able to combine independence with good manners. For Heaven's sake, I say, let us keep that reputation, though at great cost! But let us at the same time face the certainty that, when we begin to take pay for entertaining strangers it will be a hard reputation to keep. Were it within human capacity to decide between a revival of our ancient industries, fishing and mining, and the development of this new business, our decision would be prompt enough. But it is not.

I despaired too soon. Our industries seem in a fair way to revive, and with that promise I recognise that even in despair my willingness to temporise was foolish. For my punishment—though I helped not to erect them,—hideous hotels thrust themselves insistently on my sight as I walk our magnificent northern cliffs, and with the thought of that drain leading down to Arthur's cove I am haunted by the vision of Merlin erect above it, and by the memory of Hawker's canorous lines:

> He ceased; and all around was dreamy night:
> There stood Dundagel, throned; and the great sea
> Lay, like a strong vassal at his master's gate,
> And, like a drunken giant, sobbed in sleep!

SEPTEMBER

AT the village shop you may procure milk, butter, eggs, peppermints, trowsers, sun-bonnets, marbles, coloured handkerchiefs, and a number of other necessaries, including the London papers. But if you wish to pick and choose, you had better buy trowsers than the London papers; for this is less likely to bring you into conflict with the lady who owns the shop and asserts a prior claim on its conveniences. One of us (I will call him X) went ashore and asked for a London 'daily.' 'Here's *Lloyd's Weekly News* for you,' said the lady; 'but you can't have the daily, for I haven't finished reading it myself.' 'Very well,' said I, when this was reported; 'if I cannot read the news I want, I will turn to and write it.' So I descended to the shop, and asked for a bottle of ink; since, oddly enough, there was none to be found on board. The lady produced a bottle and a pen. 'But I don't want the pen,' I objected. 'They go together,' said she: 'Whatever use is a bottle of ink without a pen?' For the life of me I could discover no answer to this. I paid my penny, and on returning with my purchases to the boat, I propounded the following questions:

(1) *Quære.* If, as the lady argued, a bottle of ink be useless without a pen, by what process of reasoning did she omit a sheet of paper from her pennyworth?

(2) Suppose that I damage or wear out this pen before exhausting the bottle of ink, can she reasonably insist on my taking a second bottle as a condition of acquiring a second pen?

(3) Suppose, on the other hand, that (as I compute) one pen will outlast two and a half bottles of ink; that one bottle will distil thirty thousand words; and that the late James Anthony Froude (who lived close by) drew his supply of writing materials from this shop: how many unused pens (at a guess) must that distinguished man have accumulated in the process of composing his *History of England?*

We sailed into Salcombe on Saturday evening, in a hired yacht of twenty-eight tons, after beating around the Start and Prawl against a sou'westerly wind and a strong spring tide. Now the tide off the Start has to be studied. To begin with, it does not coincide in point of time with the tide inshore. The flood, or east stream, for instance, only starts to run there some three hours before it is high water at Salcombe; but, having started, runs with a vengeance, or, to be more precise, at something like three knots an hour during the high springs; and the consequence is a very lively race. Moreover, the bottom all the way from Start Point to Bolt Tail is extremely rough and irregular, which means that some ten or twelve miles of vicious seas can be set going on very short notice. Altogether you may spend a few hours here as uncomfortably as anywhere up or down Channel, with the single exception of Portland Race. If you turn aside for Salcombe, there is the bar to be considered; and Salcombe bar is a danger to be treated with grave respect. *The Channel Pilot* will tell us why:

There is 8 ft. water at L.W. springs on the bar at the entrance, but there are patches of 6 ft. Vessels drawing 20 ft. can cross it (*when the sea is smooth*) at H.W. springs, and those of 16 ft. at H.W. neaps. In S. gales there is a breaking, heavy sea, and no vessel should then attempt the bar; in moderate S. winds vessels may take it at high water.

The bearing of these observations on the present narrative will appear anon. For the present, entering Salcombe with plenty of water and a moderate S.W. breeze, we had nothing to distract our attention from the beauty of the spot. I suppose it to be the most imposing river-entrance on the south coast; perhaps the most imposing on any of the coasts of Britain. But being lazy and by habit a shirker of word-painting, I must have recourse to the description given in Mr Arthur Underhill's *Our Silver Streak*, most useful and pleasant of handbooks for yachtsmen cruising in the Channel:

As we approach Salcombe Head (part of Bolt Head), its magnificent form becomes more apparent. It is said to be about four hundred and thirty feet in height, but it looks very much more. Its base is hollowed out into numerous caverns, into which the sea dashes, while the profile of the head, often rising some forty or fifty feet sheer from the water, slopes back at an angle of about forty-five degrees in one long upward sweep, broken in the most fantastic way into numerous pinnacles and needles, which remind one forcibly of the *aiguilles* of the valley of Chamounix. I do not think that any headland in the Channel is so impressive as this.

As we passed it, its needles stood out darkly against a rare amber sky—such a glow as is only seen for a brief while before a sunset following much rain; and it had been raining, off and on, for a week past. I daresay that to the weatherwise this glow signified yet dirtier weather in store; but we surrendered ourselves to the charm of the hour. Unconscious of their doom the little victims played. We crossed the bar, sailed past the beautiful house in which Froude spent so many years, sailed past the little town, rounded a point, saw a long quiet stretch of river before us, and cast anchor in deep water. The address at the head of this paper is no sportive invention of mine. You may verify it by the Ordnance Map. We were in the Bag.

I awoke that night to the hum of wind in the rigging and the patter of rain on deck. It blew and rained all the morning, and at noon took a fresh breath and began to blow viciously. After luncheon we abandoned our project of walking to Bolt Head, and chose such books from the cabin library as might decently excuse an afternoon's siesta. A scamper of feet fetched me out of my berth and up on deck. By this time a small gale was blowing, and to our slight dismay the boat had dragged her anchors and carried us up into sight of Kingsbridge. Luckily our foolish career was arrested for the moment; and, still more luckily, within handy distance of a buoy—laid there, I believe, for the use of vessels under quarantine. We carried out a hawser to this buoy, and waited until the tide should ease and allow us to warp down to it. Our next business was with the peccant anchors. We had two down—the best anchor and kedge; and supposed at first that the kedge must have parted. But a couple of minutes at the capstan reassured us. It was the kedge which had been holding us, to the extent of its small ability. And the Bag is an excellent anchorage after all, but not if you happen to get your best anchor foul of its chain. We hauled up, cleared, warped down to the buoy; and then, hoisting mizzen and headsails, cast loose and worked back to our old quarters.

The afternoon's amusement, though exciting enough in its way, was not what we had come to Salcombe to seek.

And since the weather promised nothing better, and already a heap of more or less urgent letters must be gathering dust in the post office at Plymouth, we resolved to beat over the bar at high water next morning (*this* morning), and, as Mr Lang puts it, 'know the brine salt on our lips, and the large air again': for there promised to be plenty of both between Bolt Head and the Mewstone.

*   *   *   *   *

'Shun delays, they breed remorse,' and 'Time wears all his locks before' (or, as the Fourth-form boy translated it in pentameter, '*Tempus habet nullas posteriori comas*'). The fault was mine for wasting an invaluable hour among the 'shy traffickers' of Salcombe. By the time we worked down to the bar the tide had been ebbing for an hour and a half. The wind still blew strong from the south-west, and the seas on the bar were not pleasant to contemplate. Let alone the remoter risk of scraping on one of the two shallow patches which diversify the west (and only practicable) side of the entrance, if one of those big fellows happened to stagger us at the critical moment of 'staying' it would pretty certainly mean disaster. Also the yacht (as I began by saying) was a hired one, and the captain tender about his responsibility. Rather ignominiously, therefore, we turned tail; and just as we did so, a handsome sea, arched and green, the tallest of the lot, applauded our prudence. All the same, our professional pride was wounded. To stay at anchor is one thing: to weigh and stand for the attempt and then run home again 'hard up,' as a sailor would say, is quite another. There was a Greek mariner, the other day, put on his trial with one or two comrades for murder and mutiny on the high seas. They had disapproved of their captain's altering the helm, and had pitched him incontinently overboard. On being asked what he had to say in his defence, the prisoner merely cast up his hands and sobbed, 'Oh, cursed hour in which we put about!' We recalled this simple but apposite story.

Having seen to our anchor and helped to snug down the mainsail, I went below in the very worst of tempers, to find the cabin floor littered with the contents of a writing-case and a box of mixed biscuits, which had broken loose in company. As I stooped to collect the *débris*, this appeal (type-written) caught my eye:

Dear Sir,—Our paper is contemplating a Symposium of literary and eminent men—

(Observe the distinction.)

—on the subject of 'What is your favourite Modern Lyric?' I need not say how much interest would attach to the opinion of one who, etc.

I put my head up the companion and addressed a friend who was lacing tight the cover of the mainsail viciously, with the help of his teeth.

'Look here, X,' I said. 'What is your favourite Modern Lyric?'

'That one,' he answered (still with the lace between his teeth), 'which begins—

> Curse the people, blast the people,
> Damn the lower orders!'

X as a rule calls himself a Liberal-Conservative: but a certain acerbity of temper may be forgiven in a man who has just assisted (against all his instincts) in an act of poltroonery. He explained, too, that it was a genuine, if

loosely remembered, quotation from Ebenezer Elliott, the
Corn Law Rhymer. 'Yet in circumstances of peril,' he
went on, 'and in moments of depression, you cannot think
what sustenance I have derived from those lines.'

'Then you had best send them up,' said I, 'to *The Daily
Post*. It is conducting a Symposium.'

'If two wrongs do not make a right,' he answered tartly,
'even less will an assembly of deadly dry persons make
something to drink.'

*   *   *   *   *

That evening, in the cabin, we held a symposium on our
own account and in the proper sense of the term, while
the rain drummed on the deck and the sky-lights.

X said, 'The greatest poem written on love during these
fifty years—and we agree to accept love as the highest
theme of lyrical poetry—is George Meredith's "Love in the
Valley." I say this and decline to argue about it.'

'Nor am I disposed to argue about it,' I answered, 'for
York Powell—peace to his soul for a great man gone—held
that same belief. In his rooms in Christ Church, one night
while *The Oxford Book of Verse* was preparing and I had
come to him, as everyone came, for counsel. . . . I take it,
though, that we are not searching for the absolute best
but for our own prime favourite. You remember what
Swinburne says somewhere of Hugo's *Gastibelza*:

> Gastibelza, l'homme à la carabine,
> > Chantait ainsi:
> Quelqu'un a-t-il connu Doña Sabine?
> > Quelqu'un d'ici?
> Dansez, chantez, villageois! la nuit gagne
> > Le mont Falou—
> Le vent qui vient à travers la montagne
> > Me rendra fou!

'"The song of songs which is Hugo's," he calls it; and goes on to ask how often one has chanted or shouted or otherwise declaimed it to himself, on horseback at full gallop or when swimming at his best as a boy in holiday time; and how often the matchless music, ardour, pathos of it have not reduced his own ambition to a sort of rapturous and adoring despair—yes, and requickened his old delight in it with a new delight in the sense that he will always have this to rejoice in, to adore, and to recognise as something beyond the reach of man. Well, that is the sense in which our poem should be our favourite poem. Now, for my part, there's a page or so of Browning's "Saul"——'

'What do you say to Meredith's "Phœbus with Admetus?"' interrupted X.

I looked up at him quickly, almost shamefacedly. 'Now, how on earth did you guess——'

X laid down his pipe, stared up at the sky-light, and quoted, almost under his breath:

> Bulls that walk the pasture in kingly-flashing coats!
> Laurel, ivy, vine, wreath'd for feasts not few!

* * * * *

Why is it possible to consider Mr Meredith—whose total yield of verse has been so scanty and the most of it so 'harsh and crabbed,' as not only 'dull fools' suppose— beside the great poets who have been his contemporaries, and to feel no impropriety in the comparison? That was the question X and I found ourselves discussing, ten minutes later.

'Because,' maintained X, 'you feel at once that with Meredith you have hold of a man. You know—as surely, for example, as while you are listening to Handel—that the stuff is masculine, and great at that.'

'That is not all the secret,' I maintained, 'although it gets near to the secret. Why is it possible to consider Coleridge alongside of Wordsworth and Byron, yet feel no impropriety? Coleridge's yield of verse was ridiculously scanty beside theirs, and a deal more sensuous than Wordsworth's, at any rate, and yet more manly, in a sense, than Byron's, which again was thoroughly manly within the range of emotion? Why? Because Coleridge and Meredith both have a philosophy of life: and he who has a philosophy of life may write little or much; may on the one hand write "Christabel" and leave it unfinished and decline upon opium; or may, on the other hand, be a Browning or a Meredith, and "keep up his end" (as the saying is) nobly to the last, and vex us all the while with his asperities; and yet in both cases be as certainly a masculine poet. Poetry (as I have been contending all my life) has one right background and one only: and that background is philosophy. You say, Coleridge and Meredith are masculine. I ask, Why are they masculine? The answer is, They have philosophy.'

'You are on the old tack again: the old τὸ καθόλου!'

'Yes, and am going to hold upon it until we fetch land, so you may e'en fill another pipe and play the interlocutor. . . . You remember my once asking why our Jingo poets write such rotten poetry (for that their stuff is rotten we agreed). The reason is, they are engaged in mistaking the part for the whole, and that part a non-essential one; they are setting up the present potency of Great Britain as a triumphant and insolent exception to laws which (if we believe in any gods better than anarchy and chaos) extend at least over all human conduct and may even regulate "the most ancient heavens." You may remember my expressed contempt for a recent poem which lauded Henry VIII because—

> He was lustful, he was vengeful, he was hot
>   and hard and proud;
> But he set his England fairly in the sight of
>   all the crowd.

—a worse error, to my mind, than Froude's, who merely idolised him for chastising the clergy. Well, after our discussion, I asked myself this question: "Why do we not as a great Empire-making people, ruling the world for its good, assassinate the men who oppose us?" We do not; the idea revolts us. But why does it revolt us?

'We send our armies to fight, with the certainty (if we think at all) that we are sending a percentage to be killed. We recently sent out two hundred thousand with the sure and certain knowledge that some thousands must die; and these (we say) were men agonising for a righteous cause. Why did it not afflict us to send them?—whereas it would have afflicted us inexpressibly to send a man to end the difficulty by putting a bullet or a knife into Mr Kruger, who *ex hypothesi* represented an unrighteous cause, and who certainly was but one man.

'Why? Because a law above any that regulates the expansion of Great Britain says, "Thou shalt do no murder." And that law, that Universal, takes the knife or the pistol quietly, firmly, out of your hand. You send a battalion, with Tom Smith in it, to fight Mr Kruger's troops; you know that some of them must in all likelihood perish; but, thank your stars, you do not know their names. Tom Smith, as it happens, is killed; but had you known with absolute certainty that Tom Smith would be killed, you could not have sent him. You must have withdrawn him, and substituted some other fellow concerning whom your prophetic vision was less uncomfortably definite. You can kill Tom Smith if he has happened to kill Bob Jones: you are safe

enough then, being able to excuse yourself—how? By
Divine law again (as you understand it). Divine law says
that whoso sheddeth man's blood, by man shall his blood
be shed—that is to say, by you: so you can run under cover
and hang Tom Smith. But when Divine law does not
protect you, you are powerless. At the most you can send
him off to take his ten-to-one chance in a battalion, and
when you read his name in the returns, come mincing up
to God and say: "So poor old Tom's gone! How the
deuce was *I* to know?"

'I say nothing of the cowardice of this, though it smells
to Heaven. I merely point out that this law "Thou shalt
do no murder"—this Universal—must be a tremendous
one, since even you, my fine swashbuckling, Empire-
making hero, are so much afraid of it that you cannot
send even a Reservist to death without throwing the responsibility on luck—*nos te, nos facimus, Fortuna, deam*—
and have not even the nerve, without its sanction, to stick
a knife into an old man whom you accuse as the wicked
cause of all this bloodshed. If you believed in your accusa-
tions, why couldn't you do it? Because a universal law
forbade you, and one you have to believe in, truculent
Jingo though you be. Why, consider this; your poets are
hymning King Edward the Seventh as the greatest man on
earth, and yet, if he might possess all Africa to-morrow at
the expense of signing the death-warrant of one innocent
man who opposed that possession, he could not write his
name. His hand would fall numb. Such power above
kings has the Universal, though silly poets insult it who
should be its servants.

'Now of all the differences between men and women
there is none more radical than this: that a man naturally
loves law, whereas a woman naturally hates it and never

sees a law without casting about for some way of dodging it. Laws, universals, general propositions—her instinct with all of them is to get off by wheedling the judge. So, if you want a test for a masculine poet, examine first whether or no he understands the Universe as a thing of law and order.'

'Then, by your own test, Kipling—the Jingo Kipling— is a most masculine poet, since he talks of little else.'

'I will answer you, although I believe you are not serious. At present Mr Kipling's mind, in search of a philosophy, plays with the contemplation of a world reduced to law and order; the law and order being such as universal British rule would impose. There might be many worse worlds than a world so ruled, and in verse the prospect can be made to look fair enough:

> Keep ye the Law—be swift in all obedience—
> Clear the land of evil, drive the road and bridge the ford.
>> Make ye sure to each his own
>> That he reap where he hath sown;
> By the peace among Our peoples let men know
>> we serve the Lord!

Clean and wholesome teaching it seems, persuading civilised men that, as they are strong, so the obligation rests on them to set the world in order, carry tillage into its wildernesses, and clean up its bloodstained corners. Yet as a political philosophy it lacks the first of all essentials, and as Mr Kipling develops it we begin to detect the flaw in the system:

> The 'eathen in 'is blindness bows down to wood and stone;
> 'E don't obey no orders unless they is his own;
> 'E keeps 'is side-arms awful: 'e leaves 'em all about,
> An' then comes up the regiment an' pokes the 'eathen out.
>> All along o' dirtiness, all along o' mess,
>> All along o' doin' things rather-more-or-less. Etc.

'What is wrong with this? Why, simply that it leaves Justice altogether out of account. The system has no room for it; even as it has no room for clemency, mansuetude, forbearance towards the weak. My next-door neighbour may keep his children in rags and his house in dirt, may be a loose liver with a frantically foolish religious creed; but all this does not justify me in taking possession of his house, and either poking him out or making him a serf on his own hearthstone. If there be such a thing as universal justice, then all men have their rights under it—even verminous persons. We are obliged to put constraint upon them when their habits afflict us beyond a certain point. And civilised nations are obliged to put constraint upon uncivilised ones which shock their moral sense beyond a certain point—as by cannibalism or human sacrifice. But such interference should stand upon a nice sense of the offender's rights, and in practice does so stand. The custom of polygamy, for instance (as practised abroad), horribly offends quite a large majority of His Majesty's lieges; yet Great Britain tolerates polygamy even in her own subject races. Neither polygamy nor uncleanliness can be held any just excuse for turning a nation out of its possessions.

'And another reason for insisting upon the strictest reading of justice in these dealings between nations is the temptation which the least laxity offers to the stronger—a temptation which Press and Pulpit made no pretence of resisting during the late war. "We are better than they," was the cry; "we are cleanlier, less ignorant; we have arts and a literature, whereas they have none; we make for progress and enlightenment, while they are absurdly conservative, if not retrogressive. Therefore the world will be the better by our annexing their land, and substituting our government for theirs. Therefore our cause, too, is the juster." But therefore it is nothing of the sort. A dirty man may be in the right, and a clean man in the wrong; an ungodly man in the right, and a godly man in the wrong; and the most specious and well-intentioned system which allows justice to be confused with something else will allow it to be stretched, even by well-meaning persons, to cover theft, lying, and flat piracy.'

'Are you trying to prove,' demanded X, 'that Mr Kipling is a feminine poet?'

'No, but I am about to bring you to the conclusion that in his worse mood he is a sham-masculine one. The "Recessional" proves that, man of genius that he is, he rises to a conception of Universal Law. But too often he is trying to dodge it with sham law. A woman would not appeal to law at all: she would boldly take her stand on lawlessness. He, being an undoubted but misguided man, has to find some other way out; so he takes a twopenny-halfpenny code as the mood seizes him—be it the code of a barrack or of a Johannesburg Jew—and hymns it lustily against the universal code: and the pity and the sin of it is that now and then by flashes—as in "The Tale óf Purun Bhagat"—he sees the truth.

'You remember the figure of the Cave which Socrates invented and explained to Glaucon in Plato's "Republic"? He imagined men seated in a den which has its mouth open to the light, but their faces are turned to the wall of the den, and they sit with necks and legs chained so that they cannot move. Behind them, and between them and the light, runs a raised way with a low wall along it, "like the screen over which marionette-players show their puppets." Along this wall pass men carrying all sorts of vessels and statues and figures of animals. Some are talking, others silent; and as the procession goes by the chained prisoners see only the shadows passing across the rock in front of them, and, hearing the voices echoed from it, suppose that the sound comes from the shadows.

'To explain the fascination of Mr Kipling's verse one might take this famous picture and make one fearsome addition to it. There sits (one might go on to say) among the prisoners a young man different from them in voice and terribly different to look upon, because he has two pairs of eyes, the one turned towards the light and realities, the other towards the rock-face and the shadows. Using, now one, now the other of these two pairs of eyes, he never knows with which at the moment he is gazing, whether on the realities or on the shadows, but always supposes what he sees at the moment to be the realities, and calls them "Things as They Are." Further, his lips have been touched with the glory of the greater vision, and he speaks enchantingly when he discourses of the shadows on the rock, thereby deepening the delusion of the other prisoners whom his genius has played the crimp to, enticing them into the den and hocussing and chaining them there. For, seeing the shadows pass to the interpretation of such a voice, they are satisfied that they indeed behold Things as They Are, and that these are the only things worth knowing.

'The tragedy of it lies in this, that Mr Kipling in his greater moments cannot help but see that he, with every inspired singer, is by right the prophet of a law and order compared with which all the majestic law and order of the British Empire are but rags and trumpery:

> I ha' harpit ye up to the throne o' God,
>   I ha' harpit your midmost soul in three;
> I ha' harpit ye down to the Hinges o' Hell,
>   And—ye—would—make—a Knight o' me!

*　　*　　*　　*　　*

'Not long ago an interviewer called on Mr Meredith, and brought away this for his pains:

> I suppose I should regard myself as getting old—I am seventy-four. But I do not feel to be growing old either in heart or mind. I still look on life with a young man's eye. I have always hoped I should not grow old as some do—with a palsied intellect, living backwards, regarding other people as anachronisms because they themselves have lived on into other times, and left their sympathies behind them with their years.

'He never will. He will always preserve the strength of manhood in his work because hope, the salt of manhood, is the savour of all his philosophy. When I think of his work as a whole—his novels and poems together—this confession of his appears to me, not indeed to summarise it —for it is far too multifarious and complex—but to say the first and the last word upon it. In poem and in novel he puts a solemnity of his own into the warning, *ne tu pueri contempseris annos*. He has never grown old, because his hopes are set on the young; and his dearest wish, for those who can read beneath his printed word, is to leave the world not worse, but so much the better as a man may, for the generations to come after him. To him this is "the cry of the conscience of life":

> Keep the young generations in hail,
> And bequeath them no tumbled house.

To him this is at once a duty and a "sustainment supreme," and perhaps the bitterest words this master of Comedy has written are for the seniors of the race who—

> On their last plank,
> Pass mumbling it as nature's final page,

and cramp the young with their rules of "wisdom," lest,
as he says scornfully:

> Lest dreaded change, long dammed by dull decay,
> Should bring the world a vessel steered by brain,
> And ancients musical at close of day.

"Earth loves her young," begins his next sonnet:

> Her gabbling grey she eyes askant, nor treads
> The ways they walk; by what they speak oppressed.

But his conviction, if here for a moment it discharges gall,
is usually cheerful with the cheerfulness of health. Sometimes he consciously expounds it; oftener he leaves you to
seek and find it, but always (I believe) you will find this
happy hope in youth at the base of everything he writes.

'The next thing to be noted is that he does not hope in
youth because it is a period of license and waywardness,
but because it is a period of imagination—

> Days, when the ball of our vision
> Had eagles that flew unabashed to sun,

and because it therefore has a better chance of grasping
what is Universal than has the prudential wisdom of age
which contracts its eye to particulars and keeps it alert
for social pitfalls—the kind of wisdom seen at its best (but
its best never made a hero) in Bubb Doddington's verses:

> Love thy country, wish it well,
> *Not with too intense a care;*
> 'Tis enough that, when it fell,
> Thou its ruin didst not share.

Admirable caution! Now contrast it for a moment with,
let us say, the silly quixotic figure of Horatius with the
broken bridge behind him:

> Round turned he, as not deigning
>   Those craven ranks to see:
> Nought spake he to Lars Porsena,
>   To Sextus nought spake he;
> But he saw on Palatinus
>   The white porch of his home—

'I protest I have no heart to go on with the quotation: so unpopular is its author, just now, and so certainly its boyish heroism calls back the boyish tears to my eyes. Well, this boyish vision is what Mr Meredith chooses to trust rather than Bubb Doddington's, and he trusts it as being the likelier to apprehend universal truths: he believes that Horatius with an army in front and a broken bridge behind him was a nobler figure than Bubb Doddington wishing his country well but not with too intense a care; and not only nobler but—this is the point—more obedient to divine law, more expressive of that which man was meant to be. If Mr Meredith trusts youth, it is as a time of imagination; and if he trusts imagination, it is as a faculty for apprehending the Universal in life—that is to say, a divine law behind its shows and simulacra.

'In "The Empty Purse" you will find him instructing youth towards this law; but that there may be no doubt of his own belief in it, as an order not only controlling men but overriding angels and demons, first consider his famous sonnet, "Lucifer in Starlight"—to my thinking one of the finest in our language:

> On a starred night Prince Lucifer uprose.
>   Tired of his dark dominion swung the fiend
>   Above the rolling ball in cloud part screened,
> Where sinners hugged their spectre of repose.
> Poor prey to his hot fit of pride were those.

And now upon his western wing he leaned,
Now his huge bulk o'er Afric's sands careened,
Now the black planet shadowed Arctic snows.
　　Soaring through wider zones that pricked his scars
　　　With memory of the old revolt from Awe,
　　He reached a middle height, and at the stars,
Which are the brain of Heaven, he looked, and sank.
Around the ancient track marched, rank on rank,
　　The army of unalterable law.

　　*　　*　　*　　*　　*

　'Suppose my contention—that poetry should concern
itself with universals—to be admitted: suppose we all agreed
that Poetry is an expression of the universal element in
human life, that (as Shelley puts it) "a poem is the very
image of life expressed in its eternal truth." There remains
a question quite as important: and that is, How to recognise
the Universal when we see it? We may talk of a divine
law, or a divine order—call it what we will—which
regulates the lives of us poor men no less than the motions
of the stars, and binds the whole universe, high and low,
into one system: and we may have arrived at the blessed
wish to conform with this law rather than to strive and kick
against the pricks and waste our short time in petulant
rebellion. So far, so good: but how are we to know the
law? How, with the best will in the world, are we to
distinguish order from disorder? What assurance have we,
after striving to bring ourselves into obedience, that we
have succeeded? We may agree, for example, with Wordsworth that Duty is a stern daughter of the Voice of God,
and that through Duty "the most ancient heavens," no less
than we ourselves, are kept fresh and strong. But can we
always discern this Universal, this Duty? What is the

criterion? And what, when we have chosen, is the sanction of our choice?

'A number of honest people will promptly refer us to revealed religion. "Take (they say) your revealed religion on faith, and there you have the law and the prophets, and your universals set out for you, and your principles of conduct laid down. What more do you want?"

'To this I answer, "We are human, and we need also the testimony of Poetry; and the priceless value of poetry for us lies in this, that it does *not* echo the Gospel like a parrot. If it did, it would be servile, superfluous. It is ministerial and useful because it approaches truth by another path. It does not say ditto to Mr Burke—it corroborates. And it corroborates precisely because it does not say ditto, but employs a natural process of its own which it employed before ever Christianity was revealed. You may decide that religion is enough for you, and that you have no need of poetry; but if you have any intelligent need of poetry it will be because poetry, though it end in the same conclusions, reaches them by another and separate path."

'Now (as I understand him) Mr Meredith connects man with the Universal, and teaches him to arrive at it and recognise it by strongly reminding him that he is a child of Earth. "You are amenable," he says in effect, "to a law which all the firmament obeys. But in all that firmament you are tied to one planet, which we call Earth. If therefore you would apprehend the law, study your mother, Earth, which also obeys it. Search out her operations; honour your mother as legitimate children, and let your honour be the highest you can pay—that of making yourself docile to her teaching. So will you stand the best chance, the only likely chance, of living in harmony with that Will which over-arches Earth and us all."

'In this doctrine Mr Meredith believes passionately; so let there be no mistake about the thoroughness with which he preaches it. Even prayer, he tells us in one of his novels, is most useful when like a fountain it falls back and draws refreshment from Earth for a new spring heavenward:

> And there vitality, there, there solely in song
>> Besides, where earth and her uses to men, their needs,
> Their forceful cravings, the theme are: there is it strong,
>> The Master said: and the studious eye that reads,
> (Yea, even as earth to the crown of Gods on the mount),
>> In links divine with the lyrical tongue is bound.
> Pursue thy craft: it is music drawn of the fount
>> To spring perennial; well-spring is common ground.

And it follows that to one who believes in the teaching of Earth so whole-heartedly Earth is not a painted back-cloth for man to strut against and attitudinise, but a birth-place from which he cannot escape, and in relation with which he must be considered, and must consider himself, on pain of becoming absurd. Even

> His cry to heaven is a cry to her
> He would evade.

She is a stern mother, be it understood, no coddling one:

> He may entreat, aspire,
> He may despair, and she has never heed,
> She, drinking his warm sweat, will soothe his need,
> Not his desire.

When we neglect or misread her lessons, she punishes; at the best, she offers no fat rewards to the senses, but—

> The sense of large charity over the land;
> Earth's wheaten of wisdom dispensed in the rough,
> And a bell ringing thanks for a sustenance meal.

("Lean fare," as the poet observes; and unpalatable, for instance, to our Members of Parliament, to whom our Mr Balfour one evening paid the highest compliment within their range of apprehension by assuming that quite a large number of them could write cheques for £69,000 without inconvenience.) At the best, too, she offers, with the loss of things we have desired, a serene fortitude to endure their loss:

> Love born of knowledge, love that gains
>   Vitality as Earth it mates,
> The meaning of the Pleasures, Pains,
>   The Life, the Death, illuminates.
>
> For love we Earth, then serve we all;
>   Her mystic secret then is ours:
> We fall, or view our treasures fall,
>   Unclouded—as beholds her flowers.
>
> Earth, from a night of frosty wreck,
>   Enrobed in morning's mounted fire,
> When lowly, with a broken neck,
>   The crocus lays her cheek to mire.

But at least it is the true milk for man that she distils—

> From her heaved breast of sacred common mould;

the breast (to quote from another poem)—

> Which is his well of strength, his home of rest,
> And fair to scan.

And so Mr Meredith, having diagnosed our disease, which is Self—our "distempered devil of Self," gluttonous of its own enjoyments and therefore necessarily a foe to law, which rests on temperance and self-control—walks among

men like his own wise physician, Melampus, with eyes that
search the book of Nature closely, as well for love of her
as to discover and extract her healing secrets.

> With love exceeding a simple love of the things
>> That glide in grasses and rubble of woody wreck;
> Or change their perch on a beat of quivering wings
>> From branch to branch, only restful to pipe and peck;
> Or, bristled, curl at a touch their snouts in a ball;
>> Or cast their web between bramble and thorny hook;
> The good physician Melampus, loving them all,
>> Among them walked, as a scholar who reads a book.
>
> For him the woods were a home and gave him the key
>> Of knowledge, thirst for their treasures in herbs and flowers.
> The secrets held by the creatures nearer than we
>> To earth he sought, and the link of their life with ours....

'Here by another road we come to a teaching which is
also the Gospels': that to apprehend the highest truth one
must have a mind of extreme humility. "Blessed are the
meek, for they shall inherit the earth," "Neither shall they
say, Lo here! or Lo there! for behold the kingdom of
God is within you," "And He took a little child and set
him in the midst of them," etc. Poetry cannot make these
sayings any truer than they are, but it can illuminate for
us the depths of their truth, and so (be it humbly said) can
help their acceptance by man. If they come down from
heaven, derived from arguments too high for his ken,
poetry confirms them by arguments taken from his own
earth, instructing him the while to read it as—

> An Earth alive with meanings, wherein meet
> Buried, and breathing, and to be,

and teaching him, "made lowly wise," that the truth of
the highest heavens lies scattered about his feet.

Melampus dwelt among men, physician and sage,
　He served them, loving them, healing them; sick or
　　maimed,
Or them that frenzied in some delirious rage
　Outran the measure, his juice of the woods reclaimed.
He played on men, as his master Phœbus on strings
　Melodious: as the God did he drive and check,
Through love exceeding a simple love of the things
　That glide in grasses and rubble of woody wreck.

'I think, if we consider the essence of this teaching,
we shall have no difficulty now in understanding why
Mr Meredith's hopes harp so persistently on the "young
generations," why our duty to them is to him "the cry of
the conscience of life," or why, as he studies Earth, he
maintains that—

Deepest at her springs,
Most filial, is an eye to love her young.

*　　*　　*　　*　　*

'But Meredith, if a true poet, is also and undeniably
a hard one: and a poet must not only preach but persuade.
"He dooth not only show the way," says Sidney, "but
giveth so sweet a prospect into the way as will intice any
man to enter into it."

'Here, my dear X, I lay hands on you and drag you in
as the Conscientious Objector. "How?" you will ask. "Is
not the plain truth good enough for men? And if poetry
must win acceptance for her by beautiful adornments,
alluring images, captivating music, is there not something
deceptive in the business, even if it be not downright
dishonest?" Well, I think you have a right to be
answered.'

'Thank you,' said X.

'And I don't think you are convincingly answered by Keats'—

> Beauty is truth, truth beauty—that is all
> Ye know on earth, and all ye need to know.

With all respect to the poet, we don't know it; and if we did it would come a long way short of all we need to know. The Conscientious Objector will none the less maintain that truth and beauty have never been recognised as identical, and that, in practice, to employ their names as convertible terms would lead to no end of confusion. I like the man (you will be glad to hear), because on an important subject he will be satisfied with nothing less than clear thinking. My own suspicion is that, when we have yielded him the inquiry which is his due into the relations between truth and beauty, we shall discover that spiritual truth—with which alone poetry concerns itself—is less a matter of ascertained facts than of ascertained harmonies, and that these harmonies are incapable of being expressed otherwise than in beautiful terms. But pending our inquiry (which must be a long one) let us put to the objector a practical question: "What forbids a man, who has the truth to tell, from putting it as persuasively as possible? Were not the truths of the Gospel conveyed in parables? And is their truth diminished because these parables are exquisite in form and in language? Will you only commend persuasiveness in a sophist who engages to make the worst argument appear the better, and condemn it in a teacher who employs it to enforce truth?" The question, surely, is answered as soon as we have asked it.

'And the further particular question, Is Mr Meredith a persuasive poet? will be answered as promptly by us. He can be—let us grant—a plaguily forbidding one. His philosophy is not easy; yet it seems to me a deal easier than many of his single verses. I hope humbly, for instance, one of these days, to discover what is meant by such a verse as this:

> Thou animatest ancient tales,
>   To prove our world of linear seed;
> Thy very virtue now assails
>   A tempter to mislead.

Faint, yet pursuing, I hope; but I must admit that such writing does not obviously allure, that it rather dejects the student by the difficulty of finding a stool to sit down and be stoical on. "Nay," to parody Sidney, "he dooth as if your journey should lye through a fayre Vineyard, at the first give you a handful of nuts, forgetting the nut-crackers." He is, in short, half his time forbiddingly difficult, and at times to all appearance so deliberately and yet so wantonly difficult, that you wonder what on earth you came out to pursue and why you should be tearing your flesh in these thickets.

'And then you remember the swinging cadences of "Love in the Valley"—the loveliest love-song of its century. Who can forget it?:

> Lovely are the curves of the white owl sweeping
>   Wavy in the dusk lit by one large star,
> Lone on the fir-branch, his rattle-note unvaried,
>   Brooding o'er the gloom, spins the brown evejar.
> Darker grows the valley, more and more forgetting;
>   So were it with me if forgetting could be willed.
> Tell the grassy hollow that holds the bubbling well-spring,
>   Tell it to forget the source that keeps it filled.

And you swear that no thickets can be so dense but you will wrestle through them in the hope of hearing that voice again, or even an echo of it.

"'Melampus,'' ''The Nuptials of Attila,'' ''The Day of the Daughter of Hades,'' ''The Empty Purse,'' ''Jump-to-Glory Jane,'' and the splendid ''Phœbus with Admetus''—you come back to each again and again, compelled by the wizardry of single lines and by a certain separate glamour which hangs about each of them. Each of them is remembered by you as in its own way a superb performance; lines here and there so haunt you with their beauty that you must go back and read the whole poem over for the sake of them. Other lines you boggle over, and yet cannot forget them; you hope to like them better at the next reading; you re-read, and wish them away, yet find them, liked or disliked, so embedded in your memory that you cannot do without them. Take, for instance, the last stanza of ''Phœbus with Admetus'':

> You with shelly horns, rams! and promontory goats,
>   You whose browsing beards dip in coldest dew!
> Bulls that walk the pasture in kingly-flashing coats!
>   Laurel, ivy, vine, wreathed for feasts not few!
> You that build the shade-roof, and you that court the rays,
>   You that leap besprinkling the rock stream-rent;
> He has been our fellow, the morning of our days;
>   Us he chose for house-mates, and this way went.

The first thing that made this stanza unforgettable was the glorious third line: almost as soon ''promontory goats'' fastened itself on memory; and almost as soon the last two lines were perceived to be excellent, and the fourth also. These enforced you, for the pleasure of recalling them, to recall the whole, and so of necessity to be hospitably minded toward the fifth and sixth lines, which at first repelled as being too obscurely and almost fantastically expressed. Having once passed it in, I find ''You that leap besprinkling the rock stream-rent,'' with its delicate labial pause and its delicate consonantal chime, one of the most fascinating lines in the stanza. And since, after being the hardest of all to admit, it has become one of the best liked, I am forced in fairness to ask myself if hundreds of lines of Mr Meredith's which now seem crabbed or fantastic may not justify themselves after many readings.

'The greatest mistake, at all events, is to suppose him ignorant or careless of the persuasiveness which lies in technical skill; though we can hardly be surprised that he has not escaped a charge which was freely brought against Browning, than whom, perhaps, no single poet was ever more untiring in technical experiment. Every poem of Browning's is an experiment—sometimes successful, sometimes not—in wedding sense with metre; and so is every poem of Mr Meredith's (he has even attempted galliambics), though he cannot emulate Browning's range. But he, too, has had his amazing successes—in the long, swooping lines of "Love in the Valley":

> Shy as the squirrel and wayward as the swallow,
>   Swift as the swallow along the river's light,
> Circleting the surface to meet his mirrored winglets,
>   Fleeter she seems in her stay than in her flight.

—in the "Young Princess," the stanzas of which are a din of nightingales' voices; in "The Woods of Westermain" and "The Nuptials of Attila," where the ear awaits the burthen, as the sense awaits the horror, of the song, and the poet holds back both, increasing the painful expectancy; or in the hammered measure of "Phœbus with Admetus"—a real triumph. Of each of these metres you have to admit at once that it is strange and arresting, and that you cannot conceive the poem written in any other.

And, as I have said, their very asperities tend, with repetition, to pass into beauties.

'But, in the end, he is remembered best for his philosophy, as the poet who tells us to have courage and trust
in Nature, that thereby we may attain whatever heaven
may be. "Neither shall they say, Lo, here! or Lo, there!
for behold the kingdom of heaven is within you"—yes,
and hell, too, Mr Meredith wants us:

> In tragic life, God wot,
> No villain need be! Passions spin the plot:
> We are betrayed by what is false within.

So, again, in "The Woods of Westermain," we are warned
that the worst betrayal for man lies in the cowardice of his
own soul:

> But have care.
> In yourself may lurk the trap.

Are you at heart a poltroon or a palterer, cruel, dull,
envious, full of hate? Then Nature, the mother of the
strong and generous, will have no pity, but will turn and
rend you with claws. "Trust her with your whole heart,"
says Mr Meredith, "and go forward courageously until
you follow

> Where never was track
> On the path trod of all.

The fight is an ennobling one, when all is said: rejoice
in it, because our children shall use the victory.

> Take stripes or chains;
> Grip at thy standard reviled.
> And what if our body be dashed from the steeps?
> Our spoken in protest remains.
> A younger generation reaps.'

*   *   *   *   *

From a Cornish Window,

Thursday, Sept. 2nd

Hoist up sail while gale doth last....

I do not call this very sound advice: but we followed it,
and that is the reason why I am able to send off my monthly
packet from the old address. Also it came very near to
being a reason why I had no letter to send. The wind
blew as obstinately as ever on the Tuesday morning; but
this time we arranged our start more carefully, and beat
out over the bar in comparatively smooth water. The seas
outside were not at all smooth, but a Newlyn-built boat
does not make much account of mere seas, and soon after
midday we dropped anchor in Plymouth Cattewater, and
went ashore for our letters.

We were sworn to reach home next day, and somehow
we forgot to study the barometer, which was doing its best
to warn us. The weather was dirtier than ever and the wind
harder. But we had grown accustomed to this: and persuaded ourselves that, once outside of the Rame, we could
make a pretty fetch of it for home and cover the distance
at our best speed—which indeed we did. But I confess
that as we passed beyond the breakwater, and met the
Plymouth trawlers running back for shelter, I began to
wonder rather uneasily how the barometer might be behaving, and even dallied with the resolution to go below
and see. We were well dressed down, however—double-
reefed mainsail, reefed mizzen, foresail and storm jib—
and after our beating at Salcombe none of us felt inclined
to raise the question of putting back. There was nothing
to hurt, as yet: the boat was shaking off the water like
a duck, and making capital weather of it; we told each
other that once beyond the Rame, with the sea on our

quarter, we should do handsomely. And the gale—the newspapers called it a hurricane, but it was merely a gale —waited patiently until we were committed to it. Half an hour later we took in the mizzen, and, soon after, the foresail: and even so, and close-hauled, were abreast of Looe Island just forty-seven minutes after passing the Rame— nine miles. For a 28-ton cruiser this will be allowed to be fair going. For my own part I could have wished it faster: not from any desire to break 'records,' but because, should anything happen to our gear, we were uncomfortably close to a lee-shore, and the best behaved of boats could not stand up against the incessant shoreward thrust of the big seas crossing us. Also, to make matters worse, the shore itself now and then vanished in the 'dirt.' On the whole, therefore, it was not too soon for us that we opened the harbour and

> saw on Palatinus
> The white porch of our home,

though these were three or four times hidden from us by the seas over which we toppled through the harbour's mouth and into quiet water. While the sails were stowing I climbed down the ladder, and sat in front of the barometer, and wondered how I should like this sort of thing if I had to go through it often, for my living.

OCTOBER

Season of mists and mellow fruitfulness....

I HAVE been planting a perennial border in the garden
and consulting, with serious damage to the temper, a
number of the garden-books now in fashion. When a man
drives at practice—when he desires to know precisely at
what season, in what soil, and at what depth to plant his
martagon lilies, to decide between *Ayrshire Ruga* and
Fellenberg for the pillar that requires a red rose, to fix
the right proportion of sand and leaf-mould to suit his
carnations—when 'his only plot' is to plant the bergamot—
he resents being fobbed off with prattle:

My squills make a brave show this morning, and the little
petticoated Narcissus Cyclamineus in the lower rock-garden
(surely Narcissus ought to have been a girl!) begins to 'take the
winds of March with beauty.' I am expecting visitors, and hope
that mulching will benefit the Yellow Pottebakkers, which I
don't want to flower before Billy comes home from school, etc.

But the other day, in 'The Garden's Story,' by Mr George
H. Ellwanger, I came upon a piece of literary criticism
which gave me a pleasurable pause in my search for quite
other information. Mr Ellwanger, a great American
gardener, has observed that our poets usually sing of
autumn in a minor key, which startles an American who,
while accustomed to our language, cannot suit this mourn-
fulness with the still air and sunshine and glowing colour
of his own autumn. With us, as he notes, autumn is a dank,

sodden season, bleak or shivering. 'The sugar and scarlet maple, the dogwood and sumac, are wanting to impart their warmth of colour; and St Martin's summer somehow fails to shed a cheerful influence' comparable with that of the Indian summer over there. The Virginia creeper which reddens our Oxford walls so magnificently in October is an importation of no very long standing—old enough to be accepted as a feature of the place, not yet old enough to be inseparably connected with it in song. Yet—

Of all odes to autumn, Keats's, I believe, is most universally admired. This might almost answer to our own fall of the leaf, and is far less sombre than many apostrophes to the season that occur throughout English verse.

From this Mr Ellwanger proceeds to compare Keats' with the wonderful 'Ode to Autumn' which Hood wrote in 1823 (each ode, by the way, belongs to its author's twenty-fourth year), less perfect, to be sure, and far less obedient to form, but with lines so haunting and images so full of beauty that they do not suffer in the comparison. Listen to the magnificent opening:

> I saw old Autumn in the misty morn
> Stand shadowless like Silence, listening
> To silence, for no lonely bird would sing
> Into his hollow ear from woods forlorn,
> Nor lonely hedge, nor solitary thorn....

I had never (to my shame) thought of comparing the two odes until Mr Ellwanger invited me. He notes the felicitous use of the O-sounds throughout Hood's ode, and points out, shrewdly as correctly, that the two poets were contemplating two different stages of autumn. Keats, more sensuous, dwells on the stage of mellow fruitfulness, and

writes of late October at the latest. Hood's poem lies close
'on the birth of trembling winter': he sings more austerely
of November's desolation:

> Where is the pride of Summer—the green prime—
>   The many, many leaves all twinkling?—Three
> On the moss'd elm; three on the naked lime
>   Trembling,—and one upon the old oak tree!
>   Where is the Dryad's immortality?
> Gone into mournful cypress and dark yew,
> Or wearing the long gloomy Winter through
>   In the smooth holly's green eternity.
>
> The squirrel gloats o'er his accomplish'd hoard,
> The ants have brimm'd their garners with ripe grain,
>   And honey bees have stored
> The sweets of summer in their luscious cells;
> The swallows all have wing'd across the main;
> But here the Autumn melancholy dwells,
>   And sighs her tearful spells
> Amongst the sunless shadows of the plain.
>   Alone, alone
>   Upon a mossy stone
> She sits and reckons up the dead and gone
> With the last leaves for a love-rosary....

The last image involves a change of sex in personified
Autumn: an awkwardness, I allow. But if the awkwardness
of the change can be excused, Hood's lines excuse it:

> O go and sit with her and be o'er-shaded
>   Under the languid downfall of her hair;
> She wears a coronal of flowers faded
>   Upon her forehead, and a face of care;
> There is enough of wither'd everywhere
> To make her bower,—and enough of gloom....

*   *   *   *   *

In spite of its ambiguity of sex and in spite of its irregular
metre, I find, with Mr Ellwanger, more force of poetry
in Hood's ode than in Keats'; and this in spite of one's
prejudice in favour of the greater poet. It came on me
with a small shock therefore to find that Mr Bridges, in
his already famous Essay on Keats, ranks 'Autumn' as the
very best of all Keats' Odes.

Now whether one agrees with him or not, there is no
loose talk in Mr Bridges' criticism. He tells us precisely
why he prefers this poem to that other: and such definiteness
in critical writing is not only useful in itself but perhaps
the severest test of a critic's quality. No task can well be
harder than to take a poem, a stanza, or a line, to decide
'Just here lies the strength, the charm; or just here the
looseness, the defect.' In any but the strongest hands these
methods ensure mere niggling ingenuity, in which all
appreciation of the broader purposes of the author—of
Aristotle's 'universal'—disappears, while the critic reveals
himself as an industrious pick-thank person concerned with
matters of slight and secondary importance. But if well
conducted such criticism has a particular value. As
Mr Bridges says:

If my criticism should seem sometimes harsh, that is, I
believe, due to its being given in plain terms, a manner which
I prefer, because by obliging the writer to say definitely what
he means, it makes his mistakes easier to point out, and in this
way the true business of criticism may be advanced; nor do
I know that, in a work of this sort, criticism has any better
function than to discriminate between the faults and merits
of the best art: for it commonly happens, when any great
artist comes to be generally admired, that his faults, being
graced by his excellences, are confounded with them in the
popular judgment, and being easy of imitation, are the points
of his work which are most liable to be copied.

Further, Mr Bridges leaves us in no doubt that he considers the Odes to be in many respects the most important division of Keats' poetry. 'Had Keats,' he says, 'left us only his Odes, his rank among the poets would be not lower than it is, for they have stood apart in literature, at least the six most famous of them.'

These famous six are: (1) 'Psyche,' (2) 'Melancholy,' (3) 'Nightingale,' (4) 'Grecian Urn,' (5) 'Indolence,' (6) 'Autumn'; and Mr Bridges is not content until he has them arranged in a hierarchy. He draws up a list in order of merit, and in it gives first place—'for its perfection'—to 'Autumn':

> This is always reckoned among the faultless masterpieces of English poetry; and unless it be objected as a slight blemish that the words 'Think not of them' in the second line of the third stanza are somewhat awkwardly addressed to a personification of Autumn, I do not know that any sort of fault can be found in it.

But though 'Autumn' (1) is best as a whole, the 'Nightingale' (2) altogether beats it in splendour and intensity of mood; and, after pointing out its defects, Mr Bridges confesses, 'I could not name any English poem of the same length which contains so much beauty as this ode.' Still, it takes second place, and next comes 'Melancholy' (3). 'The perception in this ode is profound, and no doubt experienced'; but in spite of its great beauty 'it does not hit so hard as one would expect. I do not know whether this is due to a false note towards the end of the second stanza, or to a disagreement between the second and third stanzas.' Next in order come 'Psyche' (4) and, disputing place with it, the 'Grecian Urn' (5). 'Indolence' (6) closes the procession; and I dare say few will dispute her title to the last place.

But with these six odes we must rank (*a*) the fragment of the 'May Ode,' immortal on account of the famous passage of inimitable beauty descriptive of the Greek poets—

> Leaving great verse unto a little clan.—

and (*b*), (*c*) the Odes to 'Pan' and to 'Sorrow' from 'Endymion.' Of the latter Mr Sidney Colvin has written:

His later and more famous lyrics, though they are free from the faults and immaturities which disfigure this, yet do not, to my mind at least, show a command over such various sources of imaginative and musical effect, or touch so thrillingly so many chords of the spirit. A mood of tender irony and wistful pathos like that of the best Elizabethan love-songs; a sense as keen as Heine's of the immemorial romance of India and the East; a power like that of Coleridge, and perhaps caught from him, of evoking the remotest weird and beautiful associations almost with a word; clear visions of Greek beauty and wild wood-notes of Celtic imagination; all these elements come here commingled, yet in a strain perfectly individual.

With this Mr Bridges entirely agrees; but adds:

It unfortunately halts in the opening, and the first and fourth stanzas especially are unequal to the rest, as is again the third from the end, 'Young Stranger,' which for its matter would with more propriety have been cast into the previous section; and these impoverish the effect, and contain expressions which might put some readers off. If they would begin at the fifth stanza and omit the third from the end, they would find little that is not admirable.

Now, for my part, when in book or newspaper I come upon references to Isaiah lxi. 1–3, or Shakespeare, *K. Henry IV*, Pt. ii, Act 4, Sc. 5, l. 163, or the like, I have to drop my reading at once and hunt them up. So

I hope that these references of Mr Bridges will induce the
reader to take his Keats down from the shelf. And I hope
further that, having his Keats in hand, the reader will
examine these odes again and make out an order for himself, as I propose to do.

*   *   *   *   *

Mr Bridges' order of merit was: (1) 'Autumn,' (2) the
'Nightingale,' (3) 'Melancholy,' (4) 'Psyche,' (5) 'Grecian
Urn,' (6) 'Indolence'; leaving us to rank with these
(a) the fragment of the 'May Ode,' and (b), (c) the Odes
to 'Pan' and to 'Sorrow' from 'Endymion.'

Now of 'Autumn,' to which he gives the first place 'for
its perfection,' one may remark that Keats did not entitle
it an Ode, and the omission may be something more than
casual. Certainly its three stanzas seem to me to exhibit
very little of that *progression* of thought and feeling which
I take to be one of the qualities of an ode as distinguished
from an ordinary lyric. The line is notoriously hard to
draw: but I suppose that in theory the lyric deals summarily with its theme, whereas the ode treats it in a sustained
progressive manner. But sustained treatment is hardly
possible within the limits of three stanzas, and I can discover no progression. The first two stanzas elaborate a
picture of Autumn; the third suggests a reflection—

Where are the songs of Spring? Ay, where are they?
Think not of them, thou hast thy music too—

and promptly, with a few added strokes, all pictorial, the
poet works that reflection into decoration. A sonnet could
not well be more summary. In fact, the poem in structure
of thought very closely resembles a sonnet; its first two
stanzas corresponding to the octave, and its last stanza to
the sestet.

This will perhaps be thought very trivial criticism of a poem which most people admit to be, as a piece of writing, all but absolutely flawless. But allowing that it expresses perfectly what it sets out to express, I yet doubt if it deserve the place assigned to it by Mr Bridges. Expression counts for a great deal: but ideas perhaps count for more. And in the value of the ideas expressed I cannot see that 'Autumn' comes near to rivalling the 'Nightingale' (for instance) or 'Melancholy.' The thought that Autumn has its songs as well as Spring has neither the rarity nor the subtlety nor the moral value of the thought that

> In the very temple of Delight
> Veil'd Melancholy has her sovran shrine,
>> Though seen of none save him whose strenuous tongue
>> Can burst Joy's grape against his palate fine;
> His soul shall taste the sadness of her might,
>> And be among her cloudy trophies hung.

To test it in another way:—It is perfect, no doubt; but it has not the one thing that now and then in poetry rises (if I may use the paradox) above perfection. It does not contain, as one or two of the Odes contain, what I may call the Great Thrill. It nowhere compels that sudden 'silent, upon a peak in Darien' shiver, that awed surmise of the magic of poetry which arrests one at the seventh stanza of the 'Nightingale' or before the closing lines of 'Psyche.' Such verse as

> Perhaps the self-same song hath found a path
>> Through the sad heart of Ruth, when, sick for home,
>>> She stood in tears amid the alien corn;
>>>> The same that oft-times hath
>> Charm'd magic casements, opening on the foam
>>> Of perilous seas, in faery lands forlorn—

reaches beyond technical perfection to the very root of all tears and joy. Such verse links poetry to Love itself—

> Half angel and half bird,
> And all a wonder and a wild desire.

The 'Ode on a Grecian Urn' does not perhaps quite reach this divine thrill: but its second and third stanzas have a rapture that comes very near to it (I will speak anon of the fourth stanza); and I should not quarrel with one who preferred these two stanzas even to the close of 'Psyche.'

Now it seems to me that the mere touching of this poetic height—the mere feat of causing this most exquisite vibration in the human nerves—gives a poem a quality and a rank apart; a quality and a rank not secured to 'Autumn' by all its excellence of expression. I grant, of course, that it takes two to produce this thrill—the reader as well as the poet. And if any man object to me that he, for his part, feels a thrill as poignant when he reads stanza 2 of 'Autumn' as when he reads stanza 7 of the 'Nightingale,' then I confess that I shall have some difficulty in answering him. But I believe very few, if any, will assert this of themselves. And perhaps we may get at the truth of men's feelings on this point in another way. Suppose that of these four poems, 'Autumn,' 'Nightingale,' 'Psyche,' and 'Grecian Urn,' one were doomed to perish, and fate allowed us to choose which one should be abandoned. Sorrowful as the choice must be, I believe that lovers of poetry would find themselves least loth to part with 'Autumn'; that the loss of either of the others would be foreseen as a sharper wrench.

For the others lie close to human emotion; are indeed interpenetrated with emotion; whereas 'Autumn' makes but an objective appeal, chiefly to the visual sense. It is,

as I have said, a decorative picture; and even so it hardly
beats the pictures in stanza 4 of the 'Grecian Urn'—

> What little town by river or sea-shore,
> Or mountain, built with peaceful citadel,
> Is emptied of its folk, this pious morn?

though Keats, to be sure, comes perilously near to spoiling
these lines by the three answering ones—

> And, little town, thy streets for evermore
> Will silent be; and not a soul to tell
> Why thou art desolate, can e'er return

—which, though beautiful in themselves, involve a confusion of thought; since (in Mr Colvin's words) 'they
speak of the arrest of life as though it were an infliction
in the sphere of reality, and not merely a necessary condition in the sphere of art, having in that sphere its own
compensations.'

But it is time to be drawing up one's own order for the
Odes. The first place, then, let us give to the 'Nightingale,'
for the intensity of its emotion, for the sustained splendour
and variety of its language, for the consummate skill with
which it keeps the music matched with the mood, and
finally because it attains, at least twice, to the 'great thrill.'
Nor can one preferring it offend Mr Bridges, who confesses that he 'could not name any English poem of the
same length which contains so much beauty as this ode.'

For the second place, one feels inclined at first to bracket
'Psyche' with the 'Grecian Urn.' Each develops a
beautiful idea. In 'Psyche' the poet addresses the loveliest
but latest-born vision 'of all Olympus's faded hierarchy,'
and promises her that, though born

> Too late for antique vows,
> Too, too late for the fond believing lyre,

she shall yet have a priest, the poet, and a temple built in some untrodden region of his mind—

> And in the midst of this wide quietness
> A rosy sanctuary will I dress
> With the wreath'd trellis of a working brain,
>   With buds, and bells, and stars without a name,
> With all the gardener Fancy e'er could feign,
>   Who breeding flowers, will never breed the same:
> And there shall be for thee all soft delight
>   That shadowy thought can win,
> A bright torch, and a casement ope at night,
>   To let the warm Love in!

The thought of the 'Grecian Urn' is (to quote Mr Bridges) 'the supremacy of ideal art over Nature, because of its unchanging expression of perfection.' And this also is true and beautiful. Idea for idea, there is little to choose between the two odes. Each has the 'great thrill,' or something very like it. The diction of 'Psyche' is more splendid; the mood of the 'Grecian Urn' happier and (I think) rarer. But 'Psyche' asserts its superiority in the orderly development of its idea, which rises steadily to its climax in the magnificent lines quoted above, and on that note triumphantly closes: whereas the 'Grecian Urn' marches uncertainly, recurs to its main idea without advancing it, reaches something like its climax in the middle stanza, and tripping over a pun (as Mr Bridges does not hesitate to call 'O Attic shape! fair attitude!') at the entrance of the last stanza, barely recovers itself in time to make a forcible close.

(1) 'Nightingale,' (2) 'Psyche,' (3) 'Grecian Urn.' Shall the next place go to 'Melancholy'? The idea of this ode (I contrasted it just now with the idea of 'Autumn') is particularly fine; and when we supply the first stanza

which Keats discarded we see it to be well developed. The discarded stanza lies open to the charge of staginess. One may answer that Keats meant it to be stagey: that he deliberately surrounded the quest of the false Melancholy with those paste-board 'properties'—the bark of dead men's bones, the rudder of a dragon's tail 'long severed, yet still hard with agony,' the cordage woven of large uprootings from the skull of bald Medusa'—in order to make the genuine Melancholy more effective by contrast[1]. Yet, as Mr Bridges points out, the ode does not hit so hard as one would expect: and it has seemed to me that the composition of Dürer's great drawing may have something to do with this. Dürer *did* surround his Melancholia with 'properties,' and he *did* evoke a figure which all must admit to be not only tremendously impressive but entirely genuine, whatever Keats may say; a figure so haunting, too, that it obtrudes its face between us and Keats' page and scares away his delicate figure of

> Joy, whose hand is ever at his lips
> Bidding adieu...—

reducing him to the pettiness of a Chelsea-china shepherd. Mr Bridges, too, calls attention to a false note in the second stanza:

[1] The discarded opening stanza ran:

> Though you should build a bark of dead men's bones,
>   And rear a phantom gibbet for a mast,
> Stitch shrouds together for a sail, with groans
>   To fill it out blood-stainèd and aghast;
> Although your rudder be a dragon's tail
>   Long-sever'd, yet still hard with agony,
>   Your cordage large uprootings from the skull
> Of bald Medusa, certes you would fail
>   To find the Melancholy—whether she
>   Dreameth in any isle of Lethe dull.

> Or if thy mistress some rich anger shows,
> Emprison her soft hand, and let her rave,
> And feed, feed deep upon her peerless eyes.

So prone was Keats to sound this particular false note that
Mr Bridges had to devote some three pages of his essay
to an examination of the poet's want of taste in his speech
about women and his lack of true insight into human
passion. The worst trick this disability ever played upon
Keats was to blind him to his magnificent opportunity in
'Lamia'—an opportunity of which the missing is felt as
positively cruel: but it betrayed him also into occasional
lapses and ineptitudes which almost rival Leigh Hunt's—

> The two divinest things the world has got—
> A lovely woman in a rural spot.

This blemish may, perhaps, condemn it to a place below
'Autumn'; of which (I hope) reason has been shown why
it cannot rank higher than (4). And (6) *longo intervallo*
comes 'Indolence,' which may be fearlessly called an
altogether inferior performance.

The 'May Ode' stands by itself, an exquisite fragment.
But the two odes from "Endymion" may be set well above
'Indolence,' and that to 'Sorrow,' in my opinion, above
'Autumn,' and only a little way behind the leaders.

*   *   *   *   *

But the fall of the year is marked for us by a ceremony
more poignant, more sorrowfully seasonable than any
hymned by Hood or by Keats. Let us celebrate—

LAYING UP THE BOAT

There arrives a day towards the end of October—or
with luck we may tide over into November—when the
wind in the mainsail suddenly takes a winter force, and

we begin to talk of laying up the boat. Hitherto we have
kept a silent compact and ignored all change in the season.
We have watched the blue afternoons shortening, fading
through lilac into grey, and let pass their scarcely per-
ceptible warnings. One afternoon a few kittiwakes appeared. A week later the swallows fell to stringing themselves like beads along the coastguard's telephone-wire on
the hill. They vanished, and we pretended not to miss
them. When our hands grew chill with steering we rubbed
them by stealth or stuck them nonchalantly in our pockets.
But this vicious unmistakable winter gust breaks the spell.
We take one look around the harbour, at the desolate buoys
awash and tossing; we cast another seaward at the thick
weather through which, in a week at latest, will come
looming the earliest of the Baltic merchantmen, our
November visitors—bluff vessels with red-painted channels,
green deckhouses, white top-strakes, wooden davits over-
hanging astern, and the Danish flag fluttering aloft in the
haze. Then we find speech; and with us, as with the
swallows, the move into winter quarters is not long delayed
when once it comes into discussion. We have dissembled
too long; and know, as we go through the form of debating
it, that our date must be the next spring-tides.

This ritual of laying up the boat is our way of bidding
farewell to summer; and we go through it, when the day
comes, in ceremonial silence. *Favete linguis!* The hour
helps us, for the spring-tides at this season reach their height
a little after night-fall, and it is on an already slackening
flood that we cast off our moorings and head up the river
with our backs to the waning sunset. Since we tow a
dinghy astern and are ourselves towed by the silent yachtsman, you may call it a procession. She has been stripped,
during the last two days, of sails, rigging, and all spars but

the mainmast. Now we bring her alongside the town quay and beneath the shears—the abhorrèd shears—which lift this too out of its step, dislocated with a creak as poignant as the cry of Polydorus. We lower it, lay it along the deck, and resume our way; past quay doors and windows where already the townsfolk are beginning to light their lamps; and so by the jetties where foreign crews rest with elbows on bulwarks and stare down upon us idly through the dusk. She is after all but a little cutter of six tons, and we might well apologise, like the Athenian, for so diminutive a corpse. But she is our own; and they never saw her with jackyarder spread, or spinnaker or jib-topsail delicate as samite—those heavenly wings!—nor felt her gallant spirit straining to beat her own record before a tense northerly breeze. Yet even to them her form, in pure white with gilt fillet, might tell of no common obsequies.

For in every good ship the miracle of Galatea is renewed; and the shipwright who sent this keel down the ways to her element surely beheld the birth of a goddess. He still speaks of her with pride, but the conditions of his work keep him a modest man; for he goes about it under the concentred gaze of half a dozen old mariners hauled ashore, who haunt his yard uninvited, slow of speech but deadly critical. Nor has the language a word for their appalling candour. Often, admiring how cheerfully he tolerates them, I have wondered what it would feel like to compose a novel under the eyes of half a dozen reviewers. But to him, as to his critics, the ship was a framework only until the terrible moment when with baptism she took life. Did he in the rapture, the brief ecstasy of creation, realise that she had passed from him? Ere the local artillery band had finished 'Rule Britannia,' and while his friends were still shaking his hands and drinking to him,

did he know his loss in his triumph? His fate is to improve
the world, not to possess; to chase perfection, knowing
that under the final mastering touch it must pass from his
hand; to lose his works and anchor himself upon the
workmanship, the immaterial function. For of art this is
the cross and crown in one; and he, modest man, was born
to the sad eminence.

She is ours now by purchase, but ours, too, by something better. Like a slave's her beautiful untaught body
came to us; but it was we who gave wings to her, and with
wings a soul, and a law to its grace, and discipline to its
vital impulses. She is ours, too, by our gratitude, since the
delicate machine

> Has like a woman given up its joy;

and by memories of her helpfulness in such modest perils
as we tempt, of her sweet companionship through long
days empty of annoyance—land left behind with its striving
crowds, its short views, its idols of the market-place, its
sordid worries; the breast flung wide to the horizon, swept
by wholesome salt airs, void perhaps, but so beatifically
clean! Then it was that we learned her worth, drinking in
the knowledge without effort, lulled hour after hour by her
whisperings which asked for no answer, by the pulse of
her tiller soft against the palm. Patter of reef-points, creak
of cordage, hum of wind, hiss of brine—I think at times
that she has found a more human language. Who that has
ever steered for hours together cannot report of a mysterious
voice 'breaking the silence of the seas,' as though a friend
were standing and speaking astern? or has not turned his
head to the confident inexplicable call? The fishermen fable
of drowned sailors 'hailing their names.' But the voice is
of a single speaker; it bears no likeness to the hollow tones

of the dead; it calls no name; it utters no particular word. It merely speaks. Sometimes, ashamed at being tricked by an illusion so absurd, I steal a glance at the yatchsman forward. He is smoking, placidly staring at the clouds. Patently he was not the speaker, and patently he has heard nothing. Was it Cynthia, my dearer shipmate? She, too, knows the voice; even answered it one day, supposing it mine, and in her confusion I surprised our common secret. But we never hear it together. She is seated now on the lee side of the cockpit, her hands folded on the coaming, her chin rested on them, and her eyes gazing out beneath the sail and across the sea from which they surely have drawn their wine-coloured glooms. She has not stirred for many minutes. No, it was not Cynthia. Then either it must be the wild, obedient spirit who carries us, straining at the impassable bar of speech, to break through and be at one with her master, or else—Can it have been Ariel, perched aloft in the shrouds, with mischievous harp?

> That was the chirp of Ariel
> You heard, as overhead it flew,
> The farther going more to dwell
> And wing our green to wed our blue;
> But whether note of joy or knell
> Not his own Father-singer knew;
> Nor yet can any mortal tell,
> Save only how it shivers through;
> The breast of us a sounded shell,
> The blood of us a lighted dew.

Perhaps; but for my part I believe it was the ship; and if you deride my belief, I shall guess you one of those who need a figure-head to remind them of a vessel's sex. There are minds which find a certain romance in figure-heads.

To me they seem a frigid, unintelligent device, not to say idolatrous. I have known a crew to set so much store by one that they kept a tinsel locket and pair of ear-rings in the forecastle and duly adorned their darling when in port. But this is materialism. The true personality of a ship resides in no prefiguring lump of wood with a sightless smile to which all seas come alike and all weathers. Lay your open palm on the mast, rather, and feel life pulsing beneath it, trembling through and along every nerve of her. Are you converted? That life is yours to control. Take the tiller, then, and for an hour be a god! For indeed you shall be a god, and of the very earliest. The centuries shall run out with the chain as you slip moorings—run out and drop from you, plumb, and leave you free, winged! Or if you cannot forget in a moment the times to which you were born, each wave shall turn back a page as it rolls past to break on the shore towards which you revert no glance. Even the romance of it shall fade with the murmur of that coast.

> Sails of silk and ropes of sendal,
>   Such as gleam in ancient lore,
> And the singing of the sailor,
>   And the answer from the shore—

these shall pass and leave you younger than romance—a child open-eyed and curious, pleased to meet a sea-parrot or a rolling porpoise, or to watch the gannets diving—

> As Noah saw them dive
> O'er sunken Ararat.

Yes, and sunset shall bring you, a god, to the gates of a kingdom I must pause to describe for you, though when you reach it you will forget my description and imagine yourself its first discoverer. But that is a part of its charm.

Walter Pater, reading the *Odyssey*, was brought up (as we say) 'with a round turn' by a passage wherein Homer describes briefly and with accuracy how some mariners came to harbour, took down sail, and stepped ashore. It filled him with wonder that so simple an incident—nor to say ordinary—could be made so poetical; and, having pondered it, he divided the credit between the poet and his fortunate age—a time (said he) in which one could hardly have spoken at all without ideal effect, or the sailors pulled down their sail without making a picture 'in the great style' against a sky charged with marvels.

You will discover, when you reach the river-mouth of which I am telling, and are swept over the rolling bar into quiet water—you will discover (and with ease, being a god) that Mr Pater was entirely mistaken, and the credit belongs neither to Homer nor to his fortunate age. For here are woods with woodlanders, and fields with plough-men, and beaches with fishermen hauling nets; and all these men, as they go about their work, contrive to make pictures 'in the great style' against a sky charged with marvels, obviously without any assistance from Homer, and quite as if nothing had happened for, say, the last three thousand years. That the immemorial craft of sea-faring has no specially 'heroic age'—or that, if it have, that age is yours—you will discover by watching your own yachtsman as he moves about lowering foresail and pre-paring to drop anchor.

It is a river of gradual golden sunsets, such as Wilson painted—a broad-bosomed flood between deep and tranquil woods, the main banks holding here and there a village as in an arm maternally crook'd, but opening into creeks where the oaks dip their branches in the high tides, where the stars are glassed all night long without a ripple, and where you may spend whole days with no company but herons and sandpipers. Even by the main river each separate figure—the fisherman on the shore, the plough-man on the upland, the ferryman crossing between them— moves slowly upon a large landscape, while, permeating all, 'the essential silence cheers and blesses.' After a week at anchor in the heart of this silence Cynthia and I compared notes, and set down the total population at fifty souls; and even so she would have it that I had included the owls. Lo! the next morning an unaccustomed rocking awoke us in our berths, and, raising the flap of our dew-drenched awning, we 'descried at sunrise an emerging prow' of a peculiarly hideous excursion steamboat. She blew no whistle, and we were preparing to laugh at her grotesque temerity when we became aware of a score of boats putting out towards her from the shadowy banks. Like spectres they approached, reached her, and discharged their comple-ments, until at last a hundred and fifty passengers crowded her deck. In silence—or in such silence as a paddle-boat can achieve—she backed, turned, and bore them away: on what festal errand we never discovered. We never saw them return. For aught I know they may never have returned. They raised no cheer; no band accompanied them; they passed without even the faint hum of conversa-tion. In five minutes at most the apparition had vanished around the river-bend seawards and out of sight. We stared at the gently heaving water, turned, and caught sight of Euergetes, his head and red cap above the forecastle hatch. (I call our yachtsman Euergetes because it is so unlike his real name that neither he nor his family will recognise it.) 'Why, Euergetes,' exclaimed Cynthia, 'wher-ever did they all come from?' 'I'm sure I can't tell you, ma'am,' he answered, 'unless 'twas from the woods'—

giving us to picture these ardent holiday-makers roosting all night in the trees while we slumbered. But the odd thing was that the labourers manned the fields that day, the fishermen the beach that evening, in undiminished numbers. We landed, and could detect no depletion in the village. We landed on subsequent days, and discovered no increase. And the inference, though easy, was startling.

I suppose that 'in the great style' could hardly be predicated of our housekeeping on these excursions; and yet it achieves, in our enthusiastic opinion, a primitive elegance not often recaptured by mortals since the passing of the Golden Age. We cook for ourselves, but bring a fine spirit of emulation both to *cuisine* and service. We dine frugally, but the claret is sound. From the moment when Euergetes awakes us by washing down the deck, and the sound of water rushing through the scuppers calls me forth to discuss the weather with him, method rules the early hours, that we may be free to use the later as we list. First the cockpit beneath the awning must be prepared as a dressing-room for Cynthia; next Euergetes summoned on deck to valet me with the simple bucket. And when I am dressed and tingling from the *douche*, and sit me down on the cabin top, barefooted and whistling, to clean the boots, and Euergetes has been sent ashore for milk and eggs, bread and clotted cream, there follows a peaceful half-hour until Cynthia flings back a corner of the awning and, emerging, confirms the dawn. Then begins the business, orderly and thorough, of redding up the cabin, stowing the beds, washing out the lower deck, folding away the awning, and transforming the cockpit into a breakfast-room, with table neatly set forth. Meanwhile Euergetes has returned, and from the forecastle comes the sputter of red mullet cooking. Cynthia clatters the cups and saucers, while in the well by

the cabin door I perform some acquired tricks with the
new-laid eggs. There is plenty to be done on board a
small boat, but it is all simple enough. Only, you must not
let it overtake you. Woe to you if it fall into arrears!

By ten o'clock or thereabouts we have breakfasted, my
pipe is lit, and a free day lies before us—

> All the wood to ransack,
> All the wave explore.

We take the dinghy and quest after adventures. The nearest
railway lies six miles off, and is likely to deposit no one in
whom we have the least concern. The woods are deep,
we carry our lunch-basket and may roam independent of
taverns. If the wind invite, we can hoist our small sail;
if not, we can recline and drift and stare at the heavens,
or land and bathe, or search in vain for curlews' or king-
fishers' nests, or in more energetic moods seek out a
fisherman and hire him to shoot his seine. Seventy red
mullet have I seen fetched at one haul out of those delectable
waters, remote and enchanted as the lake whence the fisherman at the genie's orders drew fish for the young king of
the Black Isles. But such days as these require no filling,
and why should I teach you how to fill them?

Best hour of all perhaps is that before bed-time, when
the awning has been spread once more, and after long hours
in the open our world narrows to the circle of the reading-
lamp in the cockpit. Our cabin is prepared. Through the
open door we see its red curtain warm in the light of the
swinging lamp, the beds laid, the white sheets turned back.
Still we grudge these moments to sleep. Outside we hear
the tide streaming seawards, light airs play beneath the
awning, above it rides the host of heaven. And here, gathered
into a few square feet, we have home—larder, cellar,

library, tables, and cupboards; life's small appliances with
the human comradeship they serve, chosen for their service
after severely practical discussion, yet ultimately by the
heart's true nesting-instinct. We are isolated, bound even
to this strange river-bed by a few fathoms of chain only.
To-morrow we can lift anchor and spread wing; but we
carry home with us.

> I will make you brooches and toys for your delight
> Of bird-song at morning and star-shine at night;
> I will make a palace fit for you and me
> Of green days in forests and blue days at sea.
>
> I will make my kitchen and you shall keep your room
> Where white flows the river and bright blows the broom;
> And you shall wash your linen and keep your body white
> In rainfall at morning and dewfall at night.

You see now what memories we lay up with the boat.
Will you think it ridiculous that after such royal days of
summer, her inconspicuous obsequies have before now
put me in mind of Turner's 'Fighting *Téméraire*'? I declare, at any rate, that the fault lies not with me, but with
our country's painters and poets for providing no work of
art nearer to my mood. We English have a great seafaring
and a great poetical past. Yet the magic of the sea and
shipping has rarely touched our poetry, and for its finest
expression we must still turn to an art in which as a race
we are less expert, and stand before that picture of Turner's
in the National Gallery. The late Mr Froude believed in
a good time coming when the sea-captains of Elizabeth
are to find their bard and sit enshrined in 'a great English
national epic as grand as the *Odyssey*.' It may be, but as
yet our poets have achieved but a few sea-fights, marine
adventures, and occasional pieces, which wear a spirited
but accidental look, and suggest the excursionist. On me,

at any rate, no poem in our language—not even *The Ancient Mariner*—binds as that picture binds, the

> Mystic spell,
> Which none but sailors know or feel,
> And none but they can tell—

if indeed they *can* tell. In it Turner seized and rolled together in one triumphant moment the emotional effect of noble shipping and a sentiment as ancient and profound as the sea itself—human regret for transitory human glory. The great warship, glimmering in her Mediterranean fighting-paint, moving like a queen to execution; the pert and ignoble tug, itself an emblem of the new order, eager, pushing, ugly, and impatient of the slow loveliness it supersedes; the sunset hour, closing man's labour; the fading river-reach—you may call these things obvious, but all art's greatest effects are obvious when once genius has discovered them. I should know well enough by this time what is coming when I draw near that picture, and yet my heart never fails to leap with the old wild wonder. There are usually one or two men standing before it—I observe that it affects women less—and I glance at them furtively to see how *they* take it. If ever I surprise one with tears in his eyes, I believe we shall shake hands. And why not? For the moment we are not strangers, but men subdued by the wonder and sadness of our common destiny: 'we feel that we are greater than we know.' We are two Englishmen, in one moment realising the glories of our blood and state. We are alone together, gazing upon a new Pacific, 'silent, upon a peak in Darien.'

For—and here lies his subtlety—in the very flush of amazement the painter flatters you by whispering that for *you* has his full meaning been reserved. The *Téméraire* goes to her doom unattended, twilit, obscure, with no pause

in the dingy bustle of the river. You alone have eyes for
the passing of greatness, and a heart to feel it.

There's a far bell ringing,

but you alone hear it tolling to evensong, to the close of
day, the end of deeds.

So, as we near the beach where she is to lie, a sense of
proud exclusiveness mingles with our high regret. Astern.
the jettymen and stevedores are wrangling over their latest
job; trains are shunting, cranes working, trucks discharging
their cargoes amid clouds of dust. We and we only assist
at the passing of a goddess. Euergetes rests on his oars,
the tow-rope slackens, she glides into the deep shadow of
the shore, and with a soft grating noise—ah, the eloquence
of it!—takes ground. Silently we carry her chain out and
noose it about a monster elm; silently we slip the legs under
her channels, lift and make fast her stern moorings, lash
the tiller for the last time, tie the coverings over cabintop
and well; anxiously, with closed lips, praetermitting no
due rite. An hour, perhaps, passes, and November darkness
has settled on the river ere we push off our boat, in a last
farewell committing her—our treasure 'locked up, not
lost'—to a winter over which Jove shall reign genially

Et fratres Helenae, lucida sidera.

As we thread our dim way homeward among the riding-
lights flickering on the black water, the last pale vision
of her alone and lightless follows and reminds me of the
dull winter ahead, the short days, the long nights. She is
haunting me yet as I land on the wet slip strewn with dead
leaves to the tide's edge. She follows me up the hill, and
even to my library door. I throw it open, and lo! a bright
fire burning, and, smiling over against the blaze of it,
cheerful, companionable, my books have been awaiting me.

NOVEMBER

WILL the reader forgive, this month, a somewhat more serious gossip?

In my childhood I used to spend long holidays with my grandparents in Devonshire, and afterwards lived with them for a while when the shades of the prison-house began to close and I attended my first 'real' school as a day-boy. I liked those earlier visits best, for they were holidays, and I had great times in the hayfields and apple orchards, and rode a horse, and used in winter-time to go shooting with my grandfather and carry the powder-flask and shot-flask for his gun—an old muzzle-loader. Though stern in his manner, he was (as I grew to learn) extraordinarily, even extravagantly, kind; and my grandmother lived for me, her eldest grandchild. Years afterwards I gathered that in the circle of her acquaintance she passed for a satirical, slightly imperious, lady: and I do seem to remember that she suffered fools with a private reserve of mirth. But she loved her own with a thoroughness which extended—good housewife that she was—down to the last small office.

In short, here were two of the best and most affectionate grandparents in the world, who did what they knew to make a child happy all the week. But in religion they were strict evangelicals, and on Sunday they took me to public worship and acquainted me with Hell. From my eighth to my twelfth year I lived on pretty close terms with Hell, and would wake up in the night and lie awake with the horror of it upon me. Oddly enough, I had no very vivid fear for myself—or if vivid it was but occasional and rare.

Little pietistic humbug that I was, I fancied myself among the elect: but I had a desperate assurance that both my parents were damned, and I loved them too well to find the conviction bearable. To this day I wonder what kept me from tackling my father on the state of his soul. The result would have been extremely salutary for me: for he had an easy sense of humour, a depth of conviction of his own which he united with limitless tolerance, and a very warm affection for his mother-in-law. Let it suffice that I did not: but for two or three years at least my childhood was tormented with visions of Hell derived from the pulpit and mixed up with two terrible visions derived from my reading—the ghost of an evil old woman in red-heeled slippers from Sir Walter Scott's story, *The Tapestried Room*, and a jumble of devils from a chapter of Samuel Warren's *Diary of a Late Physician*. I had happened on these horrors among the dull contents of my grandfather's book-case.

For three or four years these companions—the vision of Hell particularly and my parents in it—murdered my childish sleep. Then, for no reason that I can give any account of, it all faded, and boy or man I have never been troubled at all by Hell or the fear of it.

The strangest part of the whole affair is that no priest, from first to last, has ever spoken to me in private of any life but this present one, or indeed about religion at all. I suppose there must be some instinct in the sacerdotal mind which warns it off certain cases as hopeless from the first. . .and yet I have always been eager to discuss serious things with the serious.

There has been no great loss, though—apart from the missing of sociableness—if one may judge the arguments that satisfy my clerical friends from the analogies they use

in the pulpit. The subject of a future life is one, to be sure,
which can hardly be discussed without resort to analogy.
But there are good and bad analogies, and of all bad ones
that which grates worst upon the nerves of a man who will
have clear thinking (to whatever it lead him) is the common
one of the seed and the flower.

> The flowers that we behold each year
> In chequer'd meads their heads to rear,
>   New rising from the tomb;
> The eglantines and honey daisies,
> And all those pretty smiling faces
>   That still in age grow young—
>   Even those do cry
>   That though men die,
>   Yet life from death may come,

wrote John Hagthorpe in verses which generations of
British schoolboys have turned into Latin alcaics; and how
often have we not 'sat under' this argument in church at
Easter or when the preacher was improving a Harvest
Festival? Examine it, and you see at once that the argument is not *in pari materiâ*; that all the true correspondence
between man and the flower-seed begins and ends in this
world. As the seed becomes a plant, blossoms and leaves
the seeds of other flowers, so of seed man is begotten,
flourishes and dies, leaving his seed behind him—all in
this world. The 'seed' argument makes an illicit jump
from one world to another after all its analogies have been
met and satisfied on this side of the grave. If flowers went
to heaven and blossomed there (which is possible indeed,
but is not contended) it might be cogent. As things are,
one might as validly reason from the man to prove that
flowers go to heaven, as from the flower to prove that man
goes thither. St Paul (as I do not forget) uses the similitude

of the seed: but his argument is a totally different one. St Paul bids us not be troubled in what form the dead shall be raised; for as we sow 'not the body that shall be, but bare grain, it may chance of wheat or of some other grain,' so God will raise the dead in what form it pleases Him: in other words, he tells us that since bare grain may turn into such wonderful and wonderfully different things as wheat, barley, oats, rye, in this world, we need not marvel that bare human bodies planted here should be raised in wonderful form hereafter. Objections may be urged against this illustration: I am only concerned to point out that it illustrates an argument entirely different from the common pulpit one, which (I suspect) we should have to endure far less frequently were it our custom to burn our dead, and did not interment dig a trap for facile rhetoric.

Further, St Paul's particular warning, if it do not consciously contain, at least suggests, a general warning against interpreting the future life in terms of this one, whereas its delights and pains can have little or nothing in common with ours. We try to imagine them by expanding or exaggerating and perpetuating ours—or some of them; but the attempt is demonstrably foolish, and leads straight to its own defeat. It comes of man's incapacity to form a conception of Eternity, or at any rate to grasp and hold it long enough to reason about it; by reason of which incapacity he falls back upon the easier, misleading conception of 'Everlasting Life.' In Eternity time is not: a man dies into it to-day and awakes (say) yesterday, for in Eternity yesterday and to-day and to-morrow are one, and ten thousand years is as one day. This vacuum of time you may call 'Everlasting Life,' but it clearly differs from what men ordinarily and almost inevitably understand by 'Everlasting Life,' which to them is an endless prolongation of time. Therefore, when they imagine heaven as consisting of an endless prolongation and exaggeration or rarefication of such pleasures as we know, they invite the retort, 'And pray what would become of any one of our known pleasures, or even of our conceivable pleasures, if it were made everlasting?' As Jowett asked, with his usual dry sagacity, in his Introduction to the *Phædo*—

What is the pain that does not become deadened after a thousand years? or what is the nature of that pleasure or happiness which never wearies by monotony? Earthly pleasures and pains are short in proportion as they are keen; of any others which are both intense and lasting we have no experience and can form no idea.... To beings constituted as we are the monotony of singing psalms would be as great an affliction as the pains of hell, and might even be pleasantly interrupted by them.

This is trenchant enough, and yet we perceive that the critic is setting up his rest upon the very fallacy he attacks— the fallacy of using 'Eternity' and 'Everlasting Life' as convertible terms. He neatly enough reduces to absurdity the prolongation, through endless time, of pleasures which delight us because they are transitory: he does not see, or for the moment forgets, that Eternity is not a prolongation of time at all, but an absolute negation of it.

There seems to be no end to the confusion of men's thought on this subject. Take, for example, this extract from our late Queen's private journal (1883):

After luncheon saw the great poet Tennyson in dearest Albert's room for nearly an hour; and most interesting it was. He is grown very old, his eyesight much impaired. But he was very kind. Asked him to sit down. He talked of many friends he had lost, and what it would be if he did not feel

and know that there was another world where there would be
no partings: and then he spoke with horror of the unbelievers
and philosophers who would make you believe that there was
no other world, no immortality, who tried to explain all away
in a miserable manner. We agreed that, were such a thing
possible, God, who is Love, would be far more cruel than
any human being.

It was, no doubt, a touching and memorable interview—
these two, aged and great, meeting at a point of life when
grandeur and genius alike feel themselves to be lonely,
daily more lonely, and exchanging beliefs upon that unseen
world where neither grandeur nor genius can plead more
than that they have used their gifts for good. And yet was
not Tennyson yielding to the old temptation to interpret
the future life in terms of this one? Speculation will not
carry us far upon this road; yet, so far as we can, let us
carry clear thinking with us. Cruelty implies the infliction
of pain: and there can be no pain without feeling. What
cruelty, then, can be inflicted on the dead, if they have
done with feeling? Or what on the living, if they live in
a happy delusion and pass into nothingness without discovering the cheat? Let us hold most firmly that there has
been no cheat; but let us also be reasonable and admit
that, if cheat there be, it cannot also be cruel, since everything that would make it a cheat would also blot out
completely all chance of discovery, and therefore all pain
of discovering.

*   *   *   *   *

This is a question on which, beyond pleading that what
little we say ought to be (but seldom is) the result of clear
thinking, I propose to say little, not only because here is

not the place for metaphysics, but because—to quote Jowett again—'considering the "feebleness of the human faculties and the uncertainty of the subject," we are inclined to believe that the fewer our words the better. At the approach of death there is not much said: good men are too honest to go out of the world professing more than they know. There is perhaps no important subject about which, at any time, even religious people speak so little to one another.'

I would add that, in my opinion, many men fall into this reticence because as they grow older the question seems to settle itself without argument, and they cease by degrees to worry themselves about it. It dies in sensible men almost insensibly with the death of egoism. At twenty we are all furious egoists; at forty or thereabouts—and especially if we have children, as at forty every man ought—our centre of gravity has completely shifted. We care a great deal about what happens to the next generation, we care something about our work, but about ourselves and what becomes of us in the end I really think we care very little. By this time, if we have taken account of ourselves, ourselves are by no means so splendidly interesting as they used to be, but subjects rather of humorous and charitable comprehension.

Of all the opening passages in Plato—master of beautiful openings—I like best that of the *Laws*. The scene is Crete; the season, midsummer; and on the long dusty road between Cnosus and the cave and temple of Zeus the three persons of the dialogue—strangers to one another, but bound on a common pilgrimage—join company and fall into converse together. One is an Athenian, one a Cretan, the third a Lacedæmonian, and all are elderly. Characteristically, the invitation to talk comes from the Athenian.

'It will pass the time pleasantly,' he suggests; 'for I am told that the distance from Cnosus to the cave and temple of Zeus is considerable, and doubtless there are shady places under the lofty trees which will protect us from the scorching sun. Being no longer young, we may often stop to rest beneath them, and get over the whole journey without difficulty, beguiling the time by conversation.'

'Yes, Stranger,' answers Cleinias the Cretan, 'and if we proceed onward we shall come to groves of cypresses, which are of rare height and beauty, and there are green meadows in which we may repose and converse.'

'Very good.'

'Very good indeed; and still better when we see them. Let us move on cheerily.'

So, now walking, anon pausing in the shade to rest, the three strangers beguile their journey, which (as the Athenian was made, by one of Plato's cunning touches, to foresee) is a long one; and the dialogue, moving with their deliberate progress, extends to a length which no doubt in the course of some 2300 years has frightened away many thousands of general readers. Yet its slow amplitude, when you come to think of it, is appropriate; for these elderly men are in no hurry, although they have plenty to talk about, especially on the subjects of youth and religion. 'They have,' says Jowett, 'the feelings of old age about youth, about the state, about human things in general. Nothing in life seems to be of much importance to them: they are spectators rather than actors, and men in general appear to the Athenian speaker to be the playthings of the gods and of circumstances. Still they have a fatherly care of the young, and are deeply impressed by sentiments of religion. . . .'

'Human affairs,' says the Athenian, 'are hardly worth con-

sidering in earnest, and yet we must be in earnest about them—
a sad necessity constrains us.... And so I say that about serious
matters a man should be serious, and about a matter which
is not serious he should not be serious; and that God is the
natural and worthy object of our most serious and blessed
endeavours. For man, as I said before, is made to be the play-
thing of God, and this, truly considered, is the best of him;
wherefore also every man and woman should walk seriously
and pass life in the noblest of pastimes, and be of another
mind from what they are at present.'

But on the subject of youth, too, our Athenian is anxiously,
albeit calmly, serious: and especially on the right education
of youth, 'for,' says he, 'many a victory has been and will
be suicidal to the victors; but education is never suicidal.'
By education he explains himself to mean—

that education in virtue from youth upwards which makes a
man eagerly pursue the ideal perfection of citizenship, and
teaches him how rightly to rule and how to obey. This is the
only education which, upon our view, deserves the name; and
that other sort of training which aims at the acquisition of
wealth or bodily strength, or mere cleverness apart from intelligence and justice is mean and illiberal, and is not worthy
to be called education at all.

Plato wrote this dialogue when over seventy, an age
which for many years (if I live) I shall be able to contemplate as respectable. Yet, though speaking at a guess,
I say pretty confidently that the talk of these three imaginary
interlocutors of his upon youth, and the feeling that colours
it, convey more of the truth about old age than does Cicero's
admired treatise on that subject or any of its descendants.
For these treatises start with the false postulate that age is
concerned about itself, whereas it is the mark of age to be
indifferent about itself, and this mark of indifference

deepens with the years. Nor did Cicero once in his
De Senectute get hold of so fine or so true a thought as
Plato's Athenian lets fall almost casually—that a man should
honour an aged parent as he would the image of a God
treasured up and dwelling in his house.

The outlook of Plato's three elderly men, in fact, differs
little, if at all, from Mr Meredith's, as you may see for
yourself by turning back to the top of p. 210 of this book
and reading the two or three pages which follow it.
Speaking as a parent, I say that this outlook is—I won't
say the right one, though this too I believe—the outlook
a man *naturally* takes as he grows older: naturally, because
it is natural for a man to have children, and he who has
none may find alleviations, but must miss the course of
Nature. As I write there comes back to me the cry of my
old schoolmaster, T. E. Brown, protesting from the grave—

> But when I think if we must part
>   And all this personal dream be fled—
> O, then my heart! O, then my useless heart!
>   Would God that thou wert dead—
> A clod insensible to joys or ills—
> A stone remote in some bleak gully of the hills!

I hear the note of anguish: but the appeal itself passes
me by. 'All this personal dream' must flee: it is better that
it should flee; nay, much of our present bliss rests upon its
transitoriness. But we can continue in the children.

I think that perhaps the worst of having no children
of their own is that it makes, or tends to make, men and
women indifferent to children in general. I know, to be
sure, that thousands of childless men and women reach
out (as it were) wistfully, almost passionately towards the
young. Still, I know numbers who care nothing for

children, regard them as nuisances, and yet regard themselves as patriots—though of a state which presumably is to disappear in a few years, and with their acquiescence. I own that a patriotism which sets up no hope upon its country's continuous renewal and improvement, or even upon its survival beyond the next few years, seems to me as melancholy as it is sterile.

Some of these good folk, for example, play the piano more sedulously than that instrument, in my opinion, deserves; yet are mightily indignant, in talk with me, at what they call the wickedness of teaching multitudes of poor children to play upon pianos provided by the rates. As a historical fact, very few poor children play or have ever played on pianos provided by the rates. But I prefer, passing this correction over, to point out to my indignant friends that the upper and middle classes in England are ceasing to breed, and that therefore, unless the Anglo-Saxon race is to lose one of its most cherished accomplishments—unless we are content to live and see our national music ultimately confined to the jews' harp and penny whistle—we must endow the children of the poor with pianos—or perhaps as 'labour certificates' abbreviate the years at our disposal for instruction, with pianolas, and so realise the American sculptor's grand allegorical conception of 'Freedom presenting a Pianola to Fisheries and the Fine Arts.'

*   *   *   *   *

To drop irony—and indeed I would expel it, if I could, once and for all from these pages—I like recreation as much as most men, and have grown to find it in the dull but deeply absorbing business of sitting on Education Committees. Some fifteen years ago, in the first story in my

first book of short stories, I confessed to being haunted by
a dreadful sound: 'the footfall of a multitude more terrible
than an army with banners, the ceaseless pelting feet of
children—of Whittingtons turning and turning again.'
Well, I still hear that footfall: but it has become less terrible
to me, though not one whit less insistent: and it began to
grow less terrible from the hour I picked up and read a
certain little book, *The Invisible Playmate*, to the author
of which (Mr William Canton) I desire here to tender my
thanks. In a little chapter of that little book Mr Canton
tells of an imaginary poem written by an imaginary Arm.
(Arminius?) Altegans, an elderly German cobbler of 'the
village of Wieheisstes, in the pleasant crag-and-fir region
of Schlaraffenland.' Its name is the 'Erster Schulgang,'
and I will own, and gratefully, that few real poems by real
'classics' have so sung themselves into my ears, or so
shamed the dulness out of drudgery, as have the passages
which I here set down for the mere pleasure of transcribing
them:

The poem opens with a wonderful vision of children;
delightful as it is unexpected; as romantic in presentment as
it is commonplace in fact. All over the world—and all under
it, too, when their time comes—the children are trooping to
school. The great globe swings round out of the dark into
the sun; there is always morning somewhere; and for ever in
this shifting region of the morning-light the good Altegans sees
the little ones afoot—shining companies and groups, couples
and bright solitary figures; for they all seem to have a soft
heavenly light about them!

He sees them in country lanes and rustic villages; on lonely
moorlands, where narrow brown foot-tracks thread the ex-
panse of green waste, and occasionally a hawk hovers overhead,
or a mountain-ash hangs its scarlet berries above the huge

fallen stones set up by the Druids in the old days; he sees them on the hillsides, in the woods, on the stepping-stones that cross the brook in the glen, along the sea-cliffs and on the wet ribbed sands; trespassing on the railway lines, making short cuts through the corn, sitting in ferry-boats: he sees them in the crowded streets of smoky cities, in small rocky islands, in places far inland where the sea is known only as a strange tradition.

The morning-side of the planet is alive with them; one hears their pattering footsteps everywhere. And as the vast continents sweep 'eastering out of the high shadow which reaches beyond the moon,' and as new nations, with *their* cities and villages, their fields, woods, mountains and seashores, rise up into the morning-side, lo! fresh troops, and still fresh troops, and yet again fresh troops of 'these small school-going people of the dawn!'...

What are weather and season to this incessant panorama of childhood? The pigmy people trudge through the snow on moor and hillside; wade down flooded roads; are not to be daunted by wind or rain, frost or the white smother of 'millers and bakers at fisticuffs.' Most beautiful picture of all, he sees them travelling schoolward by that late moonlight which now and again in the winter months precedes the tardy dawn.

My birthday falls in November month. Here, behind this Cornish window, we are careful in our keeping of birthdays; we observe them solemnly, stringent in our cheerful ritual;—and this has been my birthday sermon!

DECEMBER

HARD by the edge of the sand-hills, and close beside the high road on the last rise before it dips to the coast, stands a turfed embankment surrounded by a shallow fosse. This is none of our ancient camps ('castles' we call them in Cornwall), as you perceive upon stepping within the enclosure, which rises in a complete circle save for two entrances cut through the bank and facing one another. You are standing in a perfectly level area a hundred and thirty feet in diameter; the surrounding rampart rises to a height of eight or nine feet, narrowing towards the top, where it is seven feet wide; and around its inner side you may trace seven or eight rows of seats cut in the turf, but now almost obliterated by the grass.

This Round (as we call it) was once an open-air theatre or planguary (*plain-an-guaré*, place of the play). It has possibly a still older history, and may have been used by the old Cornish for their councils and rustic sports; but we know that it was used as a theatre, perhaps as early as the fourteenth century, certainly as late as the late sixteenth: and, what is more, we have preserved for us some of the plays performed in it.

They are sacred or miracle plays, of course. If you draw a line from entrance to entrance, then at right angles to it there runs from the circumference towards the centre of the area a straight shallow trench, terminating in a spoon-shaped pit. The trench is now a mere depression not more than a foot deep, the pit three feet: but doubtless time has levelled them up, and there is every reason to suppose that the pit served to represent Hell (or, in the drama of The Resurrection, the Grave), and the trench allowed the performers, after being thrust down into perdition, to regain the green-room unobserved—either actually unobserved, the trench being covered, or by a polite fiction, the audience pretending not to see. My private belief is that, the stage being erected above and along the trench, they were actually hidden while they made their exit. Where the trench meets the rampart a semi-circular hollow, about ten feet in diameter, makes a breach in the rows of seats. Here, no doubt, stood the green-room.

The first notice of the performance of these plays occurs in Carew's *Survey of Cornwall*, published in 1602:

Pastimes to delight the mind, the Cornishmen have guary miracles and three-men's songs: and for exercise of the body hunting, hawking, shooting, wrestling, hurling, and such other games.

The guary miracle, in English a miracle play, is a kind of Interlude compiled in Cornish out of some scripture history with that grossness which accompanied the Romans' *vetus comedia*. For representing it they raise an earthen amphitheatre in some open field, having the diameter of this inclosed plain some forty or fifty foot. The country people flock from all sides, many miles off, to hear and see it; for they have therein devils and devices to delight as well the eye as the ear; the players con not their parts without book, but are prompted by one called the Ordinary, who followeth at their back with the book in his hand and telleth them softly what they must pronounce aloud.

Our Round, you observe, greatly exceeds the dimensions given by Carew. But there were several in the west: one for instance, traceable fifty years ago, at the northern end of the town of Redruth, which still keeps the name of

Planguary; and another magnificent one, of stone, near the church-town of St Just by the Land's End. Carew may have seen only the smaller specimens.

As for the plays—well, they are by no means masterpieces of literature, yet they reveal here and there perceptions of beauty such as go with sincerity even though it be artless. Beautiful for instance is the idea, if primitive the writing, of a scene in one, *Origo Mundi*, where Adam, bowed with years, sends his son Seth to the gate of Paradise to beg his release from the weariness of living (I quote from Norris' translation):

> O dear God, I am weary,
> Gladly would I see once
>   The time to depart.
> Strong are the roots of the briars,
> That my arms are broken
>   Tearing up many of them.
>
> Seth my son I will send
> To the gate of Paradise forthwith,
>   To the Cherub, the guardian.
> Ask him if there will be for me
> Oil of mercy at the last
>   From the Father, the God of Grace.

Seth answers that he does not know the road to Paradise. 'Follow,' says Adam—

> Follow the prints of my feet, burnt;
> No grass or flower in the world grows
> In that same road where I went—
>   I and thy Mother surely also—
>   Thou wilt see the tokens.

Fine too is the story, in the *Passio Domini Nostri*, of the blind soldier Longius, who is led forward and given a

lance, to pierce Christ's body on the Cross. He thrusts and
the holy blood heals him of his blindness. Local colour
is sparingly imported. One of the executioners, as he bores
the Cross, says boastfully:

> I will bore a hole for the one hand,
> There is not a fellow west of Hayle
> Who can bore better.

—and in the *Resurrectio* Pilate rewards the gaoler for his
trustiness with the Cornish manors of 'Fekenal, Carvenow
and Merthyn,' and promises the soldiers by the Sepulchre
'the plain of Dansotha and Barrow Heath.' A simplicity
scarcely less refreshing is exhibited in *The Life of S
Meriasec* (a play recently recovered) by a scholar whom a
pompous pedagogue is showing off. He says:

> God help A, B, and C!
> The end of the song is D:
> No more is known to me,

but promises to learn more after dinner.

*   *   *   *   *

Enthusiasts beg us to make the experiment of 'reviving'
these old plays in their old surroundings. But here I pause,
while admitting the temptation. One would like to give
life again, if only for a day, to the picture which Mr Norris
conjures up:

The bare granite plain of St Just, in view of Cape Cornwall
and of the transparent sea which beats against that magnificent
headland.... The mighty gathering of people from many
miles around hardly showing like a crowd in that extended
region, where nothing ever grows to limit the view on any
side, with their booths and tents, absolutely necessary where
so many people had to remain three days on the spot, would

give a character to the assembly probably more like what we hear of the so-called religious revivals in America than of anything witnessed in more sober Europe.

But alas! I foresee the terrible unreality which would infect the whole business. Very pretty, no doubt, and suggestive would be the picture of the audience arrayed around the turf benches—

> In gradibus sedit populus de cespite factis—

but one does not want an audience to be acting; and this audience would be making-believe even more heroically than the actors—that is, if it took the trouble to be in earnest at all. For the success of the experiment would depend on our reconstructing the whole scene—the ring of entranced spectators as well as the primitive show; and the country-people would probably, and not entirely without reason, regard the business as 'a stupid old May game.' The only spectators properly impressed would be a handful of visitors and solemn antiquarians. I can see those visitors. If it has ever been your lot to witness the performance of a 'literary' play in London and cast an eye over the audience it attracts, you too will know them and their stigmata— their ineffable attire, their strange hirsuteness, their air of combining instruction with amusement, their soft felt hats indented along the crown. No! We may, perhaps, produce new religious dramas in these ancient Rounds: decidedly we cannot revive the old ones.

* * * * *

While I ponder these things, standing in the deserted Round, there comes to me—across the sky where the plovers wheel and flash in the wintry sunshine—the sound of men's voices carolling at an unseen farm. They are

singing 'The First Nowell'; but the fourth Nowell—the
fourth of the refrain—is the *clou* of that most common, most
excellent carol, and gloriously the tenors and basses rise to
it. No, we cannot revive the old Miracle Plays: but here
in the Christmas Carols we have something as artlessly
beautiful which we can still preserve, for with them we
have not to revive, but merely to preserve, the conditions.

*   *   *   *   *

In a preface to a little book of carols chosen (and with
good judgment) some years ago by the Rev. H. R. Bramley,
of Magdalen College, Oxford, and well edited in the
matter of music by Sir John Stainer, I read that—

The time-honoured and delightful custom of thus cele-
brating the Birthday of the Holy Child seems, with some change
of form, to be steadily and rapidly gaining ground. Instead
of the itinerant ballad-singer, or the little bands of wandering
children, the practice of singing carols in Divine Service, or
by a full choir at some fixed meeting, is becoming prevalent.

Since Mr Bramley wrote these words the practice has
grown more prevalent, and the shepherds of Bethlehem
are in process of becoming thoroughly sophisticated and
self-conscious. For that is what it means. You may (as
harassed bishops will admit) do a number of irrelevant
things in church, but you cannot sing the best carols there.
You cannot toll in your congregation, seat your organist
at the organ, array your full choir in surplices, and tune
up to sing, for example—

> Rise up, rise up, brother Dives,
>   And come along with me;
> There's a place in Hell prepared for you
>   To sit on the serpent's knee.

Or this—

> In a manger laid and wrapped I was—
>   So very poor, this was my chance—
> Between an ox and a silly poor ass,
>   To call my true love to the dance.

Or this—

> Joseph did whistle and Mary did sing,
> And all the bells on earth did ring
>   On Christmas Day in the morning.

These are verses from carols, and from excellent carols:
but I protest that with 'choirs and places where they sing'
they will be found incongruous. Indeed, Mr Bramley
admits it. Of his collection 'some,' he says, 'from their
legendary, festive or otherwise less serious character, are
unfit for use within the church.'

Now since, as we know, these old carols were written
to be sung in the open air, or in the halls and kitchens of
private houses, I prefer to put Mr Bramley's proposition
conversely, and say that the church is an unsuitable place
for carol singing. If the clergy persist in so confining it,
they will no doubt in process of time evolve a number of
new compositions which differ from ordinary hymns sufficiently to be called carols, but from which the peculiar
charm of the carol has evaporated. This charm (let me
add) by no means consists in mere primitiveness or mere
archaism. Genuine carols (if we could only get rid of
affectation and be honest authors in our own century
without straining to age ourselves back into the fifteenth)
might be written to-day as appropriately as ever. 'Joseph
did whistle,' etc., was no less unsuited at the date of its
composition to performance by a full choir in a chancel
than it is to-day. But whatever the precise nature of the

charm may be, you can prove by a very simple experiment
that such a performance tends to impair it. Assemble a
number of carollers about your doorstep or within your
hall, and listen to their rendering of 'The first good joy,'
or 'The angel Gabriel'; then take them off to church and
let them sing these same ditties to an organ accompaniment.
You will find that, strive against it as they may, the tune
drags slower and slower; the poem has become a spiritless
jingle, at once dismal and trivial. Take the poor thing out
into the fresh air again and revive it with a fife and drum;
stay it with flagons and comfort it with apples, for it is
sick of improper feeding.

No, no: such a carol as 'God rest you, merry gentlemen,'
has a note which neither is suited by, nor can be suited to,
what people call 'the sacred edifice': while 'Joseph was
an old man,' 'I saw three ships' and 'The first good joy'
are plainly impossible. Associate them with organ and
surpliced choir, and you are mixing up things that differ.
Omit them, at the same time banning the house-to-house
caroller, and you tyrannically limit men's devotional impulses. I am told that the clergy frown upon house-to-
house carolling, because they believe it encourages drunken-
ness. Why then, let them take the business in hand and
see that too much drink is neither taken nor offered. This
ought not to be very difficult. But, as with the old plays,
so with carol-singing, it is easier and more consonant with
the Puritan temper to abolish a practice than to elevate
it and clear away abuses: and the half-instructed mind is
taught with fatal facility to condemn use and abuse in a
lump, to believe carol-singing a wile of the Evil One
because Bill once went around carol-singing and came
home drunk.

In parishes where a more tolerant spirit prevails I am

glad to note that the old custom, and even a taste for the
finer ditties, seem to be reviving. Certainly the carollers
visit us in greater numbers and sing with more evidence
of careful practice than they did eight or ten years ago:
and friends in various parts of England have a like story
to tell. In this corner the rigour of winter does not usually
begin before January, and it is no unusual thing to be able
to sit out of doors in sunshine for an hour or so in the
afternoon of Christmas Day. The vessels in sight fly their
flags and carry bunches of holly at their topmast-heads: and
I confess the day is made cheerfuller for us if they are
answered by the voices of carollers on the waterside, or if,
walking inland, I hear the note of the clarionet in some
'town-place' or meet a singing-party tramping between
farm and farm.

*   *   *   *   *

That the fresh bloom of the carol was evanescent and
all too easily destroyed I always knew; but never realised
its extreme fugacity until, some five years ago, it fell to
me to prepare an anthology, which, under the title of
The Oxford Book of English Verse, has since achieved some
popularity. I believed that previous English anthologists
had unjustly, even unaccountably, neglected our English
carols, and promised myself to redress the balance. I hunted
through many collections, and brought together a score or
so of pieces which, considered merely as carols, were gems
of the first water. But no sooner did I set them among our
finer lyrics than, to my dismay, their colours vanished;
the juxtaposition became an opposition which killed them,
and all but half a dozen had to be withdrawn. There are
few gems more beautiful than the amethyst: but an amethyst
will not live in the company of rubies. A few held their
own—the exquisite 'I sing of a Maiden' for instance—

I sing of a Maiden
   That is makeles;[1]
King of all kings
   To her son she ches.[2]

He came al so still
   There his mother was,
As dew in April
   That falleth on the grass.

He came al so still
   To his mother's bour,
As dew in April
   That falleth on the flour.

He came al so still
   There his mother lay
As dew in April
   That falleth on the spray.

Mother and maiden
   Was never none but she;
Well may such a lady
   Goddes mother be.

or 'Lestenyt, lordings,' or 'Of one that is so fair and bright';
and my favourite, 'The Seven Virgins,' set among the
ballads lost none of its lovely candour. But on the whole,
and sorely against my will, it had to be allowed that our
most typical carols will not bear an ordeal through which
many of the rudest ballads pass safely enough. So it will
be found, I suspect, with the carols of other nations. I take
a typical English one, exhumed not long ago by Professor
Flügel from a sixteenth century MS. at Balliol College,
Oxford, and pounced upon as a gem by two such excellent

[1] Without a mate.   [2] Chose.

judges of poetry as Mr Alfred W. Pollard and Mr F. Sidgwick:

> *Can I not sing but Hoy!*
> *The jolly shepherd made so much joy!*

> The shepherd upon a hill he sat,
> He had on him his tabard[1] and his hat,
> His tar-box, his pipe and his flagat;[2]
> And his name was callèd jolly, jolly Wat,
>> For he was a good herd's-boy,
>>> Ut hoy!
>> For in his pipe he made so much joy.

> The shepherd upon a hill was laid
> His dog to his girdle was tayd,
> He had not slept but a little braid
> But *Gloria in excelsis* was to him said
>>> Ut hoy!
>> For in his pipe he made so much joy.

> The shepherd on a hill he stood,
> Round about him his sheep they yode,[3]
> He put his hand under his hood,
> He saw a star as red as blood.
>>> Ut hoy!
>> For in his pipe he made so much joy.

The shepherd of course follows the star, and it guides him to the inn and the Holy Family, whom he worships:

> 'Now farewell, mine own herdsman Wat!'
> 'Yea, 'fore God, Lady, even so I hat:[4]
> Lull well Jesu in thy lap,
> And farewell Joseph, with thy round cap!'
>>> Ut hoy!
>> For in his pipe he made so much joy.

[1] Short coat.   [2] Flagon.   [3] Went.
[4] Am hight, called.

Set beside this the following Burgundian carol (of which, by the way, you will find a charming translation in Lady Lindsay's *A Christmas Posy*):

Giullô, pran ton tamborin;
Toi, pran tai fleùte, Rôbin.
Au son de cés instruman—
Turelurelu, patapatapan—
Au son de cés instruman
Je diron Noel gaiman.

C'étó lai môde autrefoi
De loüé le Roi dé Roi;
Au son de cés instruman—
Turelurelu, patapatapan—
Au son de cés instruman
Ai nos an fau faire autan.

Ce jor le Diale at ai cu,
Randons an graice ai Jésu;
Au son de cés instruman—
Turelurelu, patapatapan—
Au son de cés instruman
Fezon lai nique ai Satan.

L'homme et Dei son pu d'aicor
Que lai fleùte et le tambor.
Au son de cés instruman—
Turelurelu, patapatapan—
Au son de cés instruman
Chanton, danson, sautons-an!

To set either of these delightful ditties alongside of the richly-jewelled lyrics of Keats or of Swinburne, of Victor Hugo or of Gautier would be to sin against congruity, even as to sing them in church would be to sin against congruity.

*   *   *   *   *

There was one carol, however, which I was fain to set alongside of 'The Seven Virgins,' and omitted only through a scruple in tampering with two or three stanzas, necessary to the sense, but in all discoverable versions so barbarously uncouth as to be quite inadmissible. And yet 'The Holy Well' is one of the loveliest carols in the language, and I cannot give up hope of including it some day: for the peccant verses as they stand are quite evidently corrupt, and if their originals could be found I have no doubt that the result would be flawless beauty. Can any of my readers help to restore them?

'The Holy Well,' according to Mr Bramley, is traditional in Derbyshire. 'Joshua Sylvester,' in *A Garland of Christmas Carols*, published in 1861, took his version from an eighteenth-century broadsheet printed at Gravesend, and in broadsheet form it seems to have been fairly common. I choose the version given by Mr A. H. Bullen in his *Carols and Poems*, published by Nimmo in 1886:

> As it fell out one May morning,
>   And upon one bright holiday,
> Sweet Jesus asked of His dear mother
>   If He might go to play.
>
> To play, to play, sweet Jesus shall go,
>   And to play pray get you gone;
> And let me hear of no complaint
>   At night when you come home.
>
> Sweet Jesus went down to yonder town,
>   As far as the Holy Well,
> And there did see as fine children,
>   As any tongue can tell.
>
> He said, God bless you every one,
>   And your bodies Christ save and see:
> Little children shall I play with you,
>   And you shall play with Me?

So far we have plain sailing; but now, with the children's answer, comes the trouble:

> But they made answer to Him, No:
> They were lords' and ladies' sons;
> And He, the meanest of them all,
> Was but a maiden's child, born in an ox's stall.
>
> Sweet Jesus turn'd Him around,
> And He neither laughed nor smiled,
> But the tears came trickling from His eyes
> Like water from the skies.

A glance, as I contend, shows these lines to be corrupt: they were not written, that is to say, in the above form, which violates metre and rhyme-arrangement, and is both uncouth and redundant. The carol now picks up its pace again and proceeds—

> Sweet Jesus turned Him round about,
>   To His mother's dear home went He,
> And said, I have been in yonder town
>   As far as you can see.

Some versions give 'As after you can see.' Jesus repeats the story precisely as it has been told, with His request to the children and their rude answer. Whereupon Mary says:

> Though You are but a maiden's child,
>   Born in an ox's stall,
> Though art the Christ, the King of Heaven,
>   And the Saviour of them all.
>
> Sweet Jesus, go down to yonder town
>   As far as the Holy Well,
> And take away those sinful souls
>   And dip them deep in Hell.

> Nay, nay, sweet Jesus said,
>> Nay, nay, that may not be;
> There are too many sinful souls
>> Crying out for the help of Me.

On this exquisite close the carol might well end, as Mr Bullen with his usual fine judgment makes it end. But the old copies give an additional stanza, and a very silly one:

> O then spoke the angel Gabriel,
>> Upon one good St Stephen,
> Although You're but a maiden's child,
>> You are the King of Heaven.

'One good St Stephen' is obviously an ignorant misprint for 'one good set steven,' *i.e.* 'appointed time,' and so it appears in Mr Bramley's book, and in Mr W. H. Husk's *Songs of the Nativity*. But the stanza is foolish, and may be dismissed. To amend the text of the children's answer is less legitimate. Yet one feels sorely tempted; and I cannot help suggesting that the original ran something like this:

> But they made answer to Him, No:
>> They were lords and ladies all;
> And He was but a maiden's child,
>> Born in an ox's stall.

> Sweet Jesus turned Him round about,
>> And He neither laughed nor smiled,
> But the tears came trickling from His eyes
>> To be but a maiden's child....

I plead for this suggestion: (1) that it adds nothing to the text and changes but one word; (2) that it removes nothing but the weak and unrhyming 'Like water from the skies'; and (3) that it leads directly to Mary's answer:

> Though You are but a maiden's child,
>> Born in an ox's stall, etc.

But it were better to hunt out the original than to accept any emendation; and I hope you will agree that the original of this little poem, so childlike and delicately true, is worth hunting for. 'The carol,' says Mr Husk, 'has a widely-spread popularity. On a broadside copy printed at Gravesend'—presumably the one from which 'Joshua Sylvester' took his version—'there is placed immediately under the title a woodcut purporting to be a representation of the site of the Holy Well, Palestine; but the admiration excited thereby for the excellent good taste of the printer is too soon alas! dispelled, for between the second and third stanzas we see another woodcut representing a feather-clad-and-crowned negro seated on a barrel, smoking—a veritable ornament of a tobacconists' paper.'

* * * * *

One of the finest carols written of late years is Miss Louise Imogen Guiney's 'Tryste Noel.' It is deliberately archaic, and (for reasons hinted at above) I take deliberate archaism to be about the worst fault a modern carol-writer can commit. Also it lacks the fine simplicity of Christina Rossetti's 'In the bleak midwinter.' I ought to dislike it, too, for its sophisticated close. Yet its curious rhythm and curious words haunt me in spite of all prejudice:

> The Ox he openeth wide the Doore
> And from the Snowe he calls her inne;
> And he hath seen her smile therefore,
> Our Ladye without sinne.
> Now soone from Sleepe
> A Starre shall leap,
> And soone arrive both King and Hinde
> *Amen, Amen;*
> But O the Place cou'd I but finde

The Ox hath husht his Voyce and bent
Trewe eye of Pity ore the Mow;
And on his lovelie Neck, forspent,
    The Blessèd lays her Browe.
        Around her feet
        Full Warme and Sweete
His bowerie Breath doth meeklie dwell;
        Amen, Amen;
But sore am I with vaine Travel!

The Ox is Host in Juda's stall,
And Host of more than onely one,
For close she gathereth withal
    Our Lorde, her little Sonne.
        Glad Hinde and King
        Their Gyfte may bring,
But wou'd to-night my Teares were there;
        Amen, Amen;
Between her Bosom and His hayre!

    *   *   *   *   *

The days are short. I return from this Christmas ramble
and find it high time to light the lamp and pull the curtains
over my Cornish Window.

    The days are sad—it is the Holy tide:
      The Winter morn is short, the Night is long;
    So let the lifeless Hours be glorified
      With deathless thoughts and echo'd in sweet song:
    And through the sunset of this purple cup
      They will resume the roses of their prime,
    And the old Dead will hear us and wake up,
      Pass with dim smiles and make our hearts sublime!

Friends dead and friends afar—I remember you at this
season, here with the log on the hearth, the holly around
the picture frames and the wine at my elbow. One glass
in especial to you, my old friend in the far north!—

CHRISTMAS EVE

Friend, old friend in the manse by the fireside sitting,
  Hour by hour while the grey ash drips from the log,
You with a book on your knee, your wife with her knitting,
  Silent both, and between you, silent, the dog—

Silent here in the south sit I, and, leaning,
  One sits watching the fire, with chin upon hand,
Gazes deep in its heart—but ah! its meaning
  Rather I read in the shadows and understand.

Dear, kind, she is; and daily dearer, kinder,
  Love shuts the door on the lamp and our two selves:
Not my stirring awakened the flame that behind her
  Lit up a name in the leathern dusk of the shelves.

Veterans are my books, with tarnished gilding:
  Yet there is one gives back to the winter grate
Gold of a sunset flooding a college building,
  Gold of an hour I waited—as now I wait—

For a light step on the stair, a girl's low laughter,
  Rustle of silks, shy knuckles tapping the oak,
Dinner and mirth upsetting my rooms, and, after,
  Music, waltz upon waltz, till the June day broke.

Where is her laughter now? Old tarnished covers—
  You that reflect her with fresh young face unchanged—
Tell that we met, that we parted, not as lovers:
  Time, chance, brought us together, and these estranged.

Loyal we were to the mood of the moment granted,
  Bruised not its bloom, but danced on the wave of its joy;
Passion, wisdom, fell back like a wall enchanted
  Ringing a floor for us both—Heaven for the boy!

Where is she now? Regretted not, though departed,
  Blessings attend and follow her all her days!
—Look to your hound: he dreams of the hares he started,
  Whines, and awakes, and stretches his limbs to the blaze.

Far old friend in the manse, by the grey ash peeling
  Flake by flake from the heat in the Yule log's core,
Look past the woman you love—On wall and ceiling
  Climbs not a trellis of roses—and ghosts—of yore?

Thoughts, thoughts! Whistle them back like hounds re-
      turning—
  Mark how her needles pause at a sound upstairs.
Time for bed, and to leave the log's heart burning!
  Give ye good-night, but first thank God in your prayers!

THE END

Printed in the United Kingdom
by Lightning Source UK Ltd.
134536UK00001B/22-27/P

9 780521 736794